Christ Our Life

LOYOLAPRESS.
A JESUIT MINISTRY
Chicago

LOYOLA PRESS.
A JESUIT MINISTRY

3441 N. Ashland Avenue
Chicago, Illinois 60657
(800) 621-1008
www.loyolapress.com
www.christourlife.org

Acknowledgments

Excerpts from *Catechism of the Catholic Church*. English translation of the *Catechism of the Catholic Church* for the United States of America copyright © 1994, United States Catholic Conference, Inc.—Libreria Editrice Vaticana.

Excerpt from *Follow the Way of Love: A Pastoral Message from the U.S. Catholic Bishops to Families*. Copyright © 1994 United States Conference of Catholic Bishops, Inc., Washington, DC. No portion of this text may be reproduced by any means without written permission from the copyright holder.

Excerpts from the *New American Bible* with Revised New Testament and Psalms Copyright © 1991, 1986, 1970 Confraternity of Christian Doctrine, Inc., Washington, DC. All rights reserved. No portion of the *New American Bible* may be reprinted without permission in writing from the copyright holder.

Cover art: Lori Lohstoeter
Cover design: Maggie Hong, Loyola Press
Interior design: Think Design Group

ISBN 13: 978-0-8294-2529-1, ISBN 10: 0-8294-2529-2

Copyright © 2009 Loyola Press, Chicago, Illinois

All rights reserved. No part of this publication may be reproduced, stored in a retrieval system, or transmitted in any form or by any means, electronic, mechanical, photocopying, recording, or otherwise, without the prior permission of the publisher.

Printed in USA
08 09 10 11 12 13 VERSA 10 9 8 7 6 5 4 3 2 1

Table of Contents

Part Three: Additional Resources

PART 1

Welcome to *Christ Our Life*

Welcome to *Christ Our Life*

As a parent or guardian, you have a special role to play in nurturing the budding faith of your children. *Christ Our Life* will help and guide you as you invite your children to grow closer to Christ on their journey of faith.

Christ Our Life is published by Loyola Press, a Jesuit ministry dedicated to helping children and adults deepen their friendship with God. *Christ Our Life*, which set the standard for religious education, is written by the Sisters of Notre Dame of Chardon, Ohio. The program is rich in content, doctrine, and Scripture, with Jesus at the heart of every lesson.

This *Home Learning Guide*, along with the student text, makes it easy for you to pass along the Catholic faith to your children. Additional support and learning activities are available online at christourlife.org/family.

Christ Our Life is an authentic expression of the Catholic faith, and it has been found to be in conformity with the *Catechism of the Catholic Church* by the Ad Hoc Committee to Oversee the Use of the *Catechism of the Catholic Church*.

How to Use the *Home Learning Guide*

From the moment children are born, people take notice of family resemblance. "Ooo, she has her mother's eyes!" "That smile is from *our* side of the family." "He definitely has Grandpa's nose." As children grow older, observers are likely to note not only a physical likeness in family members but also similarities of personality and temperament, behavior and values. The truth is, we do take on many of the traits and characteristics of our parents. Children naturally look to the adults in their lives for clues to how they can best grow into adults. The question is, what traits and characteristics will they learn from us? Since we want our children to be formed in the faith, we will need to set examples for them and provide an environment that supports the Catholic way of life. By choosing to use this guide, you are doing just that.

The *Home Learning Guide* provides you with an opportunity to work together with your children, using the *Christ Our Life* Student Book, to grow together in faith. Whether you are doing home catechesis with your children or just seeking to be more deeply involved in your children's faith growth, this guide will give you the tools you need to jump right in.

Who This Guide Is For

The *Home Learning Guide* will assist you if you find yourself in one of the following situations:

+ In cooperation with your parish director of religious education, you have chosen to work on *Christ Our Life* lessons at home with your children as part of the parish religious education program.

+ Because of travel, illness, or injury, your children will miss parish religious education sessions and you wish to work on *Christ Our Life* lessons with your children at home in the interim.

Whatever your situation may be, it is important to remember that no family is an island. In fact, helping children to grow in faith takes place within the broader context of the parish faith community. By keeping in regular communication with your parish catechetical staff and by participating in opportunities that bring parents and children together, your family will deepen its understanding of what it means to be a member of the Body of Christ— surely one of the essential lessons of our faith.

Using the Home Learning Guide

The *Home Learning Guide* is conveniently arranged in three parts to assist you in helping your children grow in faith.

Part One—Welcome to *Christ Our Life* provides you with an introduction to the *Christ Our Life* series and describes the experience of family faith growth. It also provides you with an overview of how your children grow in faith throughout grades one to eight. Part One also includes a description of the *Christ Our Life* Student Book and a step-by-step process for going through a chapter with your children, which is summarized in a convenient shortened format on page 208.

Part Two—Working with Your Children and *Christ Our Life* includes convenient overviews of the 25 core chapters and 7 Special Seasons and Lessons chapters in the *Christ Our Life* series, grades one through eight. By using these overviews, you can easily help

your children grow in faith by using the *Christ Our Life* Student Book together with them. By following the step-by-step process on the inside of the back cover of this guide, you can go through the chapters of the Student Book with your children, either introducing or reviewing the material, depending on your situation. Part Two also includes an opening prayer service to use as you begin this family experience.

Part Three—The Additional Resources section is an informative listing of valuable materials and resources for parents that are available to you as part of the *Christ Our Life* series.

Growing in Faith as a Family

Jesus turned and saw them following him and he said to them, "What are you looking for?" (John 1:38)

We all want what is best for our children. It is no surprise, then, that many of us brought our children to the waters of Baptism shortly after they were born. We believe that living as followers of Jesus is the best thing that we can desire for our children. Yet the celebrations of our children's Baptisms are only the first steps on their lifelong journeys of following Jesus. As our children grow older, we guide their feet to the next steps. Somewhere along the way, Jesus turns to each of us, as he turned to his first disciples, and asks "What are you looking for?"

The fact that you have made a commitment to use this *Home Learning Guide* suggests that you are looking for a way to walk with your family on the journey to a life of faith and holiness.

It may come as a surprise to think of your family as holy. We tend to think that the word *holy* is reserved for saints, or for people who dedicate their lives to the Church as a priest or religious brother or sister. The Church teaches us, however, that every baptized Catholic is called to a life of holiness. Pope John Paul II taught us that "everyone in the Church, precisely because they are members, receive and thereby share in the common vocation to holiness." (*Christ's Faithful People*, 1988)

Just what is *holiness*? The Bible teaches us that God alone is holy (1 Samuel 2:2). Jesus revealed that we can share in God's holiness by following the way of love. We can live a life of holiness when we love one another as he has loved us. One of the best places to practice this lesson of love is in the family.

Since the early days of the Church, the family home has been considered a holy place where family members receive the first teachings of the faith, learn human virtues, get initiated into a life of prayer, and practice Christian charity. The Catholic Church reinforces the importance of the family by referring to the home as "the domestic church." (*Catechism of the Catholic Church*, 1666) As a Christian family, you not only belong to the Church, but your life together is an expression of what it means to *be* Church.

Surely you have recognized holiness in the life of your family—in moments of awe, such as the first time you held your child in your arms, or moments of grace in the face of terrible loss.

The challenge we offer in *Christ Our Life* is to recognize God's grace in our everyday experiences—the sorrows and the joys, the tender and the tragic, the mundane and the magnificent.

As a parent or guardian, you are called upon to create a faith community of grace and prayer and a school for learning the Catholic way of life. The profound and the ordinary moments of daily life—mealtimes, workday, vacations, expressions of love and intimacy, household chores, caring for a sick child or an elderly parent, and even conflicts over things like how to celebrate holidays, discipline children, or spend money—are the threads from which you can weave a pattern of holiness.

It is the family, then, that prepares our children to take their rightful place within the larger Christian community, namely, the parish and the diocese, as followers of Jesus. This *Home Learning Guide* recognizes and honors the role of your family, your domestic church, in your children's faith growth.

What does a family growing in faith look like? Families, like all members of the Church, are not perfect, but rather struggle every day to become more faithful followers of Jesus. Here are some of the ways that your family can grow in faith

> A family is holy not because it is perfect but because God's grace is at work in it, helping it to set out anew everyday on the way of love.
>
> *Follow the Way of Love,*
> U.S. Catholic Bishops

and participate in the mission of the Church in daily living.

Growing in Love and Forgiveness

Children learn to love when they are loved and offered opportunities to love others, such as parents, grandparents, godparents, siblings, aunts, and uncles. Children can learn to form a healthy image of God and an intimate relationship with Jesus by experiencing healthy relationships in the family. Children learn about the dignity of others by seeing how you treat family members who are sick, disabled, or elderly. Likewise, when you let go of old hurts and reconcile with family members and friends, you help children to believe that forgiveness is always possible and that God's love never fails. The Family Feature pages of the *Christ Our Life* Student Book will help you and your family to consider ways to show love for others.

Growing in Trust

During times of trouble, tragedy, and struggle, or times of joy, success, and thanksgiving, turning to God, trusting in God, and believing that God cares for us can teach our families to grow in a living faith. The Family Feature pages of the *Christ Our Life* Student Book will help you to invite your family to trust God through all of life's ups and downs.

Growing in Prayer

Whether thanking God for blessings, asking for strength, or seeking guidance during difficult times, we can invite children to learn to pray and to believe that God hears our prayers and always responds. You can make a powerful statement to your family about the importance of prayer and foster an awareness of the sacred by creating a prayer center in your home with your family. A prayer center can be a small table covered by a cloth to show the liturgical season. On the table, you can place a Bible and

one or more of the following: a bowl of holy water, a crucifix, a religious image or statue, a candle, a plant, or flowers. Family members can use this space independently, and you can use it together when you gather to pray as part of teaching *Christ Our Life* chapters.

Growing in Respect for Life

When we avoid violent language and actions and seek peaceful resolutions to conflict, we can help children to become peacemakers. Likewise, by voicing opposition to anything that destroys life, such as violence, abortion, capital punishment, and poverty, we can help children to affirm life. An emphasis on Catholic Social Teaching in *Christ Our Life* will assist you in helping your family to affirm life.

Growing in Service and Justice

When you generously respond to the needs of others, your children learn to be generous. They learn that families serve not only their own needs, but also others who are in need. By reaching out to those in need, children learn to recognize Jesus in all people. Children can also learn what it means to act justly by treating others with respect; by fighting against poverty, illiteracy, and homelessness; and by taking a stand against racism and discrimination. Throughout the *Christ Our Life* Student Book and especially on the Family Feature pages, you will find opportunities to invite your family to show concern for others and make a commitment to social justice.

Growing in Celebration

When families use rituals to mark life's significant events— births, deaths, birthdays, sickness, weddings, first days of school, graduation days, ethnic traditions, job transitions, family reunions, holy days, and holidays— children learn to recognize the sacred dimension of life. They learn to celebrate that God's love is present always and everywhere. By gathering daily as a family for meals and sharing stories, we help children celebrate the ordinary events of life. The Family Feature pages of the *Christ Our Life* Student Book will help you identify opportunities to celebrate God's presence in family events.

Growing in Enthusiasm for the Faith

By taking the time to work together with your children on *Christ Our Life* chapters, and connecting those lessons to your daily life, your enthusiasm for your faith will grow. Together you will "taste and see" the goodness of following God's ways in faith, in prayer, and in service to others. By working together on *Christ Our Life* chapters, you can help your family to grow in their appreciation for God's Word in Scripture, develop a deeper life of prayer and a greater understanding of Catholic worship, create a deeper sense of your family as a domestic church, and foster a greater appreciation of cultural and spiritual diversity.

Growing in Vocation

If you share your own experience of listening for God's call in your life, you will help your children to consider their own vocation to live a life of holiness as a single or married person, priest, permanent deacon, brother, or sister. You can help your children to share in the life and mission of the Church by actively participating in Sunday Mass and in parish efforts to serve the Kingdom of God.

Your Children's Developing Faith

sn't it amazing to watch your children become capable of increasingly complex thinking and skills as they grow? From the dependence of infancy, through each stage of life, they grow and develop the capacity to comprehend ideas and concepts that were previously beyond their grasp. *Christ Our Life* links growth in faith to your children's physical, emotional, intellectual, and spiritual development by using language and activities appropriate to their ages. Here is a brief overview of the faith development of children in grades 1–8.

Profile of a First-Grade Child

(AGES 6–7)

The 1st grade, ages 6–7, can be considered, in many ways, the "golden age" of childhood. It is a time of many changes. Physically, children are growing rapidly and always seem to be losing teeth! They are very enthusiastic, industrious, active, and curious. They are experiencing an increase in motor activity and may often appear restless and easily distracted. Friendships outside of the family allow them to begin to understand the feelings of others and to develop important social skills.

Children at this age

+ are open to spiritual realities.
+ have a sense of the sacred.
+ have a sense of awe and wonder.
+ are comfortable with prayer.
+ need an atmosphere of warmth and security.
+ think of God as a provider and protector.
+ enjoy periods of silence.
+ are capable of taking simple prayers to heart.

The First-Grade Program

The first-grade program of the *Christ Our Life* series—*God Is Good*—is designed to provide a simple overview of the mysteries of our faith. Through learning of the goodness of God, who created and saved us, and the love of Jesus, your child is drawn to respond to God in friendship and in prayer.

The first-grade program lays the foundation for your child's spiritual growth and the development of his or her knowledge of the Catholic faith. Future study will build on the concepts, attitudes, and appreciations that your child will acquire now.

Unit 1 introduces Jesus, whose words and actions proclaim his Father's saving love. In and through Jesus, your child will come to know God as Jesus' loving Father, who is truly our Father too. Your child's wholesome self-image grows, as do loving relationships with God and others. Your child will see God's greatness in the gifts of life and freedom and in God's goodness in the other gifts of creation. Your child will hear of God's love calling him or her to eternal happiness with God in heaven.

Unit 2 presents the goodness and mercy of God in sending us his Son as our Savior. Your child is taught about God's gifts to Adam and Eve and their destiny to live with God forever. He or she will learn how sin changed God's plan but brought the promise of a Redeemer,

the Son of God, who would win back for the human family a share in God's life and the possibility of eternal happiness in heaven. Your child is led to share God's love with everyone but especially with the members of your family. The Advent and Christmas lessons of this unit prepare your child for a meaningful celebration of these seasons.

Unit 3 presents Jesus revealing the Father's love through the words and deeds of his public life. Your child will learn that Jesus teaches us to love God with our whole heart and to love others as he loves us. As your child sees Jesus reaching out to heal, encourage, and dispel fear, and hears him calling apostles to continue his ministry of reconciliation and healing love, he or she will be led to respond to the needs of others with Christlike concern.

Unit 4 presents the Paschal Mystery: how Christ, by his suffering, death, and Resurrection, reconciled the human family to God. Your child will learn that, because of Christ's victory over sin and death, all people can once more share in God's holiness. Your child is introduced to the mystery of the Church as the family of God, led on earth by the pope and bishops. Your child will learn that the risen Jesus is with him or her through his Spirit and that he helps us spread the Gospel message and give glory to God.

Profile of a Second-Grade Child

(AGES 7–8)

The second grade, ages 7–8, is a time of wonderful curiosity, changes, rapid growth, seemingly endless imagination, excitement, and enthusiasm. Though mostly positive and optimistic, in this grade, some children can occasionally become quite moody and like to spend some time alone. They still love structure and order, and work diligently at increasing skill in handwriting, computers, sports, and almost everything in which they are involved. This is also the time when many children prepare for First Penance and Reconciliation and First Eucharist. With all the excitement and enthusiasm they have, this can be a wonderful age for learning and faith development!

Children at this age

+ love to celebrate and enjoy ritual.
+ have a natural sense of wonder.
+ are comfortable with prayer and enjoy quiet.
+ are capable of reflecting for short periods of time.
+ are capable of praying spontaneously in a conversational style.
+ see nature as a reflection of God's love and greatness.
+ view the Church as a community of friends who help one another.
+ begin to appreciate the liturgical seasons, seasons of the year, and feasts.
+ are capable of taking simple prayers to heart.

The Second-Grade Program

The second-grade program of the *Christ Our Life* series—*God Cares for Us*—is designed to prepare your child for his or her first celebration of the Sacrament of Penance and Reconciliation and the Sacrament of the Eucharist. Your child is introduced to Jesus' willingness to forgive and to bring him or her peace in the Sacrament of Penance and Reconciliation. Your child will learn about the wonderful gift of the Eucharist, through which Jesus comes to us as food to strengthen us and unite us with him and with one another. Finally, your child will learn the meaning of the Mass, its different parts, and how to participate in it.

Unit 1 presents the image of an all-loving and gracious God, who offers the gifts of life and love and who sent his Son, Jesus Christ, so that we might enjoy deep friendship with him. Your child will become increasingly aware of how each life experience is a unique expression of God's loving care.

Unit 2 helps develop in your child a desire to grow in God's love by keeping his law. Your child will learn the essence of the Ten Commandments: to love God and to love others as God loves us. As your child understands more about Jesus' love through his words and example, he or she will be inspired to behave in ways that please Jesus. Your child will learn how to respond to God's love by praying, using God's name with love, and celebrating God's day. Your child will learn that love shows itself in words and in deeds that are obedient, kind, pure, honest, and truthful.

Unit 3 begins your child's formal catechesis for the Sacrament of Penance and Reconciliation. A good measure of your child's readiness is his or her own awareness of the need to be forgiven by Jesus. Although knowledge of the procedure for receiving the sacrament is desirable, it is not essential. Priests and catechists who understand this will respect your child's basic readiness to receive the Sacrament of Penance and Reconciliation and will guide and assist him or her gently and lovingly.

Unit 4 is devoted to the very heart of Christian life—the Eucharist. Your child will begin to appreciate the goodness of Jesus in the Sacrament of the Eucharist and will learn that in the Mass, Jesus offers himself to his heavenly Father and to us. Children come to understand that Jesus invites us to receive him under the forms of bread and wine so that he may fill us with his love. Your child's desire grows to receive Jesus and to prepare for the reception of First Communion.

Unit 5 introduces your child to the mystery of the Church—the Body of Christ—through which he remains with us and cares for us. Your child will learn how each member of the Church carries out God's plan and how leaders of the Church guide us to follow Jesus more closely.

Profile of a Third-Grade Child

(AGES 8–9)

Children at this age work diligently at increasing their skills in handwriting, computers, sports, and almost everything in which they are involved. They enjoy any kind of joke, riddle, or puzzle. While still quite imaginative, they begin to move toward realism and can think logically. They may begin to worry about the world, their friends, their families, people they know who may die or have died, and moving or changing schools. For some, this may be a time of being anxious and of lots of complaining!

Children at this age

+ begin to see prayer as less centered on the self and as more realistic.
+ are capable of praying for broader concerns.
+ begin to see connections between events.
+ enjoy ceremonies, rituals, and symbols.
+ need a sense of belonging.
+ enjoy moments of quiet.
+ are capable of reflecting for short periods of time.
+ are capable of praying spontaneously in a conversational style.
+ begin to appreciate the liturgical seasons, feasts, and seasons of the year.
+ are capable of taking somewhat more complex prayers to heart.

The Third-Grade Program

The third-grade program of the *Christ Our Life* series—*We Believe*—presents the main truths that Catholics believe and express in the Creed. Your child is learning to understand that he or she belongs to a faith community—the Church. Your child is helped to develop a clearer, deeper faith by learning about God as revealed in creation, in God's dealings with the Chosen People, and in the life and teachings of Jesus Christ.

Unit 1 encourages your child to develop a wholesome self-respect, as well as a respect for others. The program strengthens your child's trust in God, who calls him or her to be his, now and for all eternity. Your child will discover the means for following God's plan for him or her. The examples of Mary and others who have answered God's call encourage your child to trust God and to obey him freely.

Unit 2 aims to increase your child's knowledge of the sacraments, especially Baptism, Penance and Reconciliation, and the Eucharist. Your child will come to recognize these sacraments as signs of Jesus' special presence among his people. He or she will realize that Jesus is with his people in a sacramental way, guiding us and fortifying us with his life and love. Through Baptism, your child learns that Jesus takes away sin, shares his life of grace, and makes us part of his special family—the Church. Your child will discover that in the Sacrament of Penance and Reconciliation, Jesus forgives and strengthens us to lead a holy life. Learning how Jesus gave us the Eucharist prepares your child to be one with him in Holy Communion.

Unit 3 leads your child to study the basic truths of the Creed. Your child will learn about God as Creator and will be led to develop a spirit of obedience to his will. The Old Testament accounts of his saving deeds and his merciful love introduce God's relationship with his Chosen People. Your child will perceive that God, although seen in creation, is perfectly revealed in the teachings and saving deeds of Jesus.

Unit 4 focuses on the articles of the Creed related to Jesus, the Son of God. Your child will learn about his coming, his work, and his teaching and will see his mission as part of God's plan to share his life with us in eternal happiness.

Unit 5 centers on the Paschal Mystery—the Lord's passion, death, Resurrection, and ascension into glory—and on our sharing in that mystery. The goal of the unit is to foster a deeper appreciation of the great work of redemption and a desire to cooperate wholeheartedly with the Holy Spirit. The unit concludes with the study of the Communion of Saints, the family of God, whose members support and pray for one another. Mary's Assumption and her role as Queen of Heaven and Earth are also introduced.

Profile of a Fourth-Grade Child

(AGES 9–10)

The fourth grade, ages 9–10, is a relatively calm period for most children. Most children feel capable and in control as skills mastered at earlier stages grow stronger and are refined through practice. Fourth grade children are ready for solid conscience formation and are beginning to understand more clearly the role of intention in determining whether an act is right or wrong. This is what makes the fourth grade an ideal time to introduce moral concepts such as the Ten Commandments and an examination of conscience, and making moral choices.

Children at this age

- engage in hero worship.
- enjoy stories of saints and model Christians.
- have a more realistic image of Jesus as a human.
- see God as faithful, just, and fair.
- enjoy the rituals of liturgy.
- have a greater sense of God's presence.
- tend to trust that things will work out because God is in charge.
- are comfortable thanking God for positive things and asking God for help.
- are capable of reflecting for periods of time and enjoy quiet.
- are capable of taking more complex prayers to heart.

The Fourth-Grade Program

The fourth-grade program of the *Christ Our Life* series—*God Guides Us*—focuses on the Ten Commandments and the Beatitudes as guides for living. The program is designed to help your child see the Commandments and Beatitudes as guidelines given to us by our loving God, who intends for us to be happy in this life and in the next. Your child will be motivated to respond to God with faith and love, and to show his or her faith and love by observing his commands.

Unit 1 reviews our beliefs about the love of God, who reveals himself to us in creation, in Scripture, in the Church, and, most perfectly, in his Son, Jesus Christ. Your child will learn that all members of the Church are commissioned to share their faith, but that Jesus gave Saint Peter and his successors special authority to teach, govern, and lead the Church to holiness under the guidance of the Holy Spirit. Your child will be motivated to value the gift of eternal life that God promises to those who respond with faith to his love.

Unit 2 explores the means that God has given us to live as we were meant to live. First, God sent his Son, Jesus, to teach us how to love God and our neighbor. God, further, provided the Sacrament of Penance and Reconciliation to repair and strengthen our friendship with him and the Eucharist to bind us even closer to him as his people. God has also given us the Ten Commandments as well as the supreme commandment—love—to guide us in our journey on earth toward eternal life with him.

Unit 3 focuses on the first three commandments, which spell out how to love God. Your child will learn how to put God first in his or her life, how to honor him, and how to keep holy Sunday, the Lord's Day.

Unit 4 is devoted to the last seven commandments, which explain how to love our neighbor as ourselves. Your child will be guided in applying the commandments to his or her daily life and is challenged to show love for God and neighbor by keeping God's laws with courage and self-sacrifice.

Unit 5 develops an appreciation for the eight Beatitudes and a desire to live them in a spirit of hope and love. Jesus, who taught the Beatitudes by word and example, and Mary, who lived them perfectly, are presented as models to emulate. The lives of the saints, who exemplified the Beatitudes, also inspire your child to center his or her life in the practice of the Beatitudes.

Profile of a Fifth-Grade Child

(AGES 10–11)

Children at this age love to learn factual information. They have mastered the rules of most games, school, and family and are in love with order. It is a time of significant cognitive growth marked by the beginning of abstract thought. They are developing a sense of community and enjoy participating in planning. It is also a time of physical changes with the onset of puberty—especially for girls, whose physical development is normally ahead of boys. With the excitement and confusion that can occur at this time, it is a critical time for faith formation.

Children at this age

+ are interested in preparing for and participating in meaningful liturgy and prayer.
+ love symbols and ritual.
+ enjoy Bible stories (especially about Jesus) and the lives of the saints.
+ have a need for acceptance by the Church community.
+ are beginning to recognize how they can use their gifts to serve the community.
+ enjoy quiet.
+ are capable of reflecting for longer periods of time.
+ are capable of taking more complex prayers to heart.
+ have a desire to experience prayer that is focused on emotionally confusing issues and conflicts.

The Fifth-Grade Program

The fifth-grade program of the *Christ Our Life* series—*We Worship*—focuses on the sacraments, especially the Eucharist as the center of Christian life. This program is designed to help your child realize the wonderful gift God has given us in sharing his divine life. Your child is shown how to celebrate this life and deepen it through the liturgy. He or she is encouraged to foster it by following the commandments that guide us in loving our neighbor.

Unit 1 helps your child to reflect on worship. Your child will see Jesus as a model of worship, someone to follow in prayer, loving service, and sacrifice. Your child will learn how the Rite of Christian Initiation for Adults (RCIA) and the Sacraments of Initiation (Baptism, Confirmation, and the Eucharist) draw us into worship by making us children of God and members of God's holy people.

Unit 2 takes an in-depth look at the Eucharist, our most important form or worship. Your child will study the rites of our celebration of Christ's saving acts. The lessons will challenge your child to welcome the Word of God by listening to God's message and responding to it generously. He or she will be encouraged to offer thanks to God the Father through Jesus by uniting himself or herself with Jesus' sacrifice. Your child will be encouraged to live the Mass by proclaiming God's love through his or her words and deeds.

Unit 3 focuses on the Sacraments of Healing. Your child will be led to appreciate God's love and forgiveness offered in the Sacrament of Penance and Reconciliation. Your child will study the Sacrament of the Anointing of the Sick and will be encouraged to reach out with Christian love to those who are sick and elderly.

Unit 4 is devoted to everyone's call to holiness. Your child will consider how the various vocations can lead a person to holiness. As your child studies the different vocations, he or she will come to see how God helps people through prayer and the sacraments. Your child will learn about the Sacraments at the Service of Communion—Marriage and Holy Orders—and will be guided in the process of discerning his or her personal vocation.

Unit 5 develops an appreciation for living as followers of Christ and as true worshipers of the Father. Your child will review the fifth through tenth commandments and will learn about the works of mercy.

Profile of a Sixth-Grade Child
(AGES 11–12)

This is a time of significant cognitive growth, marked by the continuing development of abstract thought. It is also a time of physical changes with the onset of puberty—especially for girls whose physical development is normally ahead of boys. Becoming increasingly self-conscious about their own bodies, boys and girls gradually begin to separate. This is a time of searching for identity while experimenting with different roles and behaviors. With the changes and confusion that occur at this time, it is important to deal with these issues in an honest, direct, and loving manner.

Children at this age

+ are capable of relating messages from Scripture to their own life experiences.
+ respond well to participating in liturgical celebrations.
+ enjoy a variety of prayer forms.
+ are capable of understanding God, community, and faith in a deeper way.
+ see Jesus as an example to follow.
+ enjoy quiet.
+ are capable of reflecting for longer periods of time.
+ are capable of taking more complex prayers to heart.
+ desire to experience prayer that is focused on emotionally confusing issues.

The Sixth-Grade Program

The sixth-grade program of the *Christ Our Life* series—*God Calls a People*—is devoted to the study of God's saving love as it is revealed in the Bible, particularly the Old Testament. This program is designed to help your child increase his or her knowledge of salvation history, in order to respond to God with ever-deepening love and gratitude. As your child learns the stories of our ancestors in the faith and reads God's Word, he or she will learn to appreciate our ties to the Jewish people and deepen his or her understanding of Jesus, the one that God promised repeatedly to send to his people. Consequently, your child will come to love Jesus more ardently and serve him more generously.

Unit 1 teaches the value of reading the Old Testament. Your child will learn basic information about the Bible and will be introduced to Genesis 1–11 to study the accounts of Creation, the Fall, the promise of a Redeemer, and the spread of sin. Emphasis is placed on salvation history as the story of God's love for his people.

Unit 2 guides your child to develop an attitude of trust and an awareness of God's providential plan in his or her life and in the world. That God has a plan for his Chosen People—and a plan for us—becomes apparent as your child studies the lives of the patriarchs. Your child will see God's plan of salvation take shape in the call of Abraham, in the forming of a people of faith, and in the events in the lives of Isaac, Jacob, and Joseph.

Unit 3 develops your child's awareness of God's powerful presence among his people, of his concern and providential care, through the study of the greatest event in the history of the Israelites: the Exodus. The major episodes—the call of Moses, the deliverance from the Egyptians, the journey in the wilderness, the Covenant at Sinai, the infidelities and reconciliation, the uniting of a people, and finally the entrance into the Promised Land under Joshua—are paralleled to events in your child's life. Emphasis is given to the Covenant and the Ten Commandments, which set Israel apart as a holy nation dedicated to God.

Unit 4 develops your child's understanding of how God's providential use of persons and events furthers his plan of salvation. Your child will learn how God led, protected, and united his people through the judges and kings. The themes presented include an understanding of human weakness, of God's supportive and guiding grace, and of the ideals of leadership and loyalty as portrayed in the lives of the people of the era. Your child will learn that God makes use of both the strengths and the weaknesses of human beings in carrying out his plan.

Unit 5 introduces your child to the role and messages of the prophets. Through the prophets, God revealed his Word to his people: his call to sincere worship, to concern for those who are poor, to integrity of lifestyle, and to an unflagging trust in him. Your child will be encouraged to apply these messages to his or her own life, especially in the areas of social justice and authentic growth in and witness to the faith.

Profile of a Seventh-Grade Child

(AGES 12–13)

Seventh grade is a time of profound and rapid growth, when young people are entering a stage between childish and mature behavior. More than ever, peers are becoming a very strong influence. At the same time, key adults continue to play crucial roles in their lives, especially when they are facing a difficult situation. Moral guidance and faith tradition can provide valuable structure and stability. Girls are developing more quickly than boys, so boys sometimes struggle to behave in socially correct manners. In general, young people at this age are increasingly self-reliant and independent.

Children at this age

+ are capable of logical and abstract thinking based on concrete examples.
+ can be awkward and inconsistent as they seek self-image and self-identity.
+ appear sure of themselves yet question their own judgments.
+ tend toward hero worship and seek authentic models to imitate.
+ begin making decisions that have serious moral consequences.
+ are keenly sensitive to right and wrong.
+ experience fluctuating moods and strong emotional stress.
+ need support in their struggle to be responsible and adult.
+ withdraw to some degree from family; are critical and challenge adult authority.
+ seek peer approval and are eager to have friends, belong to a group, and be accepted.
+ can give more varied forms of service and need to be challenged to express generosity.

The Seventh-Grade Program

The seventh-grade program of the *Christ Our Life* series—*Jesus the Way, the Truth, and the Life*—is devoted to the study of God's saving love as it is revealed through his Son, Jesus. This program is designed to help your child grow in knowledge of Jesus so that he or she may love him more ardently and serve him more generously.

Unit 1 teaches the importance of reading and reflecting on the Bible, especially the Gospels. Your child will be led to see the value of prayer as a means to strengthen his or her relationship with God. As your child learns more about Jesus and the kind of person he is, your child will be asked to reflect on how to best respond to God's call to walk in his way. Your child will be guided and inspired by the witness of others who have come to know Jesus and follow him faithfully.

Unit 2 teaches your child to consider Jesus as the Truth. Your child will learn from his life and teachings to live the truth in love. Your child will study morality as given in the Ten Commandments, the Sermon on the Mount, the Beatitudes, and Christ's commandments of love. Your child will be encouraged to form his or her own conscience according to Christ's values. He or she will learn a process for making decisions.

Unit 3 guides your child to consider Jesus as the Life. He or she will study Jesus' death and Resurrection, the source of eternal life for all. Your child will see that the Holy Spirit guards and strengthens us as we form the faith community—the Church today—and carry on Christ's mission. Your child will be helped to discern the vocation in life to which God is calling him or her.

Throughout this book, your child will learn how Jesus is with us in the sacraments to sustain us in our journey to the Father. Living in the Spirit, as a member of the Church, your child will be led to work for God's kingdom of peace and justice. Like Mary, the first believer-disciple, your child will learn to strive daily to live by faith, witnessing to what God can do for those who have put their total trust in him. Your child will be taught to practice the works of mercy and become a sign of Christ's final coming—when all creation will be renewed and restored to God.

Profile of a Eighth-Grade Child

(AGES 13–14)

Young people at this age are often critical and self-absorbed as they stand on the threshold between childhood and young adulthood. This is a time of rapid growth, especially for girls, who develop more quickly than boys. Eighth-grade young people seek approval from peers and challenge authority but, at the same time, rely on key adults to continue to play crucial roles in their lives, especially when facing difficult situations. Eighth-grade young people can deal increasingly with abstractions and need to explore, reflect, and find meaning in new experiences. At the same time, they find comfort in familiar rituals and traditions.

Children at this age

+ become preoccupied with self and are strongly influenced by peers.
+ struggle for freedom and identity and need to channel idealism and energy constructively.
+ experience conflicts of conscience as a result of increasing independence.
+ are critical of adult inconsistency, but are inconsistent themselves.
+ tend toward absolutism in value judgments; are legalistic regarding religion, principles, and experience.
+ withdraw somewhat from family, yet need support and direction from significant adults.
+ need to challenge adult authority and begin to reevaluate religious notions of God, faith, and the Church.
+ respond well to heroes and role models from past and present.
+ need an atmosphere of encouragement, humor, respect, and trust with understanding of their negativity, moodiness, and regressive behavior.

The Eighth-Grade Program

The eighth-grade program of the *Christ Our Life* series—*The Church Then and Now*—is devoted to the study of God's faithful love as it is revealed in the Church founded by Jesus Christ. This program is designed to help your child grow in knowledge and love of the Church.

Unit 1 deepens your child's understanding and appreciation of the Church. Your child will explore the Church as a mystery and come to see Mary as the best image of the Church. He or she will reflect on the importance of prayer, what it is, its purposes, and various types of prayer. Likewise, your child will learn that every Christian is called to share in the mission of Christ and his Church.

Unit 2 helps your child grow in an understanding of the four marks of the Church—one, holy, catholic, and apostolic. He or she will explore the concept that all Catholics are united as one in the Church and will learn that the Church is holy because it was founded by Jesus, is guided by the Holy Spirit, is led to be holy, and is called to help carry out Christ's saving mission. Your child will examine the universal nature of the Church and will reflect on the notion that, as a follower of Christ, he or she too is called to help serve the mission of the Church.

Unit 3 is designed to help your child identify key people and events in the Church's history. Your child will learn how the Holy Spirit guided the Christians of the first century and will consider the Roman persecutions that threatened to eliminate the Church, as well as the heresy that divided it. He or she will find inspiration in the actions of the martyrs and defenders of the faith and will learn about the Church Fathers and the monks. Your child will receive an overview of the Church in the Middle Ages and see how the Church was a light for a dark world of fighting and feudal power.

Unit 4 continues to identify key people and events in the Church's history, beginning with the problems of the Great Western Schism, the Black Death, the Renaissance, and the Protestant Reformation. Your child will learn about the Catholic Reformation, the Council of Trent, the Enlightenment, and the French Revolution. He or she will focus on the Church's response to Rationalism at the First Vatican Council and on the effects of the Industrial Revolution. Your child will study some of the changes the Second Vatican Council made and become familiar with the beginnings of the Church in North America.

Unit 5 is designed to help your child realize what it means to live a Christian life. Your child will learn about his or her obligations under the New Covenant of Jesus and learn to recognize the seven capital sins and the corresponding virtues that free us from them. He or she will reflect on what it means to love God above all things and will learn about practices that are directly opposed to love of God and to love of neighbor by focusing on the Ten Commandments. Your child will consider how, as a Christian, he or she has a responsibility to work for peace, truth, and justice.

Your Children's *Christ Our Life* Book

To help your children grow in faith, your parish has provided you with the *Christ Our Life* Student Book. Together with this Home Learning Guide, the chapters in *Christ Our Life* will help you to create an environment in which you and your children can recognize God's gifts and respond from a deep sense of gratitude.

Before beginning to work with your children on *Christ Our Life* chapters, leaf through the Student Book to become more familiar with its contents. Pay particular attention to the following features:

✦ the inside of the front and back covers, which include traditional Catholic prayers appropriate for the particular grade level.

✦ the Table of Contents, which identifies the 25 core chapters and their arrangement in units as well as the Special Seasons and Lessons section that provides additional lessons. (Every grade has seven chapters devoted to seasons and feasts of the Church year: All Saints and All Souls Day, Advent, Christmas, Lent, Holy Week, Easter, and Pentecost.)

✦ the presentation of various aspects of the Catholic faith in an age-appropriate and engaging manner, which help your children learn the Catholic way of life. Extraordinary fine art, folk art, illustrations, and photographs that represent the rich diversity of the Catholic Church bring our Tradition to life. These visuals will connect you and your children to your Catholic identity, reveal your Catholic heritage, and increase your Catholic literacy.

✦ the arrangement of the book, which is presented in an inviting and thoughtful format, helping you to work with your children on lessons in a manner that is comfortable and effective. By following a step-by-step process (described in detail on pages 32 through 34), you and your children will learn to connect daily living with God's Word and, through prayerful reflection, recognize ways to act upon what you have learned.

✦ the *What Catholics Should Know* section at the back of the Student Book, which provides an overview of many aspects of the Catholic faith, including prayer, the Bible, the Sacraments, the Mass, and Catholic beliefs and practices.

✦ the Glossary, which provides hundreds of words to expand your child's Catholic vocabulary.

✦ the Student Books include pullout booklets and (in some grades) punch-out figures that supplement the lessons.

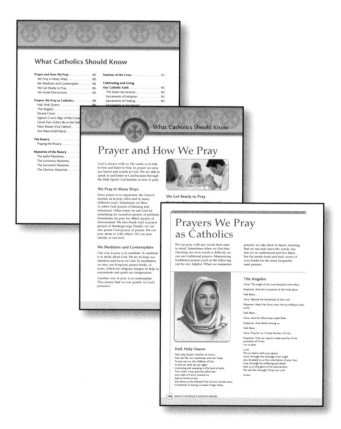

Going Through a Chapter with Your Children

Helping your children to grow in faith is a wonderful privilege for any parent or guardian. The following pages provide you with a convenient step-by-step overview of how to use the *Christ Our Life* Student Book with your children. For your convenience, the steps outlined on the following pages also appear in a convenient summarized form on page 208 of this guide.

Before You Begin

+ Work together with your parish catechetical leader (director of religious education) to set up a schedule for the year that includes the 25 core chapters, the 7 seasonal chapters, and any additional lessons at the back of the Student Book.

+ Read over the assigned chapter in the Student Book on your own to become more familiar with its content. Be sure to look for any *Note to Parents* features related to the chapter or unit and read these ahead of time as well.

+ Look over the background information provided in Part Two of this guide (pages 40–169), which includes the following:
  ◇ the chapter focus
  ◇ a summary of the content of the chapter
  ◇ Scripture in the chapter
  ◇ references to the *Catechism of the Catholic Church*
  ◇ a list of key concepts to help your child learn
  ◇ a list of vocabulary words (Words Your Child Should Know) in the chapter (See the Glossary for definitions.)
  ◇ other Key Terms for Your Information
  ◇ information about when to use pullouts and punch outs that pertain to a particular chapter (located in the back of the Student Book)

+ You may want to pray the Parent's Prayer on page 207 of this guide.

+ If you have more than one child using different grades of *Christ Our Life,* it is best to schedule separate times for working with each child individually.

+ Designate a learning space by clearing away clutter and placing in the space a Bible and one or more of the following: a crucifix, a candle, a statue, a religious image, a small bowl of holy water, a plant or flowers.

+ Prepare any materials that you will need: a Bible, the *Christ Our Life* Student Book, writing utensils, crayons, or markers.

Working on the Lesson

+ Begin by gathering together in the place that you've set aside for this special time.

+ Join together in an opening prayer:
  ◇ Invite your child to prepare together with you by slowly breathing in and out for a few seconds, becoming aware of God's presence.
  ◇ Pause for a moment of silence.
  ◇ Together, trace the Sign of the Cross with your thumb on your forehead, lips, and chest as you pray the words *"May God's Word be in my mind* (forehead), *on my lips* (mouth), *and in my heart* (chest), *Amen."*

+ Work together on the chapter in the Student Book. For variety, consider using some of the following approaches for reading the text:
  ◇ Alternate reading paragraphs aloud.
  ◇ Invite your child to read a section independently before asking him or her to summarize it.
  ◇ Read a section aloud together.
  ◇ Read a section aloud to your child.

+ In addition to reading the text, work with your child to complete any activities in the chapter.

+ Keep in mind the information from the charts in Part Two that tells you what to help your children know or do in each chapter.

+ Pause along the way to do the following:
  ◇ Talk about illustrations, pictures, and fine art depicted in the chapter.
  ◇ Point out any captions that accompany art.
  ◇ Think of questions about content just read to gauge your child's comprehension.
  ◇ Point out words that are in bold type. These are vocabulary words for the chapter (Words Your Child Should Know). Have your child find the definitions for these words in the Glossary.
  ◇ Reinforce key concepts in your own words.
  ◇ Share any stories from your own experience that reinforce the lesson.

+ Most chapters include a prayer feature titled **A Moment with Jesus** that invites your child to pray reflectively. For these features, invite your child to close his or her eyes as you slowly and prayerfully read the text. Pause for a few moments of silence with your child as you both pray quietly.

+ Occasionally, you may encounter a prayer service in a chapter. You can pray the prayer service at that time or you can save it for another opportunity.

+ Complete the Summary/Review pages that invite your child to review the main concepts taught in the chapter. In grades 1–4, the **Building Family Faith** feature provides ideas for the family to work on together. In grades 5–6, the **Things to Do at Home** feature and in grades 7–8, the **Reach Out** feature provide ideas for your child to put his or her faith into action.

+ Additional activities and assessments (quizzes) for each chapter are available on Blackline Masters at the *Christ Our Life* Web site (www.christourlife.org). To download these resources, talk to your parish catechetical leader or director of religious education about acquiring an access code from Loyola Press.

+ From time to time, supplement a chapter with a feature from the What Catholics Should Know section at the back of the Student Book. In addition, help your child take to heart (memorize) key words from the Glossary, as well as the prayers included on the inside covers of the Student Book.

+ End this time together with prayer:
  ⬦ Together with your child, prepare for prayer by slowly breathing in and out for a few seconds, becoming aware of God's presence.
  ⬦ Pause for a moment of silence.
  ⬦ Pray the Glory Be to the Father:
    Parent: *Glory be to the Father, and to the Son, and to the Holy Spirit,*
    Child: *as it was in the beginning, is now, and ever shall be, world without end.*
    Together: *Amen.*

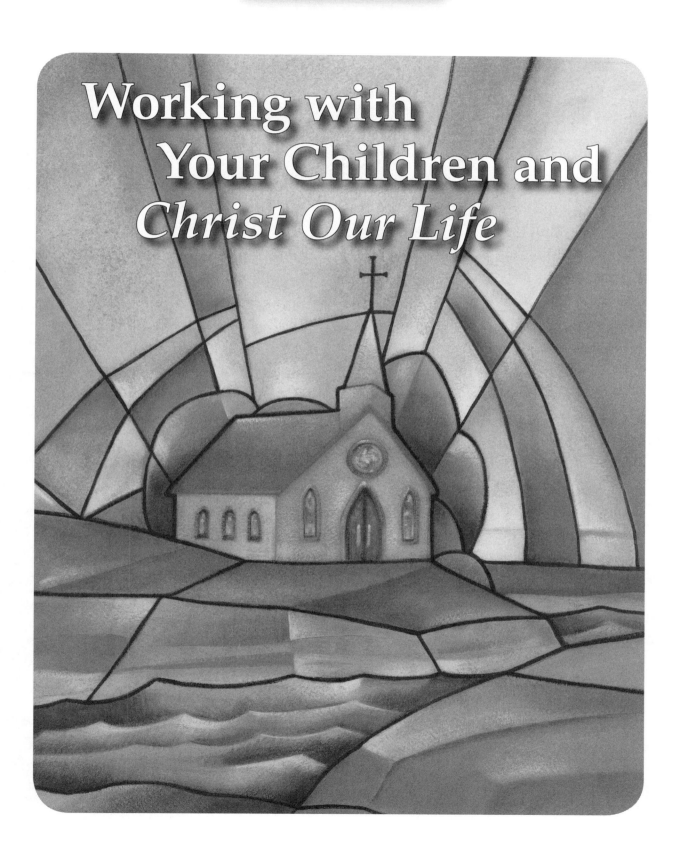

Working with
Your Children and
Christ Our Life

Opening Prayer Service

Beginnings are always important. As you and your children prepare to begin this experience of growing in faith together, gather as a family to ask for God's blessings.

Begin by choosing a place where your family can be together comfortably and free of distractions. Place your children's Christ Our Life *book or books in a prominent place.*

When the family is gathered, spend a few moments together in silence.

In your own words, introduce this important time together. Share from your heart your hopes for this year of growing in faith together. Then invite everyone to make the Sign of the Cross together.

All: In the name of the Father, and of the Son, and of the Holy Spirit. Amen.

Leader: Let us pray that we will be open to the Holy Spirit so that we may grow together in faith.

Good and gracious God, we come to you today eager to grow closer to you and your Son, Jesus. Fill us with your Holy Spirit so that our eyes may be opened and we may recognize you in all things. We ask this through Christ our Lord. Amen.

Listening to God's Word

Invite your family to listen to a story about Jesus from the Gospel of Luke that follows his experience as a child.

Read Luke 2:41–52

Sharing Faith

Invite your family to silently reflect on the following questions:

Why do you think the boy Jesus wanted to be with the teachers in the Temple?

What kinds of questions do you think he asked them?

What is one thing you hope to learn about God this year?

After a short time of silence, invite family members to share their reflections.

Presenting the *Christ Our Life* Book

Explain in your own words that the *Christ Our Life* Student Book is a way for your children to learn and share about God, just as Jesus did. To highlight the special nature and purpose of the Student Book, call your child by name to approach you as you hand out the book, saying:

_____, may Christ be your life today and every day.

Give your child a hug and then invite him or her to once again be seated.

Family Litany and Blessing

Invite your family to express their desire to learn and grow in faith together by joining in the Family Prayer found on page 207 of this guide.

After the Family Prayer, continue with the following:

Leader: God of Love, thank you for the opportunity to deepen our faith and to grow together in love of you. Bless us as we begin this sacred time together, and keep us faithful to our promise to you and to one another. We ask this through Christ our Lord. Amen.

Jesus Is Our Friend

FOCUS: In this chapter, you will be helping your child to understand that Jesus, our Savior, invites us to be his friends.

When Jesus came to bring salvation to the world, he came not only as our Lord and Savior, but also as our friend. The Lord who is above all, who is incomprehensible, and who is Holy Mystery, desires our friendship. Jesus Christ is our friend. He loves and cares for us and longs to be one with us.

Jesus considered himself a friend to us when he said, "You are my friends if you do what I command you." (John 15:14) The Gospels are rich with stories about Jesus' friendship with people from all walks of life. And Jesus especially loved children.

It is not uncommon in Catholic tradition to speak of Jesus as a friend. In being our friend, Jesus models how we are to relate to one another. Just as he calls us friend, so we are to call each of our sisters and brothers friends. We are to care for one another as Jesus cares for us.

Scripture in This Chapter
Luke 18:16 Jesus Calls the Children to Himself.

Catechism of the Catholic Church
425, 617–618, 2157

In this chapter, help your child to
* tell the story of Jesus and his love for the little children.
* explain how Jesus invites him or her to come to him.
* explain that a cross or crucifix is a visible reminder of Jesus' love as shown through his death and Resurrection.
* describe the Sign of the Cross as a blessing and a sign that Jesus' friends use to express their love for him.
* make the Sign of the Cross with reverence.

Words Your Child Should Know
* Christ
* Jesus

Key Terms for Your Information
* crucifix—an image of Jesus on the cross
* bless—to ask that the power of God's goodness come upon that person or object

God Is the Giver of Gifts

FOCUS: In this chapter, you will be helping your child to understand that we were made like God and given many gifts.

Poets capture in words the wonder of the world and the vitality of life. Their sensitivity to sights, sounds, and feelings helps us see familiar things in new ways and increases our awareness of the greatness of God.

The psalmist, reflecting on how the human person surpasses the other marvels of creation, says

> When I see your heavens, the work of your fingers,
>   the moon and stars that you set in place—
> What are humans that you are mindful of them,
>   mere mortals that you care for them?
> Yet you have made them little less than a god,
>   crowned them with glory and honor.
> You have given them rule over the works of your hands,
>   put all things at their feet:
>
> *Psalm 8:4–7*

Scripture in This Chapter
Psalm 139:14 Psalm of Praise

Catechism of the Catholic Church
299, 301, 355–358, 422

In this chapter, help your child to
* describe the gifts of God's love that are experienced each day.
* explain that God's love is known through the love of the people in their lives.
* explain that God's gifts are for sharing.
* explain that we are made in the image of God.
* describe God's never-failing care for creation.

Word Your Child Should Know
* Trinity

Key Terms for Your Information
* angels—creatures God made that are pure spirits
* creation—everything God made
* image—a likeness; something that is like another thing in form

God Calls Us

FOCUS: In this chapter, you will be helping your child to understand that we are called to believe in God and to do what God asks.

God is always calling each one of us to himself. God calls us in many different ways, even in the most ordinary situations. God's call is an election to a particular work in his plan of salvation. It is also a promise of help and blessing if we have faith in God and respond trustingly to this call. In whatever manner it is given to us, each call contains a personal challenge directed to the deepest level of our sense of moral responsibility. God awaits our response, for although God is the Lord, the events of history depend upon people's response to God's call.

Abraham and Ruth are models of fidelity to the call of God. Both Abraham and Ruth received the gift of faith. Both were blessed in many other ways, especially by progeny who were direct ancestors of Jesus. Like our ancestors in faith, we too are called to holiness, to sanctity.

Scripture in This Chapter
Genesis 12—21 God's Promises to Abraham
The Book of Ruth Ruth Responds in Faith.

Catechism of the Catholic Church
144–146, 2156–2159, 2653

In this chapter, help your child to
+ recognize the importance of his or her name and take pride in it.
+ name ways God calls and speaks to us, especially through the Bible.
+ describe the stories of Abraham and Ruth.
+ compare our journey of faith with Abraham's.
+ describe the meaning of faith.

Key Terms for Your Information
+ Abram—Abraham's name before God changed it
+ Canaan—the Promised Land
+ Haran—country from which Abram was called
+ Sarai—Sarah's name before God changed it
+ Boaz—Naomi's kinsman who marries Ruth
+ Israel—the land occupied by the descendents of Jacob (to whom God gave the name Israel)
+ Moab—ancient kingdom east of the Dead Sea

God Reveals Himself to Us Through His Son

FOCUS: In this chapter, you will be helping your child to understand that God reveals himself in many ways but especially through his Son, Jesus.

God reveals himself to us in two basic ways: natural and supernatural. In natural revelation, God makes himself known through the world of creation. In supernatural revelation, God communicates by divine speech, as he did through the prophets and through his Son, Jesus. Gerard Manley Hopkins, viewing creation with the eye of a poet and the heart of a mystic, exclaimed: "The world is charged with the grandeur of God."

from "God's Grandeur"

In supernatural communication, God speaks through others. The prophets, for example, were seers chosen by God to bring his revelation to us. In the person of Christ, however, it is not merely God speaking through someone but God himself speaking to the members of the human race.

Scripture in This Chapter
Psalm 104 Praise of God the Creator
John 20:24–29 Jesus' Appearance to Thomas

Catechism of the Catholic Church
65, 150–152, 293–294, 457–458

In this chapter, help your child to
+ explain that God is a Trinity of three Persons.
+ explain that we receive a share in God's life at Baptism.
+ explain how God reveals himself through creation and through Jesus, and how Jesus reveals the Father to us.
+ discuss how Jesus helped Thomas believe in him.
+ explain that faith is a special gift from God and describe how we come to know about God today.
+ describe how people can help him or her know and believe in Jesus.

Words Your Child Should Know
+ Hebrews
+ prophets

Key Terms for Your Information
+ deceive—to make someone believe something untrue
+ eternal life—life that will never end; living forever in heaven with God
+ faith—belief in God; a gift received at Baptism

We Are a Worshiping People

FOCUS: In this chapter, you will be helping your child to understand that we worship God through prayer, service, and sacrifices, as Jesus did.

Our highest calling as human beings is to recognize and respond to God. As we contemplate God, we are irresistibly drawn to praise him for his glory and to thank him for all he has given us. We humbly petition God, trusting that he is with us and will always help us.

The earthly life of Jesus was one of glorification of the Father. His every thought, word, and act gave praise. Indeed, Christ's last gift to us was the Eucharist, the offering of himself in joyful praise to the Father. What Jesus did we also do. We are truly a worshiping people—a people who belong to God and are aware of his creative power at work within us and among us. We give ourselves in worship to the Lord each day by our prayers and by the loving service we give to others.

Scripture in This Chapter

Deuteronomy 6:4–9 The Great Commandment
Psalm 95:1–6 A Call to Praise
Revelation 15:3–4 Giving God Praise

Catechism of the Catholic Church

2095–2100, 2104

In this chapter, help your child to

+ explain why we worship God and identify ways to praise God.
+ identify ways the Israelites responded to God's love.
+ indicate that Jesus taught Christians how to worship and identify the Eucharist as the greatest act of worship.
+ identify both personal and communal prayer as ways to worship God.
+ identify loving service, especially to those in need, as a way to worship God.

Word Your Child Should Know

+ alleluia

Key Terms for Your Information

+ synagogue—a building that is a center of Jewish prayer
+ worship—honor and praise given to God

The Bible Reveals God's Saving Love

FOCUS: In this chapter, you will be helping your child to understand that we come to know God and Jesus through Scripture.

Beginning with Abraham, God revealed himself at specific times, in specific places, to specific people, for the sake of our salvation. The record of this communication has been faithfully transmitted through the ages, first orally and then in writing. Catholic Tradition has always held that God's revelation in the Bible is true, for the Church has always believed in the divine origin of the Scriptures.

God's Word can radically change our lives—as it changed the life of Saint Augustine. After years of reckless living, Augustine's life was changed when he read the following Scripture passage:

> [L]et us conduct ourselves properly as in the day, not in orgies and drunkenness, not in promiscuity and licentiousness, not in rivalry and jealousy. But put on the Lord Jesus Christ, and make no provision for the desires of the flesh.
>
> *Romans 13:13–14*

That message was the catalyst that converted Saint Augustine, turning him away from sin and toward the Lord.

Scripture in This Chapter

Isaiah 43:1 I Have Called You By Name.
Luke 24:13–35 The Road to Emmaus
Ephesians 5:8 Live As Children of Light

Catechism of the Catholic Church

102, 151

In this chapter, help your child to

+ compare ways of coming to know people with ways of coming to know God.
+ explain that God's self-revelation is in the Bible.
+ describe how to read the Bible as a Catholic.
+ identify Scripture and Tradition as forming one sacred deposit.
+ know that God's main message in the Bible is "I love you."

Word Your Child Should Know

+ Old Testament

The Impact of Jesus— Jesus the Son of God

FOCUS: In this chapter, you will be helping your child to understand that Jesus, our Savior, is the Son of God and a human being.

Christians believe that Jesus is the Way to the Father, to eternal happiness. We believe that he is the second Person of the Trinity, the beloved Son who exists in a community of love with the Father and the Holy Spirit. These three Persons are eternal and equal. They were all present at creation, and as the One God, they achieve our salvation in history.

The love the Father has for us prompted him to send his Son to become one of us so that we could join with them. In loving obedience, the Son became incarnate in Jesus and taught us the meaning of love. Jesus revealed God to us and, through his life, suffering, death, Resurrection, and ascension, became our Savior and Lord. Now in his humanity, he is with the Father, while we are able to share in divinity through grace and the power of the Holy Spirit.

Scripture in This Chapter
John 10:30 The Father And I Are One.
Colossians 1:15 Image of the Invisible God

Catechism of the Catholic Church
464–469

In this chapter, help your child to
- express an awareness of God's unconditional love for him or her.
- relate that he or she has value and is worth loving.
- recognize the need to grow in all aspects of life.
- identify Jesus as Son of God, true God and true Man, and Savior.
- explain some of the implications of the Incarnation.
- express who Jesus is for him or her now.

Words Your Child Should Know
- eternal life   - Incarnation

Key Terms for Your Information
- Abba—Father or Daddy, how Jesus addressed God
- Jesus—the Son of God as a human being; the Savior
- Paschal Mystery—the suffering, death, Resurrection, and ascension of Jesus
- Savior—Jesus, who saved us from sin and death
- Trinity—the mystery of one God in three Persons: Father, Son, and Holy Spirit

A Community of Disciples

FOCUS: In this chapter, you will be helping your child to understand that the Church is the community of disciples, the Body of Christ, loved and redeemed by Christ.

It was Jesus' mission to reveal the mystery of God and our relationship to God. Through images, Jesus shared aspects of the mystery of the Church. He used the symbol of leaven to indicate that the kingdom would extend throughout the world. To show that we are bonded to him and find life through him, he likened our relationship with him to branches grafted to a vine. In comparing the Church to a sheepfold, Jesus emphasized his care for us.

The Church is a mystery because Christ is present in the Church and the Holy Spirit is guiding it. The Church is also a mystery because it is a sign of the Kingdom of God. Each of us is a small but vital part of the holy and splendid mystery of the Church. We are the leaven in Christ's parable; we are the living branches grafted onto Christ and rooted in him; we are the sheep of his pasture; we are the Church, and Mary is our Mother.

Scripture in This Chapter
Luke 13:20–21 The Leaven
John 10:1–16 The Sheepfold
John 15:1–8 The Vine and the Branches
1 Corinthians 12:12–31 The Body of Christ

Catechism of the Catholic Church
781–798, 829, 963–975

In this chapter, help your child to
- explain that the Church is a mystery.
- identify scriptural images of the Church.
- explain that he or she is responsible for making Christ and his Church present to others.
- explain why Mary is called the Mother of the Church.
- describe the role of the Spirit in the Church.

Words Your Child Should Know
- Church
- Communion of Saints
- Mystery
- Sanctify
- Second Vatican Council

God Is Good

FOCUS: In this chapter, you will be helping your child to understand that God made the world good.

Pausing to reflect on the intricacy, the design, the power, or the infinite variety in the created world refreshes the mind that is weary from the sound and image bombardment of our technological age. Through the psalmist, God invites us:

> Be still and confess that I am God!　*Psalm 46:11*

If only we take the time to put aside our business, the goodness of creation will captivate us and lead us to give thanks and praise to God, our good Father. We can open our senses to the warmth of the sunlight, the beauty of a rainbow, the gentleness of a refreshing breeze. We can pause to see the dew on the grass, the winged wonders in the sky, or the antics of a chipmunk scampering nearby. We can recognize the goodness of God shining through the eyes of a child and hear our creator speak in the exclamations of delight of the young at play.

Scripture in This Chapter
Genesis 1:1—2:4　First Story of Creation
Genesis 2:4–25　Second Story of Creation

Catechism Of The Catholic Church
282, 289–293, 299, 307, 2415

In this chapter, help your child to
- ✦ name some of the wonders of creation.
- ✦ tell the biblical story of creation and interpret its meaning.
- ✦ give examples of God's continuing creative activity in our world.
- ✦ see God's goodness in creation.
- ✦ suggest ways they we can care for our world.

Words Your Child Should Know
- ✦ creation
- ✦ Creator

Key Terms for Your Information
- ✦ create—to make something out of nothing
- ✦ creatures—things that God made

Jesus Is God's Best Gift

FOCUS: In this chapter, you will be helping your child to understand that God sent Jesus to die and rise in order to give us new life.

Augustine of Hippo, one of the greatest philosophers the world has ever known, tried to find happiness in the delights of the earth. Eventually, he realized that only through Jesus can a person come to enjoy the intimate and real contact with God, which alone satisfies the deepest human desires.

Jesus is the best gift of the Father, the perfect revelation of the Father, the Savior who died and rose to bring us the Father's love. To know Jesus is to know the Father, whose faithful love continually invites us to share more fully in his life. The image Jesus used to express the nature of our relationship with him expressed clearly the overwhelming bounty of God's love: Christ is the vine, and we are the branches. The branches of a vine yield a fruit that gladdens the human heart, but this delightful fruit results only when the branches remain united to the vine.

Scripture in This Chapter
John 12:23–24　A Buried Seed
John 15:5–7　The Vine and the Branches

Catechism of the Catholic Church
457, 615–618, 2157

In this chapter, help your child to
- ✦ explain that a seed dies in order to have new life as a plant.
- ✦ explain that Jesus showed the Father's love by dying and rising to give us new life.
- ✦ identify the disciples and themselves as members of the Church, and Mary as the Mother of the Church.
- ✦ explain the parable of the vine and branches.
- ✦ describe how union with Jesus brings happiness.
- ✦ make the Sign of the Cross.

Word Your Child Should Know
- ✦ disciple

Key Terms for Your Information
- ✦ crucifix—a cross with a figure of Jesus on it
- ✦ grace—the life of God in us
- ✦ Savior—Jesus, who died and rose to give us new life
- ✦ union—being one with someone; sharing the same life, ideas, and so on

CHAPTER 2   GRADE

God Gives Us Gifts

FOCUS: In this chapter, you will be helping your child to understand that we each have unique gifts to praise God and to serve others.

Though we may not know how great we can be or how much we can accomplish, we do know that we are all gifted and that God is the source of our abilities.

> There are different kinds of spiritual gifts but the same Spirit; there are different forms of service but the same Lord; there are different workings but the same God who produces all of them in everyone.
>
> *1 Corinthians 12:4–6*

Each person fulfills God's plan in a different way. God gives us the gifts and talents we need to do his will. God expects us to be responsible for them, to develop them to the best of our ability, and to use them to improve ourselves, to help others, and to praise and glorify him. By accepting our abilities as well as our limitations, we develop a healthy self-concept. This helps us respect others. We are able to appreciate successes and failures.

Scripture in This Chapter
1 Samuel 16:1–13   Samuel's Anointment of David
1 Samuel 17:4–52   David and Goliath
Matthew 25:14–29   The Parable of the Talents

Catechism of the Catholic Church
1936–1937

In this chapter, help your child to
+ describe the Parable of the Talents.
+ name some of the gifts he or she has received from God.
+ explain ways that he or she can develop his or her gifts and use them for the good of others.
+ describe how David is an example of someone who developed his talents and used them for good.
+ appreciate the abilities of others and encourage them to use their talents.

Word Your Child Should Know
+ psalm

Key Terms for Your Information
+ talents—a monetary unit used in New Testament times; natural gifts or abilities
+ anoint—to pour oil on someone as a sign that the person is chosen by God

CHAPTER 2   GRADE

God Speaks to Us in Scripture

FOCUS: In this chapter, you will be helping your child to understand that God reveals his love in the Old Testament and the New Testament.

Catholics are encouraged to direct their journey toward the Kingdom of God by reading, knowing, understanding, and loving Sacred Scripture. As parents, we have the privilege and duty of leading our children along the way, but we can do this only if we ourselves are traveling it as well. Nourished and sustained by Scripture, we can share with others the life-giving Word of God and encourage in them a love and respect for the Scriptures. The words of Saint Paul give wise counsel:

> But you, remain faithful to what you have learned and believed, because you know from whom you learned it, and that from infancy you have known [the] sacred scriptures, which are capable of giving you wisdom for salvation through faith in Christ Jesus.
>
> *2 Timothy 3:14–15*

Scripture in This Chapter
Psalm 50:15   God Our Rescuer
Wisdom 15:1   Good and True God
Philippians 4:5   Kindness of God
1 John 4:16   God in Us

Catechism of the Catholic Church
102–104, 131–133

In this chapter, help your child to
+ explain that the Old Testament and the New Testament are the two parts of Sacred Scripture.
+ discuss how Sacred Scripture is God's message that reveals his love for us.
+ describe some of the messages of Scripture.
+ explain that we show reverence for God's Word through symbolic actions,
+ explain that our faith community believes in the Bible as God's Word among us.

Words Your Child Should Know
+ Hebrews
+ inspired
+ prophet

Key Terms for Your Information
+ Israelites—God's Chosen People; the Jews
+ enthron—to put in a place of honor

PART 2 Working With Your Children and *Christ Our Life*   **45**

Jesus Calls Us to Worship

FOCUS: In this chapter, you will be helping your child to understand that we worship with Jesus by imitating his life of prayer, loving service, and sacrifice.

Jesus' life of service on earth ended with the ultimate sacrifice—the sacrifice of his life. The Resurrection was the sign that the Father accepted his Son's sacrifice. It is the Father's confirmed approval of Jesus' work on earth.

If we are to offer ourselves as a living sacrifice that is holy and pleasing to God, we must live our lives following the way led by Jesus. Through the sacraments, we receive a share in God's own life and are strengthened to do what is pleasing to God.

Scripture in This Chapter
Mark 1:35–39   Jesus Leaves Capernaum.
Mark 8:22–26   Jesus Cures the Man Who Was Blind.

Catechism of the Catholic Church
1174–1175, 1189, 1996–1997, 2009–2011

In this chapter, help your child to
+ explain that through Baptism, Jesus gives us the grace to follow him more closely.
+ locate and interpret Scripture passages.
+ identify the Sacraments of Initiation, Healing, and at the Service of Communion.
+ recognize in the New Testament how Jesus worshiped the Father.
+ understand that we worship God through prayer, loving service, and sacrifice.

Words Your Child Should Know
+ Eastern Catholic Church
+ liturgy
+ Liturgy of the Hours
+ rite
+ Sacraments at the Service of Communion
+ Sacraments of Healing
+ Sacraments of Initiation

Key Terms for Your Information
+ character—a permanent spiritual mark showing that a person has a new relationship with Jesus and a special standing in the Church
+ grace—the gift of sharing in the life of God
+ sacraments—sacred
+ Scripture reference—the code that refers to a passage in the Bible
+ verses (of Scripture)—the phrases or sentences in the Bible that are marked by numbers in a chapter

Scripture Is God's Saving Word

FOCUS: In this chapter, you will be helping your child to understand that God, the author of the Bible, speaks to us through it.

God has seen fit to preserve his gradual self-revelation to his Chosen People for all time. The Holy Scriptures were so inspired by God that God can truly be considered their principal author. God guided the minds and hearts of the human authors as they wrote those truths he wanted others to know. God did this in accordance with the personality of each author, while still allowing that person to fully exercise free will. Thus, the human authors used their own languages, their own images, and their own history to reveal God's plan.

How privileged we are to frequently hear and read the Word of God! This Word is living and active, leading to holiness those who are open to it.

Scripture in This Chapter
Psalm 119:105, 107   Your Word Is a Lamp.
Psalm 136:1–7   God's Love Endures Forever.

Catechism of the Catholic Church
104, 122, 129

In this chapter, help your child to
+ describe what *biblical inspiration* means.
+ explain that the Holy Spirit helps us to understand God's Word.
+ identify and describe the four categories of Old Testament books: Law, historical, Wisdom Literature, and prophetic.
+ explain that the books of the Bible differ in intention and style and reflect the backgrounds of their human authors.
+ locate passages in Scripture.

Words Your Child Should Know
+ Interpretation
+ Law
+ Pentateuch
+ revelation
+ Torah
+ tradition

Key Terms for Your Information
+ inspiration—God's guidance of the human authors and editors of the Bible that allowed them to pass on those truths God wanted to teach us
+ Sacred Scripture—the Bible

Friendship with Jesus— Jesus the Son of Man

FOCUS: In this chapter, you will be helping your child to understand that Jesus is truly human and that he invites us to friendship with him.

Sharing a meal is a universal sign of friendship. The word companion comes from two Latin words that mean "with bread." A companion is someone with whom we break bread. Christ wants to be our companion, our friend. He does not force us, but leaves us free to choose whether or not we will open our hearts to him.

Friendship with the living God is more than we dare to dream. The distance between God's transcendence and our limitations would seem to prevent friendship. To make matters worse, human sin widens the gap between the all-holy God and us. God, however, bridged that gap and showed the immensity of his love by becoming human, walking among us, living like us, giving us a sacred meal to celebrate with him, and ultimately, suffering and dying for us. What more proof of our Creator's love for us do we need?

Scripture in This Chapter
John 15:12–17 I Call You Friends.
Revelation 3:20 Jesus Stands at the Door.

Catechism of the Catholic Church
470–478

In this chapter, help your child to
+ discuss that Jesus is truly human and like us in all ways except sin.
+ describe how the sacraments keep us in touch with Jesus.
+ describe the privileges and responsibilities that are part of friendship.
+ identify some of Jesus' friends in Scripture.
+ understand that a relationship with Jesus is an essential part of life.
+ identify prayer and action as two ways to know Jesus better.

Key Terms for Your Information
+ faith—believing and trusting when one doesn't understand
+ Scripture—sacred writings containing God's Revelation; the written testimony of people's beliefs
+ Tradition—the Revelation of God through truths handed down by the Church from the time of the apostles in teachings, liturgy, writings, and the lives of Christians

Tracing Our Roots

FOCUS: In this chapter, you will be helping your child to understand that the Church, which began with God's Chosen People, includes all the living and dead who have responded to God's love.

All of us who share the faith can trace our spiritual roots back to not only Jesus and the apostles, but also Father Abraham, who first dealt with the Lord as a loving friend and lived a life of faith in God.

We belong to a faith family, a worshiping community that believes the same words, participates in the same sacraments, and serves the same Lord. Together we are pilgrims on a journey to the Father. In the Body of Christ, we are united not only with the living members of the Church but also with those believers who have gone before us into the next world.

Scripture in This Chapter
Acts of the Apostles 2:1–13 The Coming of the Holy Spirit
Luke 18:16 Let the Children Come to Me.

Catechism of the Catholic Church
120–133, 836–848, 2041, 2043, 2180

In this chapter, help your child to
+ recall important people and events in salvation history.
+ demonstrate greater familiarity with the books of the Bible.
+ express a commitment to read and pray the Bible.
+ identify who belongs to the Church and to the Communion of Saints, pray for the souls in purgatory, and pray to the saints.
+ describe what it means to be a good member of the Catholic Church.

Words Your Child Should Know
+ Buddhism
+ Islam (Muslims)
+ justification
+ New Testament
+ Old Testament
+ Paschal Mystery
+ purgatory
+ salvation history
+ Scripture

Key Term for Your Information
+ saint—a person in heaven who practiced virtue while on earth

God Is Our Father

FOCUS: In this chapter, you will be helping your child to understand that God loves, cares for, and forgives us like a good father.

In giving us human life, God has given us something of himself, for each person is made in God's image. God has not only loved us into life, but also continually invites us to love in return and to grow in our relationship with him and with others. We belong to God. We are loved by God and are filled with God's own life and love. God calls us to share truth and love with one another and to work for the betterment of a world where many still hunger for recognition and respect of their human rights.

When we are fully present in our experiences and in our relationship with the Lord we are, as Saint Irenaeus put it, fully alive—the glory of God. To recognize with humility the wonder of the gifts the Lord has given us as members of the human family, to develop our abilities and share them with one another—these are, in themselves, praise and thanksgiving to the Father.

Scripture in This Chapter
Genesis 1:26–27 God Made Humans in His Own Image.
Matthew 6: 25–34 Dependence on God

Catechism of the Catholic Church
302–303, 355–357, 2793

In this chapter, help your child to
+ explain that each person is unique.
+ determine his or her own special qualities and draw pictures to illustrate them.
+ express his or her belief in God's care for people today.
+ describe how God is a good father.
+ identify people who convey God's love.

Key Terms for Your Information
+ angels—messengers of God
+ guardian angels—angels who care for people

Jesus Lives in His Church

FOCUS: In this chapter, you will be helping your child to understand that through Baptism, we become members of the Church and share in God's life.

Through Baptism, each of us becomes a new creation, a new person in Christ. Each person in the Church is intimately bound to God and to others. The more everyone cooperates and supports others, the more the Church bears witness to the unity of the Body of Christ.

All the members of Christ's mystical body are called to use their gifts to serve God and his people freely, imitating Jesus, who said he "did not come to be served but to serve" (Matthew 20:28). Under Christ, the invisible head of the Church, members labor in different ways as fellow workers with God.

Scripture in This Chapter
Ephesians 2:19–22 One in Christ
1 John 3:1 Children of God

Catechism of the Catholic Church
551–552, 882, 1213, 1234–1243

In this chapter, help your child to
+ identify himself or herself as a child of God and as part of the People of God through Baptism.
+ explain that the community's love and support are expressed in the baptismal ceremony.
+ describe parts and symbols of the rite of Baptism.
+ identify the leaders of the Church.

Words Your Child Should Know
+ bishop
+ Confirmation
+ faith
+ original sin
+ priest
+ sacrament

Key Terms for Your Information
+ apostle—one of the first leaders of the Church
+ Baptism—the sacrament that gives us God's life, makes us members of the Church, and takes away sin
+ Church—the group of people who believe and follow Jesus
+ Eucharist—the sacred, sacrificial meal shared by Catholics; the sacrament in which we receive Christ and are helped by him
+ godparents—the people who promise to help parents bring up a baptized child as a Christian

We Are God's Holy People

FOCUS: In this chapter, you will be helping your child to understand that God calls us to be holy—to know, love, and serve him.

God not only calls us to be his holy people, but he gave us his Son to be "the way and the truth and the life." Jesus showed us the way by becoming one of us, by living a life of holiness among us, and by teaching us. He gave us the Church and his Holy Spirit, both of which continue to guide us on our journey, strengthen us, and form us into God's holy people.

Through Baptism, we are united with God and begin to live a new life in Christ. The Holy Spirit incorporates us into the family of the Church. Mindful of our call to holiness, we come together as God's people for each Sunday's liturgy. In and through Christ Jesus, the Church brings us to the Father.

Scripture in This Chapter

John 14:7–11 Jesus and Philip's Conversation at the Last Supper
Acts 2:42–47 The Communal Life of the Early Church
1 Peter 1:15–16 Peter Calls the Church to Be Holy.

Catechism of the Catholic Church

823–825, 2013

In this chapter, help your child to

+ describe what it means to be holy and name ways that the Church leads us to holiness.
+ relate following God's call to finding happiness.
+ tell the stories of Saints Francis and Clare.
+ apply what he or she has learned about the goodness of creation and caring for others to his or her own lives.
+ ask himself or herself questions to examine his or her consciences.

Key Terms for Your Information

+ holy—being like God; full of love
+ sacrament—a meeting with Jesus that is a visible sign of God's love and that celebrates the gift of God's life

God Speaks to Us Through the Church

FOCUS: In this chapter, you will be helping your child to understand that the pope and bishops guide the Church.

The Holy Spirit teaches us to know Jesus through his Church, the People of God. The Church is composed of people of all races, ages, and callings. This visible Church publicly helps manifest the Kingdom of God here on earth.

As Catholics, we gladly acknowledge and respect those called to lead us to live in holiness. We listen with open hearts and minds to the teachings of the pope and the bishops.

Scripture in This Chapter

Matthew 16:13–19 Peter's Confession About Jesus
John 21:1–17 The Appearance to the Seven Disciples

Catechism of the Catholic Church

552, 880–885

In this chapter, help your child to

+ describe how God speaks through the Holy Spirit working in the Church.
+ discuss how everyone in the Church has a role in spreading the Gospel message.
+ describe how, beginning with Peter, every pope has had the power to govern and teach the Church.
+ name the Holy Father and the local bishops, and explain their roles.

Key Terms for Your Information

+ authority—the right to make decisions and to command
+ bishop—the Church leader in a particular area who teaches and governs God's people
+ Church—the new People of God
+ council—a meeting of the pope and bishops from all over the world
+ deacon—ordained man that helps bishops and priests do work for the Church
+ diocese—the territory and churches for which a bishop is responsible
+ preside—to lead people in the celebration of the Eucharist
+ synod—a meeting of the pope and certain bishops to discuss a particular topic
+ Vatican Council II—a meeting of bishops in Rome from 1962 to 1965

Baptism Unites Us with the Christian Community

FOCUS: In this chapter, you will be helping your child to understand that Baptism gives us a share in God's life and makes us members of the Church.

The Sacrament of Baptism cleanses us of original sin and totally transforms us so that we may enjoy a life of intimacy with God. Baptism initiates us into the community of faith, challenging us to help bring the entire human family into communion with Christ. As we celebrate the other sacraments, we are constantly reminded of how we are to live the life we received in Baptism. Saint Paul reminds us that Baptism has made us completely new in Christ. We have entered into his Paschal Mystery, his dying and rising. We have "put on" the Lord Jesus. Now, dead to sin and risen with him, we must live as God's children. (See Ephesians 4:22–24.)

Scripture in This Chapter
John 1:35–42　The First Disciples
John 3:5　Born of Water and the Spirit

Catechism of the Catholic Church
1212–1246, 1253–1258, 1265–1274

In this chapter, help your child to
+ explain that Baptism cleanses us of original sin.
+ discuss the use of sacramentals.
+ describe the Rite of Baptism.
+ list the characteristics of a Christian.
+ describe God's special love shown in Baptism.

Words Your Child Should Know
+ catechumen (KAT-uh-KYOO-muhn)
+ Rite of Christian Initiation of Adults (RCIA)
+ chrism
+ original sin

Key Terms for Your Information
+ anoint—to sign with blessed oil
+ conversion—turning from sin to new life in Christ
+ deacon—a man ordained by the bishop to proclaim God's Word, to assist in the liturgy, and to do works of charity
+ godparent—a witness to Baptism who assumes the responsibility for helping the baptized person along the road of Christian life
+ oil of catechumens—oil blessed by the bishop used to anoint catechumens and strengthen them on their path of initiation
+ sacramentals—words, actions, or objects blessed by the Church that bring us closer to God

---

Everything God Created Is Good

FOCUS: In this chapter, you will be helping your child to understand that God created the world and all creatures and made us stewards of the world.

God's love is creative. Not only did God create everything from nothing, but God continues creative activity by bringing forth new life and sustaining all things. God invites us to participate in this creative love by using our gifts carefully and with innovation to benefit the good of all. As stewards of creation, we are tasked to protect and care for all life and the natural resources of the earth, preserving these gifts through conservation, reclamation, recycling, and other ecological methods.

With the help of science, industry, and art, we are to develop the resources of the earth, design new products, and improve the circumstances of life for all people. God, in divine power and love, not only created a beautiful world for our use and enjoyment, not only bestowed on us wonderful powers of body and mind, but also permits us to share in the very work of creation.

Scripture in This Chapter
Genesis 1:1—2:25　The Two Creation Stories
Psalm 139:14　Wonderful Are All Your Works.

Catechism of the Catholic Church
280, 283, 288–289, 294, 2415–2418

In this chapter, help your child to
+ summarize the biblical stories of Creation and explain that they are intended to teach religious truths, not scientific or historical facts.
+ explain what it means to be made in God's image.
+ describe our responsibility to use the gifts of the earth justly and creatively.
+ describe creation as a gift from God.
+ differentiate between right ways and wrong ways to care for God's creation.

Words Your Child Should Know
+ free will
+ stewardship

Key Terms for Your Information
+ evolution—a slow, continual change from a lower form of life to a higher, more complicated form
+ intellect—ability to learn, to understand, and to reason

Scripture: A Portrait of Jesus—Jesus the Messiah

FOCUS: In this chapter, you will be helping your child to understand that Scripture, God's inspired Word—especially the Gospels—helps us to know Jesus.

Decades after the Resurrection, the existing written and oral traditions of the sayings and works of Jesus were compiled into the Gospels. Under the guidance of the Holy Spirit, each evangelist shaped the Good News with a unique style and emphasis for a particular group of people. The Gospels are inexhaustible treasures that bring us closer to the Lord of life. Through the Gospels, we find the way to a full human life.

Scripture in This Chapter
John 20:30–31 Jesus the Messiah
John 21:25 Jesus' Deeds

Catechism of the Catholic Church
81–82; 124–127

In this chapter, help your child to
* describe the purpose of the Gospels and how they came to be written.
* identify the books of the New Testament.
* describe the main message of the Gospels and recognize the features of the four Gospels.
* explain that the Bible is the inspired Word of God.
* identify and describe the books of the Bible.

Words Your Child Should Know
* evangelist   * synoptic

Key Terms for Your Information
* Acts of the Apostles—book in the New Testament that describes the early Christian community
* Book of Revelation—last book in the New Testament that encourages persecuted Christians to maintain their faith and hope in Jesus
* New Testament—the 27 books of the second part of the Bible
* discourse—a long speech
* epistles— New Testament letters
* Gentile—a non-Jewish person
* Gospels—the four inspired books that give an account of the life and teachings of Jesus
* inspiration—the action of God moving the human authors of the Bible to communicate what he wanted made known

A Closer Look

FOCUS: In this chapter, you will be helping your child to understand that the Church—the community of disciples—is a herald of the Good News, a sacrament, an institution, a servant, and a mystical communion.

The Church is a community, a union of people. United in his Church, we each reflect what it is in our own lives. The Church has many aspects. As an institution, the Church has traditions, laws, and leaders. As mystical communion, we are members of the Body of Christ. As sacrament, we are signs of God's love. As herald, we are responsible for proclaiming the Good News. As servant, we are called to serve as Christ did. As a community of disciples, we declare our beliefs by professing the Creed and by living according to the teachings of Jesus and the Church.

Through the power of the Spirit, who came to remake us in Baptism and Confirmation, we increasingly assume the characteristics of the Church, and of Christ. The Spirit's grace renews the earth until that time when there will be a new heaven and a new earth and all of us, united in love, glorify God with one voice.

Scripture in This Chapter
Acts of the Apostles 1:24–26; 2:38; 2:46–47; 4:32; 5:42; 6:2–3; 11:28–29 The Experience of the Early Church.

Catechism of the Catholic Church
774–776, 787–791

In this chapter, help your child to
* describe the origins of the Church and the experience of the first Christian community.
* identify four ways that the early Christian community was one.
* name and explain the six models of the Church.
* relate the models of the Church to activities in the life of a parish.
* explain how the family can be thought of as the domestic church.

Words Your Child Should Know
* Pentecost
* canon law

Key Terms for Your Information
* domestic church—The family, the Christian home
* models—images or views of the Church proposed by theologian Avery Dulles

God Our Father Is Holy

FOCUS: In this chapter, you will be helping your child to understand that we worship God in church by words and actions.

History records the reaction of many people who have experienced God's holiness. Their awareness of the gulf between the human and the divine prompted them to acknowledge their sense of the sacred with reverent words and gestures.

Conscious of our human need to worship, people through the ages have set aside sacred space. Catholics gather to worship in the sacred space that we call "church." It is there that the Lord, who is totally other, makes himself available to us through his Son present in the Eucharist. We adore Christ present in the Blessed Sacrament and acknowledge our need for his mercy. We spend time with him, talk with him, listen to him, and rest in his presence. In this sacred space, we come to realize the great things the Almighty has done for us.

Scripture in This Chapter

Exodus 3:1–3 The Burning Bush
Exodus 33:7–23; 34:6–9 Moses' Intimacy with God

Catechism of the Catholic Church

1180–1186, 2691, 2809, 2811

In this chapter, help your child to

+ name ways to show reverence in God's presence.
+ describe how Jesus is present in the church building in a special way.
+ identify some of the important objects in a Catholic church and explain their purpose.
+ respond to God's presence in prayer.

Key Terms for Your Information

+ altar—the table on which the Eucharist is offered
+ Blessed Sacrament—the bread that has been consecrated by the priest at Mass
+ church—a sacred building where we worship
+ genuflect—to bend the right knee in adoration
+ holy—sacred; related to God
+ pew—a bench in church on which people sit
+ sanctuary—the space in church that is around the altar
+ sanctuary lamp—a light that burns continually when the Blessed Sacrament is present
+ tabernacle—a container in which the Blessed Sacrament is kept
+ worship—to praise God

God Speaks to Us

FOCUS: In this chapter, you will be helping your child to understand that Baptism is the beginning of a new way of life of service to others.

The Spirit of the Lord given to us at Baptism enlightens us and helps us see things as they really are. Saint John Chrysostom describes the new vision of those whose minds have been illumined by Christ:

> Whenever grace comes and drives out the darkness from our mind, we learn the exact nature of things; what frightened us before now becomes contemptible in our eyes. We no longer are afraid of death . . . nor are we afraid of poverty or disease or any such misfortune, because we know that we are on our way to a better life, which is impervious to death and destruction and is free from all such inequality.
>
> *Twelfth Baptismal Instruction*

With the light of Christ, we are set out on the path of love. We begin to see that Baptism is but the beginning of a new way of life, and we devote ourselves to deepening the bonds that unite us with God and with others.

Scripture in This Chapter

Mark 7:31–37 Cure of the Deaf Man

Catechism of the Catholic Church

102–105, 1503–1504

In this chapter, help your child to

+ explain that Baptism imparts grace to hear God's word and spread it to others.
+ describe how to use Scripture verses for prayer.
+ demonstrate a knowledge of Baptism and the Church.
+ propose actions that flow from Christian responsibility.
+ plan to use his or her gifts to help others

Words Your Child Should Know

+ New Testament
+ Old Testament
+ saint

God Called Mary

FOCUS: In this chapter, you will be helping your child to understand that Mary said yes to God.

From the Cross, Jesus gave us his Mother, Mary. We honor Mary with the Rosary. The basic prayer of the Rosary is the Hail Mary. The repetition of the Hail Marys is a spiritual canticle as we meditate on the mysteries of the Rosary. Beginning with the Annunciation, we contemplate Mary in the joyful, luminous, sorrowful, and glorious events of her life and the life of her Son.

As parents, we endeavor to deepen our own love for Mary so that we may be better able to fulfill our mission of teaching the special love and veneration that Mary deserves as Mother of Christ, Mother of the Church, and our spiritual Mother.

Scripture in This Chapter
Luke 1:26–38 The Annunciation
John 19:26–27 Jesus Entrusts Mary to John.

Catechism of the Catholic Church
484, 494, 971

In this chapter, help your child to
+ tell the story of the Annunciation.
+ relate Mary's yes to God's call to his or her own response to God.
+ name ways that God calls us through messengers.
+ describe Mary's message at Fatima.
+ explain the significance of the beads of a rosary and pray the Rosary.

Words Your Child Should Know
+ Annunciation
+ Rosary
+ sacramental

Key Terms for Your Information
+ angel—a spiritual creature who brings a message from God
+ Gabriel—one of three archangels mentioned in the Bible (The others are Michael and Raphael.)
+ handmaid—a servant girl
+ *Gloria Patri*—the Latin name for the Glory Be to the Father
+ decade—set of ten
+ mystery—a joyful, luminous, sorrowful, or glorious event from the life of Mary, Jesus, or the Church that is prayed about during the Rosary

God Offers Us Eternal Life

FOCUS: In this chapter, you will be helping your child to understand that knowing and loving God leads to eternal life.

We grow spiritually when we surrender ourselves completely to God's loving care and when we listen to God speaking through the Spirit, Scripture, the Church, and all creation. Filled with the gifts God alone can give, we have the strength we need to become all that we can be.

Our faith flows from an awareness of God's goodness to us. We trust in the Lord, whose love is so great that he gives us not what we feel or think we need but what will truly benefit us. Belonging to Christ and living in his love can fill us with the same deep happiness that enabled the apostle Paul to give praise to God even in the midst of suffering.

Scripture in This Chapter
Matthew 13:44 Kingdom of Heaven Parable
John 14:2–3 A Place in the Father's House

Catechism of the Catholic Church
160–163, 871–873, 2611

In this chapter, help your child to
+ explain that faith empowers Christians to live as true children of God.
+ define the concept of eternal life.
+ describe ways to show Jesus' love and goodness through his or her life.
+ explain ways we live our Catholic faith.

Confirmation Is the Sacrament of the Holy Spirit

FOCUS: In this chapter, you will be helping your child to understand that in Confirmation, we celebrate the Holy Spirit within us and renew our baptismal commitment to witness to Jesus.

In the Sacrament of Confirmation, we celebrate the fullness of the Holy Spirit within us. We give evidence of the Spirit's influence in our lives by our attentiveness and responsiveness to Jesus Christ—for the role of the Holy Spirit is to testify to Jesus.

The Holy Spirit, the Spirit of Truth, helps us to understand the mystery of Christ—his fulfillment of the Scriptures and of the Father's will, his words and actions, his death and Resurrection. The better we understand Jesus, the deeper will be our love for him and the more effective will be our witness to him and our faith in his teachings. The presence of the Holy Spirit within us makes it possible for us to lead holy lives.

Scripture in This Chapter
Acts of the Apostles 1:6–8 You Will Be My Witnesses.
Acts of the Apostles 2:1–41 The Coming of the Spirit

Catechism of the Catholic Church
1285–1289, 1293–1321

In this chapter, help your child to
+ tell the story of the coming of the Holy Spirit at Pentecost.
+ recognize the significance of Confirmation as a means to strengthen faith.
+ describe the Rite of Confirmation and the responsibilities the sacrament imposes.
+ explain the meaning of the baptismal call to give witness.
+ suggest ways to help the Church, especially by supporting the missions.

Words Your Child Should Know
+ Advocate
+ missionary
+ Gifts of the Holy Spirit

Key Terms for Your Information
+ Pentecost—Jewish feast celebrating the giving of the Ten Commandments
+ sponsor—the Catholic who helps the person to be confirmed to know and to practice the faith
+ witness—person who shows by words and actions that he or she believes in Jesus

---

God Offers Love and Mercy

FOCUS: In this chapter, you will be helping your child to understand that from the time of the first human beings, sin entered the world and spread, destroying relationships.

We Christians know the story of the Fall, and we are aware of its pain and consequences. We see the effects of sin in a war-weary world. Within each of us there is a tendency toward sin. Yet this weakness is tragedy and triumph. For sin, the "happy fault" of Adam and Eve, has occasioned the most glorious outpouring of God's love and mercy—in the person of Jesus Christ, in the mystery of the empty tomb.

With generous love and mercy, God created us and sustains us through life's journey. In Genesis, we see the reality of sin and its destructive power, but we also see that we are never abandoned.

Scripture in This Chapter
Genesis 2:4—3:24; Genesis 4:1–16; Genesis 6—9; Genesis 11:1–9 How Sin Entered the World

Catechism of the Catholic Church
376, 388–390, 404, 410–412

In this chapter, help your child to
+ identify the evil effects of sin.
+ retell the biblical stories of how sin entered the world and spread.
+ explain that God's faithful love repeatedly offers us mercy and forgiveness as a means to peace.
+ identify ways of responding to failing and faults—both one's own and the faults of others.
+ identify the components of a good moral choice.

Words Your Child Should Know
+ conscience
+ sin

Key Terms for Your Information
+ ark—a place of security or refuge; while traditionally thought of as a boat, an ark can be a container that houses something of great importance, such as the Ark of the Covenant
+ consequence—something that happens following an action or a decision
+ reconciliation—healing of the separation (caused by sin) between self and God and self and others.
+ sanctifying grace—God's life in us
+ ziggurat—a temple similar in appearance to a terraced pyramid.

The World Jesus Lived In— Jesus the Nazarene

FOCUS: In this chapter, you will be helping your child to understand that Jesus was a Jewish man who lived in first century Palestine under Roman occupation.

Before Jesus became the glorified risen Lord, he was a man of flesh and blood who experienced life much as we do. The environment in which Jesus lived influenced his teachings and his stories as well as the way people reacted to him. An understanding of the religious, social, and political world at the time of Jesus makes for a better understanding of him and his teachings. It brings the Gospel to life.

Jesus' life was limited to a particular time and place. Yet his message is for all people who would ever live on earth. Our challenge is to communicate his universal truths and values to the contemporary world. As our children become familiar with the world Jesus experienced and relate it to their own lives, Jesus becomes more real to them, someone who understands their situations and is keenly interested in them.

Scripture in This Chapter
Deuteronomy 6:4–5 The Lord Alone is God.
John 1:14 The Word Became One of Us.

Catechism of the Catholic Church
122, 423

In this chapter, help your child to
+ describe the social, geographical, political, and religious situation in Palestine at the time of Jesus.
+ explain how Jesus practiced his religion.
+ identify some of the Jewish feasts.
+ describe what daily life was like in Jesus' time.
+ apply knowledge of the world Jesus lived in to passages of the Gospels.

Words Your Child Should Know
+ Gentiles   + Pharisees

Key Terms for Your Information
+ Passover—the Jewish feast at the end of spring that commemorates the Exodus
+ Pentecost—the Jewish feast of the Ten Commandments and of thanksgiving for the harvest
+ Tabernacles (Sukkot)—the fall Jewish feast of seven or eight days to recall the time the Israelites lived in tents (booths) in the desert

A People of Prayer

FOCUS: In this chapter, you will be helping your child to understand that the Church deepens its relationship with God through prayer, especially the Eucharistic Liturgy and the Liturgy of the Hours.

One who loves needs to be with the beloved, to share thoughts and aspirations, and to listen to others. In the covenantal relationship between God and us, this openness, this sharing and listening, is called prayer. The more one prays, the greater is the desire for prayer, for ever-deeper union. The themes of prayer are beautifully expressed in the Book of Psalms. Like every Jewish person, Jesus prayed the psalms with Mary and Joseph at home, in the synagogue, and in the Temple. Jesus used psalms in his teachings and prayer. Through them, he communicated continuously with his Father.

The first Christians met for prayer at regular hours to sanctify all their activities. The Church came to consider these moments as extensions of the Eucharist. And so evolved the official prayer of the Church—the Liturgy of the Hours.

Scripture in This Chapter
Matthew 5:44 Pray For Those Who Persecute You.
Matthew 6:9 The Our Father
Mark 1:35 Jesus Went Off to Pray.
Luke 11:9 Ask and You Will Receive.

Catechism of the Catholic Church
1070–1073, 1174–1178, 1343–1344, 1396, 2607–2616

In this chapter, help your child to
+ identify and explain two types of prayer: communal and personal.
+ identify models of prayer: Jesus, Mary, and the saints.
+ assess his or her own prayer habits and practice habits that can improve his or her prayer life.
+ describe the format of the Liturgy of the Hours.

Words Your Child Should Know
+ Liturgy of the Hours
+ prayer
+ liturgy

God Shares His Life with Us

FOCUS: In this chapter, you will be helping your child to understand that through Baptism, we become children of God and Christians.

Through Baptism, we die to sin and receive a share in God's life. We have faith in Christ and no longer live our own life, but live with the life of Christ. The Spirit incorporates us into the family of the Church. This newness of life calls us to a radical change and requires that we live by the Spirit with unshakable fidelity.

The difficulty of living up to our dignity as baptized Christians prompted Saint Paul to give us signs by which we can tell if we are guided by the Spirit—"love, joy, peace, patience, kindness, generosity, faithfulness, gentleness, self-control." (Galatians 5:22) Mindful of our sinfulness, as well as of our high dignity and privilege, the priest or deacon prays during the Preparation of the Gifts:

> By the mystery of this water and wine may we come to share in the divinity of Christ, who humbled himself to share in our humanity.

Scripture in This Chapter

John 8:12 Jesus, the Light of the World

Catechism of the Catholic Church

1213, 1217–1222, 1234–1243

In this chapter, help your child to

+ identify water as a gift from God and be concerned about its proper use and care.
+ explain that water has a religious symbolic value.
+ name the major parts of the Baptism ritual.
+ appreciate the new life received at Baptism.
+ name ways they can share the light of Christ received at Baptism.

Words Your Child Should Know

+ Baptism   + Christian
+ Church

Key Terms for Your Information

+ Chi-Rho (key-ROE)—a symbol of Christ formed from the first letters of the Greek word *Christos*. The Chi (X) is superimposed on the Rho (P).
+ godparent—someone who promises at a person's Baptism to help that person be a Christian
+ saint—someone who loved like Jesus and is in heaven

Jesus Shows Us How to Love God Our Father

FOCUS: In this chapter, you will be helping your child to understand that when we obey God's commandments and love God with all our hearts, we are happy.

Jesus' mission on earth was to show us the Father's love and to bring us to him. Jesus showed us how to keep the Father's Word and how to pray. Above all, prayer is listening to God. Prayer strengthens our relationship with God. A prayerful attitude makes us aware of what the Lord has done for us. Our daily prayer is a continuation of the gift of love we offer to the Father at each Mass. As we praise God's name for that love, our lives are shaped by Christ's gift of himself, which unites us to God and to one another.

Basically, the Christian life consists of listening and responding to God as Jesus taught. To live as a Christian is to believe that the Father's love is at work in everything and to return his love by doing the things that please him. As we follow Christ, we experience the joy that comes from above, the joy that no one can take from us.

Scripture in This Chapter

Psalm 139:1–5 God's Watchfulness
Mark 12:30 Love of God
John 15:10–11 Fullness of Joy

Catechism of the Catholic Church

1166, 2143–2144, 2173, 2599, 2765

In this chapter, help your child to

+ explain that God satisfies our longing for happiness.
+ explain the first three commandments of God.
+ discuss how he or she can respond to God by prayer throughout the day.
+ explain why we use God's name reverently.
+ describe how celebrating the Lord's Day manifests love.

Words Your Child Should Know

+ commandments
+ Lord's Day
+ Ten Commandments

Key Terms for Your Information

+ Abba—a Hebrew word for *Father*
+ hallowed—holy
+ reverence—a great respect for someone or something

Jesus Calls Us to Follow

FOCUS: In this chapter, you will be helping your child to understand that Jesus called apostles, disciples, and us to carry on his work.

When Jesus called his apostles to walk in his way, he did not hide the sufferings and persecutions they would face.

> "You will be hated by all because of my name, but whoever endures to the end will be saved."
>
> *Matthew 10:22*

We have accepted Jesus as our Way, and we follow him. Jesus' call always leads to changes in our lives. We ask his help in rearranging the patterns of our lives into ones of holiness just as Saint Paul did. By loving Christ and growing in the knowledge of God's ways, we learn to love one another more.

Scripture in This Chapter
Mark 1:16–20 Jesus Called the Apostles.
Luke 10:1–2 Jesus Called Disciples.
Acts of the Apostles 9:1–19 Saul's conversion

Catechism of the Catholic Church
858–859, 873, 1506

In this chapter, help your child to
+ describe how Jesus called the apostles and disciples.
+ explain that all Christians are called by Jesus to spread the Good News and that some are called to follow him in a special way as priests, deacons, sisters, or brothers.
+ describe the conversion story of Saul.
+ recall how various people in the Bible responded to God's call.

Word Your Child Should Know
+ synagogue

Key Terms for Your Information
+ apostles—the 12 men called to be leaders of the Church
+ disciples—the people called to follow Jesus and continue his work
+ Saul—Paul's Hebrew name
+ Paul—Saul's Roman name; the name by which he identifies himself
+ Damascus—a major center of Greco-Roman culture during the time of Paul
+ Ananias—disciple of Christ living in Damascus

We Are Called to Follow Jesus

FOCUS: In this chapter, you will be helping your child to understand that Jesus shows us how to love God and to love others.

The love of God the Father becomes visible in Jesus. The Gospels show Jesus meeting each person's needs, responding to each one's unique dignity and calling each to live more fully in his love. God's love for us asks for nothing less than a total response. We are to share that love with each person we encounter in our daily lives. Jesus tells us that we are to share God's goodness with all. We are to love one another with the power we receive from him.

At each Eucharist, we express our willingness to die with Christ so that others might live. In the opening prayer of liturgies and at pastoral or spiritual meetings, the Church prays for Christlike love:

> Lord, pour out on us the spirit of understanding, truth, and peace. Help us to strive with all our hearts to know what is pleasing to you, and when we know your will, make us determined to do it.

Scripture in This Chapter
Matthew 9: 18–25 Raising of Jairus's Daughter
Mark 2:1-12 Healing of the Paralyzed Man

Catechism of the Catholic Church
1882–1885, 1889, 2447

In this chapter, help your child to
+ discuss how Jesus expressed his concern for people by relieving their sufferings.
+ explain that as Christians, we are called upon to show concern for others and try to relieve suffering.
+ explain the transforming effects of forgiveness.
+ explain that Jesus prayed to his Father.
+ explain the significance of the Lord's Prayer as a prayer taught by Jesus.

Key Terms for Your Information
+ hallowed—blessed; treated in a holy way
+ trespass—sin, fault, hurtful action

The Eucharist Is the Center of Christian Life

FOCUS: In this chapter, you will be helping your child to understand that in the Eucharist, Jesus offers himself to the Father and gives himself to us in the form of bread and wine.

The appearances of bread and wine signify the nourishing value of the Sacrament of the Eucharist. By means of the Eucharist, we are truly able to live a life in Christ. Christ comes to us as our food, communicating his life in a way that enables us to live in his love. The Eucharist brings us to a reverent awareness of Jesus' power within us. We begin to walk in spiritual communion with Christ, conscious that we have been chosen to live in God's presence.

Scripture in This Chapter
Psalm 145 The Hand of the Lord Feeds Us.
1 Corinthians 11:23–26 Institution of the Eucharist

Catechism of the Catholic Church
1322–1323, 1333, 1337, 1346–1355, 1366–1368

In this chapter, help your child to
+ explain how the Mass is our Passover meal.
+ describe how the Eucharist celebrates the Paschal Mystery and nourishes our spiritual life.
+ recall how to prepare for Holy Communion.
+ describe how the Blessed Sacrament can be taken to those who are sick and aged.
+ explain how Jesus is honored in exposition and benediction.
+ identify the sacred vessels, vestments, and roles of the Mass.

Words Your Child Should Know
+ Passover   + Real Presence

Key Terms for Your Information
+ benediction—a blessing given at the end of a eucharistic devotion
+ exposition—time when the Blessed Sacrament in a monstrance or ciborium is honored on the altar
+ fasting—not eating or drinking anything except water and medicine
+ monstrance—the sacred vessel with a metal holder used to expose the Blessed Sacrament
+ mortal sin—serious sin that separates us from God and from the Church
+ paschal lamb—the lamb whose blood saved the Israelites from death

Unit 1 Review

FOCUS: In this chapter, you will be helping your child to understand that God enters into history and carries out the divine plan to save all people.

God made us in his own image and likeness, to be his sons and daughters. If we keep our eyes on Christ throughout our lives, we will experience all that we are and all that we can be through him. We will give ourselves back to God, grateful for his loving kindness. Then our lives will truly be all that God meant them to be.

Cyril of Jerusalem, an early Christian writer who was noted for his masterly presentations on the meaning of our life in Christ, says,

> Just as a writing-pen or a dart has need of one to employ it, so also does grace have need of believing hearts. . . .
> It is God's part to confer grace, but yours to accept and guard it.
>
> *Catechetical Lectures 1*

Through daily prayer, we turn to God and express our desire to be God's very own. We remain open to God's grace, allowing divine love to lead us to God's kingdom.

Catechism of the Catholic Church
53, 287, 421, 759

In this chapter, help your child to
+ understand how Jesus relates to the year's theme.
+ review the signs of God's love in the lives of the Old Testament people studied in Unit 1.
+ review the people, things, and events through which God began unfolding his plan of love.

Key Term for Your Information
+ salvation history—story of God's love for his people, which shows how God entered into history and carried out the divine plan to save all people

The Early Life of Jesus—Jesus the Son of Mary and Joseph

FOCUS: In this chapter, you will be helping your child to understand that the Infancy Narratives reveal that Jesus is the Lord, the Son of God who saved us.

The evangelists presented the birth and infancy of Jesus not as bare historical facts, but as moving stories that touch our hearts. Skillfully, they shaped their narratives to their themes and their audience. In proclaiming Jesus as Lord to the Jewish Christians, the author of Matthew's Gospel weaves references to the Old Testament throughout his narratives. The author of Luke apparently writes for mainly Gentile Christians, teaching that salvation is extended to all people.

Those of us who have faith in the Resurrection perceive that the baby of Bethlehem, Mary's baby, is divine. We adore him and pray that the Holy Spirit who formed him in Mary's womb will form us into his image.

Scripture in This Chapter
Matthew 1:18—2:23 The Birth of Jesus.
Luke 1:5—2:25 Mary Says Yes to the Angel Gabriel. Jesus Is Born in Bethlehem.

Catechism of the Catholic Church
488, 490–499, 525–534

In this chapter, help your child to
+ explain the significance of the Infancy Narratives.
+ relate God's calling of Mary to his or her own call.
+ describe Mary's role in salvation history and her special graces.
+ apply the message of a symbol from the Infancy Narratives to his or her own life.

Words Your Child Should Know
+ inerrancy
+ doctrine
+ Infancy Narratives
+ Mother of God

Key Terms for Your Information
+ Assumption—the Catholic doctrine that Mary was assumed into heaven body and soul at the end of her life
+ Immaculate Conception—the Catholic doctrine that since the time of her conception, Mary was preserved from all sin, including original sin
+ virgin birth—the Catholic doctrine that Mary conceived and gave birth to Jesus solely through the power of the Holy Spirit

A People of Service

FOCUS: In this chapter, you will be helping your child to understand that the love of Christ is shown in the service that Church members give as they live the Beatitudes and perform works of mercy.

Jesus of Nazareth can be described as the God-man for others. He conveyed this idea when he told us his mission: "[T]he Son of Man did not come to be served but to serve." (Mark 10:45) Jesus showed us the royal dignity of serving. Jesus was God's love for men and women made visible and active. Jesus was incredibly loving and selfless, even to the point of laying down his life for others. He was unbelievably generous, as he shared with us eternal life. The awareness of God's lavish love fosters in us a desire to pass on this gift to those who come into our lives, to share in Christ's mission.

How do we, the members of the Body of Christ, carry on his mission? We are enriched supernaturally through Baptism with the gifts the Spirit gives to all members of the Church. Through the sacraments, Jesus transforms us into images of himself, and we too live as he did—for others.

Scripture in This Chapter
Matthew 5:3–10 The Beatitudes
Matthew 10:8 Without Cost You Are to Give.
Matthew 25:31–46 Corporal Works of Mercy
1 Corinthians 12:4–6 Many Gifts, One Spirit
Ephesians 2:19–22 Jesus is the Capstone.

Catechism of the Catholic Church
799–801, 876, 951, 1716–1719, 2003

In this chapter, help your child to
+ explain how Church members can be thought of as "living stones."
+ identify service and witness as ways of building Christ's Church.
+ reflect upon his or her gifts and desire to use them to serve others through his or her vocation.
+ identify and describe the Beatitudes and the Corporal Works of Mercy.
+ explain how every individual member of the Church can make a difference.

Words Your Child Should Know
+ witness
+ Corporal Works of Mercy
+ Beatitudes
+ vocation

God Speaks to Us

FOCUS: In this chapter, you will be helping your child to understand that God speaks to us in silence, in the Bible, and through helpers.

Genesis affirms the unique power of God's Word: "Then God said . . . and so it happened." Yet, throughout salvation history, men and women have hardened their hearts and resisted God's life-giving Word. The Lord does not force people to submit to his Word. God usually speaks quietly and tenderly, inviting those he has gifted with freedom to choose the path of love and peace.

God spoke to Elijah in the sound of the gentle breeze, not in the storm or the earthquake (1 Kings 19:9–13). Samuel heard the Lord in the quiet of the night (1 Samuel 3:1–18).

At each Eucharist, we celebrate God's Word in the Liturgy of the Word. We are nourished by the Word, which provides us with what we need to live as children of our heavenly Father. God reveals himself to us through his Word and his Church.

Scripture in This Chapter
1 Kings 19:9–13 God Speaks to Elijah.
Mark 9:37 The Greatest in the Kingdom

Catechism of the Catholic Church
105–107, 1880, 2717

In this chapter, help your child to
+ examine wonderful things in nature that take place silently.
+ recognize that silence promotes awareness of God and choose times of quiet to hear God speak.
+ understand that God speaks to us in a different way from the way people speak.
+ recall that the Bible is the Word of God. express reverence for God's Word.

Word Your Child Should Know
+ Bible

Key Term for Your Information
+ Elijah—Israelite prophet of the ninth century B.C.

Jesus Shows Us How to Love Others

FOCUS: In this chapter, you will be helping your child to understand that when we love others as Jesus did, we show our love for God.

To live a life deeply rooted in Christ is to see everything in the light of God's gracious love. Such a life prompts us to say with the psalmist, "How can I repay the Lord for all the good done for me?" (Psalm 116:12) Our eyes are opened to the needs of others as we listen and respond to God in the everyday happenings that reveal his presence and gifts. We see how we can relieve the needs of others by using our gifts, and we recognize and honor the gifts of others as we work together to bring Christ's love into our world.

As we try to live like Jesus, we recognize the needs of others and learn what is good, what God wants, and the perfect thing to do.

Scripture in This Chapter
Matthew 25:34–40 The Last Judgment
Mark 12:30–31 The Great Commandment
Luke 2:42–52 The Boy Jesus in the Temple

Catechism of the Catholic Church
531, 534, 678, 1823–1827

In this chapter, help your child to
+ understand that Jesus regards acts of love done for others as done for him.
+ explain Jesus' Great Commandment.
+ associate Jesus' obedience to his Father with the obedience he asks of us.
+ understand that obeying parents and others who are in charge is obeying God.
+ describe ways to make every day a kindness day.

Word Your Child Should Know
+ Great Commandment

CHAPTER 6   GRADE

We Believe in God

FOCUS: In this chapter, you will be helping your child to understand that God our Creator saved the Israelites from slavery to bring them to the Promised Land.

Indifference to the sufferings of another is a grave injustice and shows a lack of love. Words and gestures that reach out to others express love. God's promises assure us that his love will strengthen and guide us—leading us back to God when we have strayed. God's fidelity, in spite of human infidelity to God, demonstrates the wisdom of placing all our trust in God. As the psalmist reminds us, to trust in the Lord is to have chosen the right path.

> Trust in the LORD and do good
> that you may dwell in the
> land and live secure.
> *Psalm 37:3*

Scripture in This Chapter
Genesis 12:7; 15:13–16   God's Promise to Abraham
Exodus 3—15   The Plagues and the Exodus
Exodus 12:11–13   Preparation for the Passover Meal

Catechism of the Catholic Church
62, 193–195, 253–255, 1023–1029

In this chapter, help your child to
* recall the Apostles' Creed.
* describe God as three Persons in one and as our good Creator.
* explain that we can learn about God from his creation.
* describe how the Passover story shows God's faithfulness to his people.
* explain that God is true to his promises.

Words Your Child Should Know
* Apostles' Creed
* creed
* mystery
* Hebrews
* Israelites

Key Terms for Your Information
* Nicene Creed—the creed professed at Sunday Mass
* Passover—the feast celebrating the night when the Hebrews were led out of slavery in Egypt
* Red Sea—sea the Israelites crossed safely as they escaped Egypt
* Raamses—city in Egypt where the Israelites were held in slavery

CHAPTER 6   GRADE

Jesus Invites Us to Receive God's Mercy

FOCUS: In this chapter, you will be helping your child to understand that God forgives us in the Sacrament of Reconciliation.

Throughout the New Testament, we find Jesus calling God's people to change their way of life, to repent, and to believe that he has come to save them from their sins. How sad it is when those of us who most need his mercy and forgiveness assume that he is speaking to others. In the Gospel passage about the woman caught in adultery, we find the Pharisees questioning Jesus in order to trick him. Jesus responded to their question with a statement that caused all those present to examine their consciences. Having done so, each man realized his sinfulness and walked away.

This Gospel passage brings to mind two important aids to growth in friendship with Christ: a sensitive conscience and a love for the Sacrament of Reconciliation.

Scripture in This Chapter
Matthew 18:23 –25   The Unforgiving Servant
John 8:3–11   A Woman Caught in Adultery

Catechism of the Catholic Church
1448–1449, 1451, 1456, 1459, 1468–1469

In this chapter, help your child to
* describe the steps in celebrating the Sacrament of Reconciliation.
* explain that his or her conscience enables him or her to distinguish good from evil.
* explain that we should choose whatever our consciences recognize as good.
* experience Jesus' gift of forgiveness.
* discuss the special graces he or she receives from the Sacrament of Reconciliation.

Words Your Child Should Know
* examination of conscience
* mortal sin
* venial sin

Key Term for Your Information
* parable—a story that reveals a truth about God's kingdom through a comparison

Unit 1 Review

FOCUS: In this chapter, you will be helping your child to understand that we are called to worship through prayer and loving service.

We live by God's grace. Ever since the day of our Baptism, we have had the power to bring the image of Christ within us to life. Marked with the character of Christ in Baptism and Confirmation, we become most conscious of his presence and his gifts at Holy Communion. If we fix our gaze on Christ throughout life, we will experience all that we are and all that we have through him. We will give ourselves back to God by living lives of praise and thanksgiving for the ways his loving kindness is manifested to us. Our lives will truly be ones of joyful worship, united to the death and Resurrection of Jesus Christ our Savior.

> Just as a writing-pen or a dart has need of one to employ it, so also does grace have need of believing hearts. . . . It is God's part to confer grace, but yours to accept and guard it.
>
> *Cyril of Jerusalem, Catechetical Lectures 1*

Scripture in This Chapter
Psalm 139:1–5 The All-Knowing God
John 6:33,35,54–56 The Bread of Life

Catechism of the Catholic Church
2105–2106

In this chapter, help your child to
+ reflect on the key concepts in this unit.
+ evaluate how he or she puts the concepts in this unit into practice.
+ recall words and meanings related to worship and the Sacraments of Initiation.
+ describe key concepts and definitions learned in this unit.
+ participate in a prayer service.

Abraham Is Our Father in Faith

FOCUS: In this chapter, you will be helping your child to understand that Abraham made a covenant of faith with the one true God.

Abraham is a model of faith. He responded with obedience to whatever God asked of him. God rewarded Abraham's faith by renewing the covenant with him.

Through Baptism, we have entered into a covenant with God. We have been sanctified; however, we are called to give witness to that sanctification. Just as God encouraged Abraham to do his will, so God encourages us.

Scripture in This Chapter
Genesis 12, 15, 17, 22 God Calls Abraham.
Psalm 89:1–2,15–16,19,28 God's Faithfulness
James 2:14–24 Saint James Speaks About Faith.

Catechism of the Catholic Church
59–60, 144–146, 166, 762, 1080, 2100

In this chapter, help your child to
+ retell the story of Abraham's call.
+ explain that through Baptism, we have entered into God's covenant.
+ describe Abraham's faith and obedience.
+ evaluate their own ability to practice obedience.
+ explain that faith is expressed by service.

Words Your Child Should Know
+ Abraham
+ sacrifice
+ covenant

Key Terms for Your Information
+ Canaan—land located between Syria and Egypt that God promised to the descendants of Abraham
+ Chaldea—land through which Abraham journeyed when he moved from Ur to Haran
+ Chosen People—the descendants of Abraham
+ Euphrates—river that flows through the Fertile Crescent
+ Islam—along with Judaism and Christianity, a religion that professes belief in one God
+ Palestine—the land of Canaan; the Holy Land
+ Tigris—river that flows through the Fertile Crescent
+ Ur—city located in Chaldea (present-day Iraq) from which Abraham moved early in life

The Mission of Jesus— Jesus the Christ

FOCUS: In this chapter, you will be helping your child to understand that Jesus accepted his mission as Messiah at his baptism and was faithful to it during his temptation.

From time to time, we need distance from daily life in order to reflect and plan, and to renew our commitments. John the Baptist felt this need, for he prepared for his mission by living in the desert wilderness to strengthen himself for what was to come. Christ himself, in his humanity, felt the need to go into the wilderness to prepare for his mission as Messiah.

Aware of our needs, God invites us to share Jesus' desert experience when he says "Come away by yourselves to a deserted place and rest a while." (Mark 6:31)

Scripture in This Chapter
Matthew 3:1–17 John the Baptist
Matthew 4:1–11 Jesus is Tempted.

Catechism of the Catholic Church
535–540

In this chapter, help your child to
+ identify the roles of Jesus as prophet, priest, and king.
+ explain the significance of Jesus' baptism.
+ explain the significance of Jesus' temptation.
+ apply Jesus' experience of temptation to his or her own times of temptation.
+ identify types of sin and factors that lessen guilt.
+ define a good decision-making process.

Key Terms for Your Information
+ Christ—the anointed one; Messiah
+ epiphany—revelation or manifestation of God
+ king—one who has the greatest power and authority
+ mortal sin—a serious offense against God that destroys our relationship with him
+ original sin—the sin of Adam and Eve that is passed on to their descendants
+ priest—one who represents the people in offering sacrifice to God
+ prophet—one who hears and proclaims God's Word
+ sin—choosing to do what is wrong or omit what is good
+ temptation—person or thing that entices us to do what is wrong or omit what is good
+ venial sin—an offense that weakens our relationship with God

One in the Spirit

FOCUS: In this chapter, you will be helping your child to understand that the Church is one in faith, worship, governance, and charity.

Genuine unity involves love, as illustrated in the Blessed Trinity. In love, the Father eternally generates the Son; their perfect love is eternally expressed in a third Person, the Holy Spirit. This union in love among Father, Son, and Holy Spirit is so complete that they are one God while still being three distinct, divine Persons.

It is the love born of this oneness that Jesus wished to be the distinguishing mark of his disciples. The Church has clung to that oneness: oneness in doctrine, in worship, and in governance. Since God created Adam in his own image and breathed his breath of life into him, then God must be the model of spiritual union among his children and the Holy Spirit its source.

Scripture in This Chapter
+ Acts of the Apostles 4:32 The Christian Community
+ Ephesians 4:1–3 Unity in the Body
+ 1 Corinthians 12:12–20 One Body, Many Parts
+ John 17:21 That They All May Be One.

Catechism of the Catholic Church
791, 811–822, 834, 864

In this chapter, help your child to
+ define a mark of the Church.
+ describe the four ways that the Church is one.
+ describe how unity exists in the Church.
+ describe the importance of ecumenism.
+ express respect for other religious denominations, while being faithful to his or her own.
+ name practical techniques for resolving conflicts peacefully.

Words Your Child Should Know
+ Marks of the Church
+ one
+ catholic
+ holy
+ apostolic
+ ecumenism

Key Terms for Your Information
+ encyclical—a letter written by the pope to the universal church
+ charismatic gifts—Gifts of the Spirit that are to be used for the good of the entire Church

We Pray to God Our Father

FOCUS: In this chapter, you will be helping your child to understand that we listen and talk to God in many ways every day.

A person who prays enters into a love relationship with God. The listening aspect of prayer invites God to speak his thoughts, to let them influence our course of action. Our talking to God in prayer is a decision to enter into his presence and to expose the subtle ways we hinder God's action in our lives. In our relationship with God, prayer is the light that illuminates the dark corners of our being.

Prayer is a love exchange between God and us. We express our love for God by praising and thanking God, by begging for forgiveness, and by asking for all our needs. Prayer is a conscious opening up to God's presence in our lives and a recognition of God's hand in all that happens to us.

Scripture in This Chapter
1 Samuel 3   The Call of Samuel
Jeremiah 29:12   God Listens When We Pray.

Catechism of the Catholic Church
2559, 2628–2629, 2637, 2639, 2698

In this chapter, help your child to
+ know that God communicated with Samuel and continues to speak to human beings.
+ be aware of the importance of listening to God as well as speaking to God.
+ experience the presence of God in stillness.
+ pray various forms of prayer: praise, gratitude, petitions, and sorrow for sin.
+ realize that God should be thanked for his many gifts to us.
+ know appropriate prayers for the morning, for meals, and for the night.

Word Your Child Should Know
+ prayer

Key Terms for Your Information
+ bless—God's sending good things to people
+ Samuel—priest and prophet during the time of Israel's transition from judges to kings (10th century B.C.)
+ praise—to tell a person how great he or she is
+ psalm—a song-prayer in the Bible

We Give Love to Others

FOCUS: In this chapter, you will be helping your child to understand that we show love when we are kind, respectful, honest, and truthful.

When we sincerely follow every impulse of the Holy Spirit, our love embraces all of God's children. Embracing pure love helps us to cherish the good in another person. It enables us to regard that person as Christ and to treat him or her with utmost respect. It inspires commitment to that person.

Courtesy, the habit of treating others with deference and respect, flows from and nurtures an appreciation for the dignity of each person. The daily life of a Christian is dedicated to showing this respect for others. United with Christ, we gather for our eucharistic celebration and recall God's goodness; we admit our failure to love God in our brothers and sisters, and ask for mercy. The Eucharist helps us recognize God's presence in each member of the Christian community who joins us in worshiping the Father.

Scripture in This Chapter
1 John 4:16   Union in Love

Catechism of the Catholic Church
2318–2319, 2401, 2415, 2464

In this chapter, help your child to
+ name ways to treat things with respect and people with kindness.
+ name different ways to show respect.
+ explain ways to show love for others.
+ understand that he or she brings God's love to others when he or she is truthful.

Key Terms for Your Information
+ courteous—respectful and polite
+ honest—respecting what belongs to others; fair
+ precious—very special and good
+ truthful—telling what is real

God Is Powerful and Loving

FOCUS: In this chapter, you will be helping your child to understand that God shows power and love by sending manna and giving the Law.

Brought to Egypt by a famine in their own country, the Israelites were favored at first, but were eventually reduced to slavery. Led by Moses, they escaped from Egypt and fled to the Sinai desert. There God miraculously fed them and in various ways, showed love and care for these people chosen as his own. Finally, God united the Israelites to himself in a solemn Covenant. (Exodus 19:5)

We can see the parallel in our own lives: God choosing us through Baptism, delivering us from the slavery of sin, feeding us with the Bread of Heaven, continually showing love and care for us, and binding us in a covenant of love.

Scripture in This Chapter

+ Exodus 10—15:21 Crossing of the Red Sea
+ Exodus 16:1–35 God Fed the Israelites with Manna.
+ Exodus 19–24 The Covenant at Mount Sinai
+ Psalm 136 Hymn of Thanksgiving
+ John 6:51 Jesus, the Bread of Life

Catechism of the Catholic Church

218–221, 1334, 2060–2061

In this chapter, help your child to

+ tell the story of how God saved the Israelites from Pharaoh's army.
+ know that he or she can trust God in times of need.
+ respond to God's love with prayer and obedience to God's will.
+ describe what a covenant is.
+ name ways that he or she keeps the covenant God made with us at Baptism.

Words Your Child Should Know

+ covenant
+ worship

Key Terms for Your Information

+ manna—breadlike substance that God sent to the Israelites in the desert
+ Mount Sinai—mountain where God revealed himself to Moses and gave him the Ten Commandments

We Worship God

FOCUS: In this chapter, you will be helping your child to understand that we worship God by praying and through service, but especially through the Eucharist.

Saint Augustine expressed our innate need to revere and serve God when he stated, "You have made us for Yourself, and our heart is restless until it rests in You." (Confessions, Book I, Chapter 1) Every person longs to satisfy the divine call to intimacy. No amount of wealth or prestige, no number of friends or accomplishments, can ever remove our need for God. It is impossible to be truly happy unless we are living in an intimate relationship with our Creator.

God, in the mystery of divine love, draws us daily into a deeper union. God's spirit is at work within and around us, inviting us to praise him and to acclaim his greatness. We worship God in the liturgy by singing joyful praise and by rendering acts of loving service. We bless God for his gifts and use them to glorify God's name.

Scripture in This Chapter

Exodus 20:24 Sacrificial Offerings to the Lord
Hosea 6:6 Love as the Truest Offering

Catechism of the Catholic Church

1366–1368, 2099–2100, 2659–2660

In this chapter, help your child to

+ explain that worship is the human response to God's greatness and holiness.
+ describe worship as fulfilling our desire to enjoy an intimate relationship with God.
+ explain that Jesus' sacrifice on the cross was the only perfect sacrifice.
+ describe how to make each day a gift of love.
+ identify ways to honor God through lives of praise and loving service.

Word Your Child Should Know

+ adore

Key Term for Your Information

+ worship—honor and praise given to God; our response to God's greatness and love

We Come Together to Celebrate

FOCUS: In this chapter, you will be helping your child to understand that the Eucharist, a thanksgiving celebration, begins with praise and a penitential rite.

Christ is in our midst as we celebrate Mass and make it the center of our lives as Christians. Through the complete self-giving of Christ at Mass, we are made holy, and we give the Father our greatest act of worship because we offer ourselves with Jesus. Acknowledging our complete dependence on God and realizing God's goodness, we praise and thank God for the great love shown in the mystery of our salvation.

As living members of Christ's Body, the Church, we participate fully and actively in the celebration of the Eucharist with our whole being. As we share in the Eucharist, we pray that through the Holy Spirit, we will grow in unity with our risen Lord and in love for all God's people.

Scripture in This Chapter
Matthew 3:3 Prepare the Way of the Lord.
Matthew 5:23–24 Leave Your Gift at the Altar.

Catechism of the Catholic Church
1168–1173, 1345–1355, 1391, 1396

In this chapter, help your child to
+ explain why the Eucharist is a celebration.
+ identify the parts of the Introductory Rites.
+ discuss ways to make his or her participation in the Eucharist meaningful.
+ participate more fully at the beginning of the Eucharist.
+ understand the meaning of the prayers of the Introductory Rites.

Words Your Child Should Know
+ Eucharistic Liturgy
+ liturgical year
+ penitential rite
+ Sacramentary

Key Term for Your Information
+ Ordinary Time—the 33 or 34 weeks outside the year's major seasons

Jacob Is Chosen by God

FOCUS: In this chapter, you will be helping your child to understand that the Covenant promises were passed on through Jacob.

God quite obviously chooses some individuals and bestows on them special gifts of love. However, we know that God infinitely loves each human person, and wills that each one of us enjoy eternal happiness with him. We all can depend on God to give us what is needed to achieve this eternal blessing. All who have been joined through the waters of Baptism to the death and Resurrection of Jesus can consider themselves among the chosen, the elect. They can rightly join the psalmist in praise and thanksgiving:

> How can I repay the LORD
>   for all the good done for me?
> *Psalm 116:12*

The answer can be found in Jesus' teachings throughout the Gospels. He asks his chosen ones to live as true sons and daughters of their heavenly Father. He asks them to continue his life and work in today's world. In return he promises a happiness that will begin even now.

Scripture in This Chapter
Genesis 25:19–34; 27–32 The Story of Jacob
1 Peter 2:9 A Chosen Race

Catechism of the Catholic Church
3, 824–825, 2156, 2573

In this chapter, help your child to
+ identify and describe various episodes in Jacob's life.
+ describe how God guided Jacob and brought good from his deceit.
+ explain that God will guide us as he did Jacob.
+ identify his or her mission as a Christian.
+ propose Christian responses to situations.

Word Your Child Should Know
+ Israelites

Key Term for Your Information
+ birthright—special privileges that belong to the first male child born in a family, including the right to inheritance and authority over brothers and sisters

The Apostles, Mary, and Others—Jesus the Master

FOCUS: In this chapter, you will be helping your child to understand that Jesus called disciples, in particular, Mary and the apostles, to share in his mission.

Jesus called twelve disciples to carry his message to the known limits of the world. What changes people's lives is the gift of seeing, of encountering Jesus. Peter saw Jesus from afar. He encountered Jesus in moments of love and forgiveness. Nathaniel heard of Jesus through a friend. Nathaniel encountered Jesus in a penetrating look that revealed Christ's knowledge of him. Paul knew of Jesus from others, but his life was transformed as he encountered Christ in a vision's blinding light.

God always takes the first step. We don't understand why or how; but we can comprehend God's language of love: the look that frees, the touch that heals, the call that moves us out of our smallness into the vastness of Christian love. And in return, God seeks only the triumph of love in our midst.

Scripture in This Chapter
Luke 8:21   Jesus and His Family
John 1:35–39   Come and See

Catechism of the Catholic Church
494, 551–552, 857–860

In this chapter, help your child to
+ discuss how Jesus called the first disciples.
+ identify the principal characteristics of the apostles.
+ explain the role of the pope and bishops as those who carry on the teaching of the apostles.
+ explain how Mary is the first and best disciple.
+ identify the role other people have had in leading them to deeper faith.

Word Your Child Should Know
+ disciple

Key Terms for Your Information
+ apostle—one of the Twelve who were chosen by Jesus to preach the Good News and act in his name
+ college of bishops—The organization of Roman Catholic bishops together with all the other Eastern Catholic Church leaders.
+ witness—one whose life gives testimony to his or her beliefs

Made Holy in the Spirit

FOCUS: In this chapter, you will be helping your child to understand that the Church is holy in Jesus its founder, in its mission, and in its members who are called to holiness.

Jesus displayed every virtue. For the weak, he was a tower of strength; to the downtrodden, he was hope. Those who were riddled by fear and doubt gained peace and security from his wisdom and understanding. People found in him the love that the human heart craves. By his holiness, Christ restored human nature to its original wholeness. He held up himself and his Father as models of holiness. Knowing our weakness, however, he provided us with grace and promised us the Holy Spirit.

Since Christ is holy, and he enables us to follow him, holiness is one of the distinctive marks of the Church. Graced by the sacraments and gifted by the Spirit, the holy ones of God have "been Christ" to others.

Scripture in This Chapter
Isaiah 11:1–3   The Gifts of the Holy Spirit

Catechism of the Catholic Church
737–739, 768, 823–829

In this chapter, help your child to
+ describe how the Church is holy.
+ outline steps for growing in holiness.
+ name and explain the Gifts of the Holy Spirit.
+ describe how the saints responded to the Gifts of the Holy Spirit.

Words Your Child Should Know
+ Sacraments at the Service of Communion
+ Sacraments of Healing
+ Sacraments of Initiation
+ counsel (right judgment)
+ courage (fortitude)
+ Doctor of the Church
+ fear of the Lord (wonder and awe)
+ knowledge
+ piety (reverence)
+ understanding
+ wisdom

Key Terms for Your Information
+ sacrament—an outward sign signifying an inward grace and instituted by Christ to make us holy
+ Gifts of the Spirit—seven permanent, spiritual gifts of the Spirit that help us to be holy; gifts received at Baptism and strengthened at Confirmation

Jesus Teaches Us to Pray to Our Father

FOCUS: In this chapter, you will be helping your child to understand that God's family prays the Our Father that Jesus taught us.

The name we call a person expresses the relationship between us. We use intimate terms to address those united to us in love. We use more formal terms to speak to those who are business associates. When Jesus told us to call God our Father and gave us the Our Father prayer, he said a great deal about our relationship both to God and to one another.

With Christ, we acclaim God as our heavenly Father and offer God our praise and love. We express our desire for the coming of the Father's kingdom and the fulfillment of his will. We acknowledge our dependence and God's loving, forgiving, and faithful care for us. We declare our confident trust to our heavenly Father, the source of our very being, who not only can, but does, provide all that we need for our human sustenance. We express our solidarity with the human family and note how our personal well-being is inseparably linked to our forgiving and selfless concern for others.

Scripture in This Chapter
Matthew 6:9–13 The Lord's Prayer
Luke 11:1–4 The Lord's Prayer

Catechism of the Catholic Church
2759, 2761, 2765–2766

In this chapter, help your child to
+ know that Jesus gave us the Our Father.
+ understand the petitions in both halves of the Our Father.
+ pray both halves of the Our Father meaningfully.

Key Terms for Your Information
+ amen—yes; a Hebrew word meaning "it is so" or "let it be done"
+ hallowed—holy
+ heaven—the life with God that is full of happiness and never ends
+ kingdom—people and land ruled by a king
+ saints—good people who loved God on earth and are now in heavenly glory
+ temptation—something that leads us to do what is wrong
+ trespasses—wrong things we do

Jesus Calls Us to Live in Love

FOCUS: In this chapter, you will be helping your child to understand that when we love God, we follow Jesus and share his love with others.

Civil laws are usually made in order to promote the common good. They safeguard our rights and protect us. They enable us to live freely, to grow, and to contribute to the progress of humankind to the best of our abilities.

The commandments given to us by God have a similar purpose. They are not unreasonable demands made at the whim of an almighty being as an assertion of his authority over us. Rather, the commandments are presented as a light to help us see the right way to live, in fact, the only way to live happily.

God does not enforce his commands like a cruel despot. He encourages us to follow them like a loving parent who knows what is good for us. We are free to obey the commandments or not. But by not following the commandments, we foolishly go against our very nature, which is to be loving people made in the image and likeness of God.

Scripture in This Chapter
Matthew 9:9 The Calling of Matthew
John 15:9–11 The Fullness of Joy

Catechism of the Catholic Church
1430, 2052–2055

In this chapter, help your child to
+ identify in the life of Saint Thérèse, guidelines for a life of love.
+ explain why we make sacrifices for God and for the Church.
+ understand better the demands of Jesus' law of love.
+ demonstrate his or her knowledge and understanding of the Ten Commandments as taught in Unit 2.
+ understand that Jesus leaves us free to respond to his call.

Key Term for Your Information
+ sacrifice—a difficult thing that is done out of love

God Is Holy and Great

FOCUS: In this chapter, you will be helping your child to understand that our holy God is everywhere, especially with us, and knows all things.

The "Holy, Holy, Holy" acclamation that we pray at every eucharistic celebration may be routine for some Catholics. Not so for the prophet Isaiah, who heard the words from the lips of seraphim during a vision he had of the all-holy God. These words resounded with God's holiness and greatness, and Isaiah was completely awed. He was struck with fear at the realization of his own sinfulness. However, one of the seraphim came to him and purified him. Isaiah was then prepared to go forth and reflect God's holiness among the people.

Indeed, God is holy. What does holiness mean for us? How do we translate God's transcendence and otherness into our human way of life? We look to Jesus, divine teacher and model of all perfection. He calls all Christians, all who would follow him, to holiness of life. "So be perfect, just as your heavenly Father is perfect." (Matthew 5:48) Jesus is ever at work leading us to holiness.

Scripture in This Chapter
Exodus 3:1–6 The Call of Moses
Psalm 139:1–12 The All-Knowing and Ever-Present God
1 Kings 18:16–39 Elijah and the Prophets of Baal

Catechism of the Catholic Church
27, 205–209, 300, 2143–2144

In this chapter, help your child to
+ describe Moses' experience when he encountered the holiness of God.
+ identify ways people reflect God's holiness.
+ recall the Second Commandment and its meaning.
+ name ways to respond to God's holiness.
+ describe how God is all-knowing and all-present.

Word Your Child Should Know
+ Yahweh

Key Terms for Your Information
+ awe—holy fear
+ Yahweh—the Hebrew name for God

God Gave Us Laws for Living

FOCUS: In this chapter, you will be helping your child to understand that God gave us laws to be happy in this world and in the next.

The happiness we seek and for which we are created is found in Jesus. In the Old Testament, the principles governing human existence were outlined in the Ten Commandments. In the New Covenant, Jesus said:

> Whoever has my commandments and observes them is the one who loves me. And whoever loves me will be loved by my Father, and I will love him and reveal myself to him.
> *John 14:21*

God reveals to us in Jesus how we are to live. It is God's plan that we freely respond. This is not always easy, for we cannot make arbitrary decisions about what is good and bad or right and wrong. Accepting Christ's love and living according to the values he teaches enables God's reign to take root within us; we become more like him.

Scripture in This Chapter
Exodus 14, 19 God's Covenant with His People
Psalm 119:9–16 Delight in God's Laws

Catechism of the Catholic Church
2055–2063, 2072

In this chapter, help your child to
+ describe the Scripture account of Moses receiving the Ten Commandments.
+ explain that the commandments express God's love and care for us.
+ identify the Ten Commandments as laws of love.
+ explain that the commandments guide us in our duties toward God, self, and others.
+ discuss the commandments as a way to happiness and eternal life.

Word Your Child Should Know
+ moral law

Key Terms for Your Information
+ covenant—an agreement between God and human beings
+ Israelites—the Chosen People
+ Moses—a great prophet who led the Israelites out of Egypt
+ Mount Sinai—the mountain on which God gave Moses the Ten Commandments

We Listen to God's Word

FOCUS: In this chapter, you will be helping your child to understand that in the Liturgy of the Word, God speaks to us and we respond.

God spoke, and there was the beauty of creation. God called, and individuals and isolated tribes were formed into his people. The power of God's Word brings into existence the ecclesial community of both the Old Testament and the New Testament. Indeed God's Word was and always is active and alive.

No less powerful is the Word described in the New Testament by John.

> In the beginning was the Word,
> and the Word was with God,
> and the Word was God.
> *John 1:1*

Similarly, the power of God's Word touches our hearts because "he first loved us." (1 John 4:19) God's Word invites us to grow continually in God's love. We open our hearts to listen to God's Word, which beckons and commands, illumines, and inspires us. We hear the Word (or read it), and it increases our faith. It is both the sign of salvation and the grace needed to attain it.

Scripture in This Chapter
Mark 1:32–34 Jesus Heals the Sick
Luke 11:28 Blessed Are Those Who Hear the Word of God.

Catechism of the Catholic Church
1100–1102, 1346, 1349

In this chapter, help your child to
+ recognize that God speaks to us in the Scripture.
+ understand that listening to God's Word means listening with faith and paying close attention.
+ recognize that when God speaks, we are invited to respond.
+ discuss how the Word of God can be applied to life situations.
+ define the term Nicene Creed.

Word Your Child Should Know
+ Nicene Creed

The Israelites Journey to Egypt

FOCUS: In this chapter, you will be helping your child to understand that God saved the ancient world from famine through Joseph, an upright and forgiving man.

For those who believe, there is divine purpose in every moment. We brush eternity in every movement. Seemingly inconsequential events are actually charged with mystery and meaning, for we know that there is a glorious and loving divine plan. God's love combines human freedom and redemption in Christ so that our faith response to these events is not folly—it is Divine Providence. Our faith helps us know that every moment of life draws us closer to God.

We do not learn this in any book. It is revealed to us in the silence of prayer. Knowing that God is with us, watching over us and caring for us, gives us a strength and trust that know no limits.

Scripture in This Chapter
Genesis 37–50 Joseph's story
Luke 12:22–32 Trust in God

Catechism of the Catholic Church
128, 302–303, 305

In this chapter, help your child to
+ describe the story of Joseph up to the point where he is made governor of Egypt.
+ trace God's providential acts in Joseph's life.
+ identify strategies for avoiding and overcoming envy.
+ summarize the conclusion of Joseph's story.
+ identify ways to grow in a trustful acceptance of Divine Providence.

Word Your Child Should Know
+ Divine Providence

Key Terms for Your Information
+ Benjamin—youngest son of Jacob; Joseph's youngest brother
+ Judah—one of the twelve sons of Jacob (Israel), who received the special blessing that he would rule his brothers and that the Messiah would come from his tribe
+ Pharaoh—title given to the Egyptian kings or rulers
+ prefigure—to show or suggest beforehand
+ Simeon—Joseph's brother, whom he kept a prisoner until his other brothers returned to Egypt with Benjamin

Baptism and Confirmation—Jesus the Savior

FOCUS: In this chapter, you will be helping your child to understand that in the sacraments, we receive and celebrate the life that Jesus won for us.

The Rite of Christian Initiation of Adults (RCIA) is a spiritual journey through which a person enters into the Church through Baptism, Confirmation, and the Eucharist. Baptism is a sharing in the death and rising of Christ, by which we die to sin and rise to eternal life. Confirmation strengthens our baptismal call and seals us with the Holy Spirit. In the Eucharist, we are nourished with the Body and Blood of Christ.

Scripture in This Chapter
Romans 6:3–4 Life in God
1 Peter 2:9 We Live in God's Light

Catechism of the Catholic Church
1127–1129, 1212, 1239–1243, 1300–1305

In this chapter, help your child to
* express an understanding of the sacraments.
* name the three categories of sacraments and the sacraments that belong to each.
* describe the Rite of Christian Initiation of Adults.
* explain that we are reborn in Baptism, strengthened in Confirmation, and nourished by the Eucharist.

Words Your Child Should Know
* mystagogy
* Mystical Body of Christ

Key Terms for Your Information
* catechumen—a person preparing to become a member of the faith community
* elect—those who are called to the Sacraments of Initiation during the Rite of Enrollment
* exorcism—prayers of deliverance from evil in the Rite of Baptism
* Rite of Christian Initiation of Adults (RCIA)—the process through which people become members of the Church
* Rite of Enrollment—the ceremony in which catechumens become the Elect
* sacrament—an outward sign of an inward grace instituted by Christ in which we encounter him at key points in our journey of life and grow in grace
* scrutinies—petitions and exorcisms that strengthen the catechumens in their decision to live for Christ

A Church That Is Catholic

FOCUS: In this chapter, you will be helping your child to understand that the Church is catholic, or universal: for all people of all nations and all times.

In obedience to the Father and animated with the Holy Spirit, Christ entered the world as the salvation prepared for all nations. (Luke 2:30–31) He showed that no race, no nation, no individual was to be excluded from his saving mission. His love was great enough to embrace friend and foe alike, but he never forced it upon anyone.

The Holy Spirit has endowed the Church in each era with missionaries. Their efforts give the Church a marvelous diversity that emphasizes its unity. Like the tiles of a great mosaic, each race, each culture, has added its richness to the beauty of Christ's Church.

Scripture in This Chapter
Luke 14:15–24 The Great Feast
Matthew 28:18–20 Make Disciples of All Nations.
1 Corinthians 9:22–23 I Have Become All Things to All.

Catechism of the Catholic Church
830–856

In this chapter, help your child to
* explain how the Church is catholic.
* describe the universal character of the Church.
* identify the Church's responsibility to evangelize.
* express an understanding of the Eastern Catholic Churches.
* identify how he or she can participate in the mission of the Church.

Words Your Child Should Know
* culture
* interreligious dialogue

Key Terms for Your Information
* evangelization—proclaiming the Good News
* Eastern Catholic Church—a faith tradition that began in the eastern part of the Roman Empire. Its ways of worship and government are different from those of the Roman (Western) Church, though we remain in communion with each other.
* icon—traditional art representing God, Mary, or a saint that is highly honored in the Eastern Churches
* patriarch—a bishop in one of the Eastern Churches who has precedence over other bishops and the authority to settle most matters in his local churches

God Promised a Savior

FOCUS: In this chapter, you will be helping your child to understand that after Adam and Eve sinned, God promised a Savior so that we could be happy with God forever in heaven.

When Adam and Eve turned in sin from God's love, God's promise assured us of God's continued desire to share his glory with the creatures he had made in the divine likeness:

> For God so loved the world that he gave his only Son, so that everyone who believes in him might not perish but might have eternal life. *John 3:16*

God's creative love destined men and women for eternal happiness with him. Ever since our first parents' sin, salvation history records God's love in forgiving his people. Despite our own sins, we hope in God's faithful love.

Scripture in This Chapter
Genesis 1, 2 The Story of Creation
Genesis 3 The Fall

Catechism of the Catholic Church
218, 396–400, 839, 1731

In this chapter, help your child to
- know that God created humans capable of knowing and loving him.
- recognize that the first people had a loving relationship with God, with each other, and with all of creation when they were obedient to God.
- appreciate the happiness of people living in a loving relationship with God.
- understand that evil came into the world, and we are affected by it.
- be aware of the role of the Jewish people in the history of our salvation.

Words Your Child Should Know
- grace
- Savior
- heaven

Key Terms for Your Information
- Chosen people—the Jewish people
- devil—an evil spirit
- Israel—the country of the Jewish people, where the Savior was born
- sin—to disobey God; to fail to love

Our Friend Jesus Forgives Us

FOCUS: In this chapter, you will be helping your child to understand that Jesus is a good friend who forgives us as he forgave Zacchaeus.

Humble acknowledgment of one's sinfulness can strengthen bonds of love with God. Zacchaeus was conscious of the alienation caused by his sin, but in the end, he used his failings and sins to his advantage and experienced God's forgiving love.

Zacchaeus's story illustrates a dramatic conversion, or turning, toward a better way of life. The change required may be radical, as with Zacchaeus, or it may merely involve listening more attentively, responding more fully to God, and welcoming God into each moment and event. Every person has room for growth; there is always need for a greater response to God's love. The Almighty, who is always faithful and always forgiving, will do wonders for us if we acknowledge our need for forgiveness.

Scripture in This Chapter
Luke 15:1–7 The Lost Sheep
Luke 18:10–14 The Pharisee and the Tax Collector
Luke 19:1–10 Zacchaeus' Meeting with Jesus
John 15:14,16 Following Jesus

Catechism of the Catholic Church
1422, 1432, 1441–1442, 1446

In this chapter, help your child to
- understand that Jesus chose him or her as friends.
- understand the importance of reconciliation in friendship.
- explain that Jesus loves us even when we have done wrong.
- explain the difference Jesus made in the life of Zacchaeus.
- understand that we can go to Jesus for forgiveness.
- distinguish between good and bad choices.

Key Terms for Your Information
- friends—people who love one another and share one another's lives
- heaven—a place where we will be happy forever with God, Jesus, the Holy Spirit, the angels, and the saints
- I'm sorry—words that tell others we feel bad about what we've done to hurt them and wish we had not done it
- Pharisee—a member of an ancient Jewish group that stressed a strict interpretation of Mosaic law

God Is Just and Merciful

FOCUS: In this chapter, you will be helping your child to understand that our just and merciful God forgives us and asks us to show justice and mercy.

Justice and mercy are characteristics of God's love. Throughout the Bible, we see examples of justice that are modeled on God's justice. God has made a commitment to the human family and is faithful to his commitments. In our human relationships, we are called to be like God in treating one another with love and compassion. We treat one another with justice when we remove any fault or obstacle that blocks our relationships with one another and with God. The justice we find in the Old Testament always flows from love and compassion. Without justice, authentic relationships are not possible.

In the Gospels, Jesus is presented not only as a just teacher but also as the manifestation of God's justice and mercy. Through Jesus, sins are forgiven and broken relationships are healed. Those who believe in Jesus are made into a new creation.

Scripture in This Chapter
Psalm 103 Praise of Divine Goodness
Luke 15:8–10 The Parable of the Lost Coin
Luke 16:19–31 The Parable of the Rich Man and Lazarus
John 10:1–18 The Good Shepherd

Catechism of the Catholic Church
210–211, 218–219, 1465

In this chapter, help your child to
+ name ways that God shows justice and mercy.
+ recall the Good Shepherd story, which shows God's merciful love.
+ describe how Saint Vincent de Paul and Saint Louise de Marillac reflected God's love and justice.
+ describe how Saint Vincent de Paul and Saint Louise de Marillac practiced justice and mercy.
+ propose ways he or she can be just and merciful.

Word Your Child Should Know
+ justice

We Honor Mary

FOCUS: In this chapter, you will be helping your child to understand that Mary shows us how to follow Jesus.

The angel Gabriel spoke to Mary three times. First, he saluted her with deep reverence and called her "favored one." Mary was so filled with God that she surpassed all others. She was conceived immaculate from the first moment of her existence and conformed most faithfully to God's will.

The angel then announced the message with which he had been entrusted. Mary did not ask "How can this be?" because she doubted, but rather because she needed enlightenment. The angel then explained the work of the Spirit within her, making Mary the first to hear and understand the good news of the Incarnation.

Mary's prompt and unhesitating reply showed her readiness and joy, as well as her humility and obedience. Her response was the fulfillment of all the prayers and longings of all time and all creation, for with her consent, the Word was made flesh! God became a human being so that human beings might become like God.

Scripture in This Chapter
Luke 1:26–28 The Annunciation

Catechism of the Catholic Church
148, 484–485, 488, 494

In this chapter, help your child to
+ identify the Angelus as a prayer honoring the Annunciation.
+ describe the mystery of the Incarnation.
+ describe the concepts learned in Unit 2.
+ identify ways to apply to his or her lives what he or she has learned.

Word Your Child Should Know
+ Angelus

Key Terms for Your Information
+ conceived—became pregnant
+ handmaid—a female servant
+ Incarnation—the mystery of God becoming man

We Praise and Thank God

FOCUS: In this chapter, you will be helping your child to understand that in the Eucharist, bread and wine become Jesus, and we offer ourselves with Jesus to the Father.

At Mass, we offer gifts of bread and wine, which represent, not only the poverty of the gift of ourselves, but also our desire for union with Jesus and with one another. They make us aware of the wonder of this mystery in which Jesus unites human beings with himself to be offered to God our Father.

Jesus, the eternal priest, offers himself in a mysterious way so that we can join in his sacrifice on the cross. At this sacrificial banquet, we remember God's saving acts. In response, we raise our minds and hearts in praise and thanksgiving. We acclaim this mystery of our redemption whereby our sins are forgiven and we are made whole again. We pray for the unity of all people.

Scripture in This Chapter

Psalm 116:12–13,17 . Thanksgiving to God
Luke 22:14–20 The Last Supper

Catechism of the Catholic Church

1356–1361

In this chapter, help your child to

+ explain how we unite ourselves with Jesus' sacrifice at Mass.
+ identify Jesus as the perfect gift offered to the Father.
+ explain that bread and wine become the Body and Blood of Jesus at Mass.
+ define consecration and transubstantiation.
+ express an understanding and appreciation for the Eucharistic Prayer.

Words Your Child Should Know

+ consecration
+ transubstantiation

Key Terms for Your Information

+ acclamation—a short, enthusiastic response of praise
+ Eucharistic Prayer—the prayer during which bread and wine are changed into the Body and Blood of Jesus and Jesus offers himself to the Father
+ Institution Narrative—that part of the Eucharistic Prayer that describes Jesus' words and actions at the Last Supper
+ Preface—the prayer of thanksgiving that begins the Eucharistic Prayer

---

Unit 2 Review

FOCUS: In this chapter, you will be helping your child to understand that God formed the people, gradually revealing himself to them.

The book of Genesis emerged partly as the result of a people reflecting on their origins. Knowing God through gradual revelation, they sought to discern some pattern, some plan in the events of their personal history. In so doing, the book of Genesis evolved, which gave eloquent testimony to their faith. The authors of Genesis were, above all else, people who relied on God's promises.

The stories of the patriarchs told the Israelites not only who they were, but, where they were going. The patriarchs were heirs of the promise of redemption, a promise fulfilled through Jesus Christ. Now we too look to our faith origins, trying to discern the pattern of God's ways in our lives. We gain courage and hope by referring to the call we have received. God's providence is evident in our lives and frees us to be trusting people.

Catechism of the Catholic Church

218, 269

In this chapter, help your child to

+ demonstrate a comprehensive understanding of what he or she has learned in Unit 2.

Key Term for Your Information

+ sanctuary—a holy place; in a church, the area around the altar

Unit 1 Review

FOCUS: In this chapter, you will be helping your child to understand that through Jesus, we find the way to the Father.

The Scriptures tell us that following the Lord involves suffering. It entails leaving behind one way of living and adopting another. As followers of a crucified Redeemer, we choose to live the mystery of the cross, aware that accepting hardships strengthens and frees us to grow in God's life and to experience the joy of his Resurrection.

The apostles who responded to Jesus' call to follow him were ordinary people. They dreamed of greatness and pursued happiness. Like us, they needed the warmth of acceptance and the joy of accomplishment. They had the shortcomings and failings common to all members of the human family. Yet Jesus invited them. He invited them just as they were. And he invites us just as we are. All he asks is that we come with a generous spirit ready to risk all for the love of him. Membership in his Church is a commitment to follow Jesus in new and ever-changing situations.

Scripture in This Chapter
Matthew 7:21,24–27 God's Word is Our Foundation.
John 1:1–2, 10–12 Jesus is the Word.

Catechism of the Catholic Church
460, 618, 654

In this chapter, help your child to
+ recall the significant facts and basic concepts introduced in Unit 1.
+ identify material that needs more study.
+ demonstrate an understanding of the key concepts in Unit 1.
+ clarify his or her attitudes toward Jesus.
+ express through prayer a desire to be a more faithful follower of Jesus.

An Apostolic Church

FOCUS: In this chapter, you will be helping your child to understand that the Church is apostolic, carrying on the faith and the mission of the apostles under the apostles' successors.

This fidelity to apostolic instruction indicates the first Christians' esteem for the leaders of the Church and openness to the Spirit's guiding presence. What credentials did Jesus demand of Peter and his successors? Jesus simply asked Peter three times, "Simon, son of John, do you love me?" Peter answered three times, "Yes, Lord, you know that I love you." (John 21:15–17) This was all the assurance Jesus needed.

From that moment on, the intense, loyal love of Christ spurred Peter, the other apostles, and their successors to "be Christ" in the world. Like Jesus, they offer sacrifice and bring forgiveness to a suffering world. Like Jesus the master teacher, they preach his saving message—total and unchanged—to all people in all ages.

Scripture in This Chapter
Acts of the Apostles 1:15–26 The Apostles Select a Successor to Judas.

Catechism of the Catholic Church
857–865, 880–892

In this chapter, help your child to
+ identify his or her responsibilities in the Church.
+ explain how the Church is apostolic.
+ describe the role of Peter in the Church.
+ describe how Church leaders serve as Christ did, and as priest, prophet, and servant-king.
+ identify the ways in which Church leaders help him or her.

Words Your Child Should Know
+ bishops
+ infallibility
+ collegiality
+ pope diocese

Key Terms for Your Information
+ apostolic—rooted in the beliefs of the apostles and continuing their mission
+ Magisterium—the teaching authority of the Church

CHAPTER 10   **GRADE** ①

God Chose Mary and Joseph

FOCUS: In this chapter, you will be helping your child to understand that Mary consented to be the Mother of the Savior.

God chose a young Jewish woman to be the Mother of his Son. He chose Joseph to care for the mother and child. Whenever God enters people's lives, however, God respects their freedom, as God respected the freedom of Mary and Joseph. Mary listened to God's Word and offered herself freely as the Lord's faithful handmaid. With her consent, the Word became flesh. Jesus, the Son of God, entered human history.

With total receptivity, Mary listened to what God calls us to learn—how to conceive Christ in our hearts. Saint Paul explains that when you are open to God's Word, you discern what is of value so that you may be pure, filled with the fruit of righteousness that comes through Jesus.

Scripture in This Chapter

Luke 1:26–38 An Angel Announces Jesus' Birth to Mary.
Luke 1:39-56 Mary Visits Elizabeth.

Catechism of the Catholic Church

488, 494–495, 532, 534, 2220

In this chapter, help your child to

* tell the story of the Annunciation.
* associate the words of the Hail Mary prayer with Mary's visit to Elizabeth.
* identify the Hail Mary as a prayer to honor Mary.
* become acquainted with Saint Joseph, the foster father of Jesus.
* associate doing what is right with God's will.

Words Your Child Should Know

* angel
* Mary
* Joseph

Key Terms for Your Information

* Amen—yes
* Annunciation—the announcement to Mary that God had chosen her to be the mother of the Savior
* Elizabeth—Mary's relative
* foster father—man who assumes the role of father to a child
* Gabriel—angel who told Mary that she had been chosen to be the mother of the Savior
* Nazareth—town where Mary lived

CHAPTER 10   **GRADE** ②

Jesus Leads Us to His Peace

FOCUS: In this chapter, you will be helping your child to understand that after we have sinned, Jesus gives us peace through the Sacrament of Reconciliation.

On the evening of his Resurrection, Jesus greeted the apostles who had deserted him in his hours of agony with the words "Peace be with you." (John 20:19) God, in his merciful kindness, always forgives us when we express sorrow for our offenses. As soon as we utter our prayerful desire to affirm and strengthen our relationship with God, divine love forgives us our sins. This is the peace that Jesus gives. This is the reconciliation we celebrate when the Church continues the healing ministry of the Lord and calls for a deeper community and more faithful love.

Jesus leads us to God's peace; his Spirit enables us to be a reconciling community, which restores peace through mutual forgiveness. Every baptized person should repeatedly experience conversion toward God to allow the divine life received in Baptism to unfold and develop.

Scripture in This Chapter

Luke 7:36–50 Pardon of the Sinful Woman
John 20:19–23 Authority to Forgive Sin

Catechism of the Catholic Church

1423–1424, 1443, 1468, 1486

In this chapter, help your child to

* define sin as saying no to God.
* understand that accidents, mistakes, and temptations are not sins.
* understand that the Sacrament of Reconciliation is Jesus' gift for peace and spiritual growth.
* realize that Jesus forgives us through a priest in the Sacrament of Reconciliation.
* understand that by expressing sorrow for sins he or she shows his or her love for Jesus.

Words Your Child Should Know

* sin
* temptation
* reconciliation
* Sacrament of Penance and Reconciliation

Key Terms for Your Information

* sinner—a person who has offended God by failing to love
* sorrow—sadness

God Created People to Share His Life

FOCUS: In this chapter, you will be helping your child to understand that after the first people disobeyed, God continued to offer his life to us through Jesus.

Even though God has every right over us and knows that we will be truly happy only in union with him, God does not force us to choose that which would draw us into a more intimate, fulfilling relationship with him and with others. Our Creator has gifted us with the freedom to choose. No matter how foolish our choices, God always respects our liberty.

Our power to choose is real, yet is limited by the effects of sin. The wound of sin has weakened our ability to know the truth; it has lessened our innate desire to choose what is truly good. We find ourselves giving up divine truth for a lie, and worshiping and serving creatures instead of our Creator. (Romans 1:25) God's grace enables us to choose faithfully things that will bring us to fulfillment as his sons and daughters.

Scripture in This Chapter
Genesis 3 Adam and Eve Disobey God.
Psalm 8 Divine Majesty and Human Dignity

Catechism of the Catholic Church
356, 374–375, 404–407, 410, 1996–1999

In this chapter, help your child to
+ have a greater appreciation for the gift of life as well as a greater respect for the basic equality of men and women.
+ tell the story of how Adam and Eve rejected grace and how Jesus came to restore it.
+ explain that sin brought evil into our world.
+ recall that temptation is not a sin.
+ resolve to make choices pleasing to God.
+ describe the biblical account of creation and the Fall.

Words Your Child Should Know
+ charity
+ Scriptures
+ devil
+ Redeemer
+ hope

Key Terms for Your Information
+ supernatural—greater than what is natural
+ grace—a share in God's life
+ temptation—anything that urges us to do what we know is wrong

We Show Our Love for God

FOCUS: In this chapter, you will be helping your child to understand that the First Commandment tells us to adore God alone and to pray.

The history of salvation is the story of God's love for the human race; God entered into human affairs to save us from sin and to bring us closer to him. Although God cherishes each of us as a loving parent, we are sometimes tempted to allow other gods into our lives—people, places, or things that claim our first attention. That is why God's First Commandment demands that we recognize him as the one true God and worship him alone.

The worship we give to God alone is called adoration. As Supreme Lord and Creator of all, God has a right to it; as creatures totally dependent on God, we owe it to him. We express our worship of God by faith, hope, love, prayer, and sacrifice. We worship God privately and publicly. In prayers of praise, thanksgiving, contrition, and petition, we unite ourselves with the praying Jesus.

Scripture in This Chapter
Exodus 20:2–3 One God Only
Exodus 20, 23, 34 Moses' Encounters with God
Matthew 6:6 Prayer in Secret

Catechism of the Catholic Church
2096, 2629–2643, 946–948, 971

In this chapter, help your child to
+ recite the First Commandment.
+ explain the danger of worshiping God's gifts instead of God.
+ explain the purpose of prayer.
+ name the various kinds of prayer.
+ explain why we honor Mary, the angels, and the saints.

Word Your Child Should Know
+ prayer of petition

We Receive Holy Communion

FOCUS: In this chapter, you will be helping your child to understand that Jesus comes to us in Communion and unites us to himself and to one another.

When we partake of the Bread of Life in Holy Communion, we share in the fullness of Christ's love. We participate in his love for the Father and for all the members of his Mystical Body, the Church. We receive the grace that enables us to fulfill his commandment:

> I give you a new commandment: love one another. As I have loved you, so you also should love one another.
>
> *John 13:34*

In the eucharistic banquet, we anticipate the heavenly banquet in which we will join with Christ in giving eternal praise to the Father. As we receive Holy Communion, we are aware that the Eucharist spans both time and eternity. Partaking of the one bread and the one cup, we are nourished by the Body and Blood of Christ and filled with his Spirit. We grow in the divine life that Christ shares with us, and we become one body with him and with one another.

Scripture in This Chapter
+ Psalm 75:2   Song of Thanks

Catechism of the Catholic Church
1328–1332, 1384–1389

In this chapter, help your child to
+ recall that in the Eucharist, our unity with Christ and one another is expressed and brought about.
+ explain the meaning of the prayers and actions of the Communion Rite.
+ demonstrate the proper conduct for receiving Holy Communion.
+ express an understanding of the prayers that he or she prays before and after Communion.
+ recall the kinds of prayers he or she can pray to Jesus after receiving him.

God Rescues the Chosen People from Slavery

FOCUS: In this chapter, you will be helping your child to understand that God led the Hebrews out of slavery in Egypt.

Passover is a celebration that recalls the Exodus experience. However, the Exodus does not merely deal with a past event. It is a celebration of an eternal truth: God is a God who saves.

At the Last Supper, Jesus gave new meaning to the sacred Passover meal. He himself became the paschal lamb, offered in sacrifice to deliver us from the bondage of sin. Our celebration of the Eucharist, like the Jewish Passover ritual, offers praise and thanks to God for leading us from slavery to freedom from sin.

Scripture in This Chapter
+ Exodus 1–15:21   Moses and the Exodus

Catechism of the Catholic Church
62, 204–208, 1164, 1328–1330

In this chapter, help your child to
+ describe the circumstances of Moses' call.
+ retell the story of the Passover and the Exodus.
+ describe the Jewish celebration of Passover.
+ explain the purpose of the Eucharist and identify and describe the main parts of the Mass (Liturgy of the Word, Liturgy of the Eucharist).

Word Your Child Should Know
+ Exodus

Key Terms for Your Information
+ consecration—the part of the Eucharistic Prayer at which Christ's Body and Blood become present under the appearance of bread and wine
+ Liturgy of the Eucharist—second part of the Mass, in which Jesus feeds us with his Body and Blood
+ Liturgy of the Word—first part of the Mass, in which we hear the story of our salvation
+ matzoh—flat, thin pieces of unleavened bread eaten by Jewish people during Passover
+ Midian—land north of Arabia and east of Egypt
+ Nile River—river stretching from the Burundi, east Africa, to the Mediterranean Sea in northeast Egypt
+ Red Sea—an inlet of the Indian Ocean between Africa and Asia
+ unleavened—containing no yeast

Parables: Stories Jesus Told— Jesus the Storyteller

FOCUS: In this chapter, you will be helping your child to understand that some truths taught by Jesus and his Church are contained in parables.

The parables were one way Jesus revealed truths. Through parables, stories about ordinary people and things, Jesus taught truths about the kingdom of God. He taught that God was as surprising in his mercy as a king who cancels completely a servant's enormous debt. He taught that the kingdom was open to sinners, outcasts, and foreigners. He taught that in God's sight, a contrite sinner is better than a righteous Pharisee. In parables, Jesus instructed us how to walk in light: to pray with perseverance, to use our talents, to share our wealth, and to show love even to our enemies.

By applying the parables to our own lives, we will have the light of life. We will be like the five wise bridesmaids whose lamps burned brightly to greet the bridegroom. We will be as deliriously happy as the merchant who became owner of the priceless pearl.

Scripture in This Chapter
Matthew 13:3–9,18–23   Parable of the Sower
Luke 12:16–21   Parable of the Rich Fool

Catechism of the Catholic Church
543–546

In this chapter, help your child to
- identify parables as stories that convey truths about the Kingdom of God.
- compare how his or her life measures up to the teachings of Jesus contained in the parables.
- respond to a parable by determining to change an attitude or a behavior.
- demonstrate an understanding of the meaning and purpose of the parables of Jesus.

Words Your Child Should Know
- evangelization
- Magisterium

Key Terms for Your Information
- doctrine—a belief taught by the Church as true
- dogma—a truth revealed by God that is officially defined by the Church as an article of faith for Catholics
- Magisterium—the teaching authority of the Church
- parable—a story of something familiar from life experiences used to teach a truth about the kingdom

The First Years

FOCUS: In this chapter, you will be helping your child to understand that after the coming of the Holy Spirit on Pentecost, the faith spread from Jerusalem to Rome, from Jews to Gentiles, despite persecution.

New undertakings are frequently plagued with problems, and the Church was no exception. There were serious questions to answer:

> A Church for Jews alone or for all people?
> Synagogue on the Sabbath or Christian liturgy on Sunday?
> Adhere to Mosaic practices or discard them?
> Oral tradition only or something more concrete and permanent?
> Tribute to Caesar or tribute to God?
> Dispersion and flight to safety or martyrdom with loss of members?

Relying heavily on the guidance of the Holy Spirit, the apostolic Church met challenges wisely and courageously. During those difficult years after the Lord's ascension, the memory of that simple parable about the mustard seed certainly must have buoyed the spirits of the early Christians and strengthened their resolve in the face of a seemingly impossible mandate: "Go into the whole world and proclaim the gospel to every creature." (Mark 16:15)

Scripture in This Chapter
Acts of the Apostles 5—10, 15   The Beginnings of the Church

Catechism of the Catholic Church
848–850, 861–862

In this chapter, help your child to
- describe the Acts of the Apostles and the letters in Scripture.
- summarize the first days and early growth of the Church.
- describe the experience of the Christians of the first century.
- identify the virtues of the builders of the early Church.
- demonstrate an understanding of the key concepts in this chapter.

Words Your Child Should Know
- epistles
- deacon
- martyr

Jesus Our Savior Was Born in Bethlehem

FOCUS: In this chapter, you will be helping your child to understand that on Christmas, we celebrate that Jesus came to save all people.

Because of a census ordered by Caesar Augustus, the Roman Emperor, Mary and Joseph traveled from Nazareth to Bethlehem, the city of David. There, the coming of God into the world was a mere statistic.

Most of the people who had longed for a Savior were unaware of his quiet arrival. The shepherds and wise men alone responded to the significance of the event and welcomed the coming of the Lord. The shepherds hurried to find their Savior and gave praise to God. The wise men, filled with delight, followed the star's guiding light until they found the child and offered him gifts.

Scripture in This Chapter
Matthew 1:18–25 and Luke 2:1–7   The Birth of Jesus
Luke 2:8–20   The Visit of the Shepherds
Matthew 2:1–12   The Visit of the Magi

Catechism of the Catholic Church
461, 525–526, 528, 826, 1889

In this chapter, help your child to
+ tell the traditional Christmas story.
+ associate the coming of Jesus into our world with the celebration of Christmas.
+ tell the story of how the shepherds heard about Jesus' birth and visited him.
+ tell the story of the visit of the Magi (wise men).
+ know that Jesus came to save all people.

Word Your Child Should Know
+ Christmas

Key Terms for Your Information
+ Bethlehem—town located southwest of Jerusalem; birthplace of King David and later of Jesus
+ eternal life—life forever with God
+ frankincense—incense that makes a sweet-smelling smoke
+ myrrh—a type of perfume that comes from trees
+ Nazareth—town located in lower Galilee; the hometown of the Holy Family
+ swaddling clothes—strips of cloth
+ wise men, or Magi—astrologers from the East

The Spirit of Jesus Helps Us

FOCUS: In this chapter, you will be helping your child to understand that the Holy Spirit helps us examine our consciences and become better people.

The Holy Spirit is with us always, but we are not always sensitive to his presence. Just as photographic film captures elusive and fleeting impressions when it is carefully exposed to light, the human heart detects delicate and seemingly imperceptible movements of grace when it is closely attuned to the Holy Spirit.

In George Bernard Shaw's play *St. Joan*, King Charles asks Joan why she is granted heavenly revelations and he is not. Joan answers, "They do come to you, but you do not hear them. You have not sat in the field in the evening, listening for them." The inspirations of the Holy Spirit illuminate the various ways we hinder God's action in our lives. Only if we come into the healing presence of our God will we see ourselves reflected as we truly are. The more receptive we are to the Holy Spirit in our lives, the more we will experience the fruits of his presence.

Scripture in This Chapter
John 14:16,26   The Holy Spirit, Our Advocate
1 John 4:12–13   God's Spirit in Us

Catechism of the Catholic Church
1431–1433, 1454, 1695

In this chapter, help your child to
+ explain that the presence of the Holy Spirit is manifested by love, peace, and joy.
+ discuss ways to share love, peace, and joy with others.
+ explain the necessity of prayer to the Holy Spirit.
+ relate the fact that he or she can rely on the Holy Spirit's help.
+ explain how to examine his or her conscience.

Key Terms for Your Information
+ examination of conscience—looking into our hearts to see how we have loved or failed to love God and others.
+ Holy Spirit—the third Person of the Trinity sent to teach us and help us to love
+ leper—a person with leprosy, a serious disease that covers the body with sores.

God Sent His Son, Jesus, to Live Among Us

FOCUS: In this chapter, you will be helping your child to understand that Jesus, the Light of the World, leads us to God.

When we ponder the monumental national and international problems that confront countries today, the upheavals and uncertainties faced by families, or the personal problems that abide within our own hearts, we might be tempted to respond with fear or even despondency. If, however, we can focus the light of Christ on these problems, his love, his wisdom, his providence, and his power will fill the darkest corners with hope. The fire of Christ's love will burn ever more brightly in our hearts, radiating hope to those around us as they begin to see things in his light.

With trust in Christ's guidance, they can face these issues calmly and prudently. It is hoped that they will see the light of Christ's love reflected back to them through the loving respect of their children.

Scripture in This Chapter
Luke 2:1–14 The Birth of Jesus
Luke 2:15–20 The Visit of the Shepherds
Luke 2:22–38 The Presentation in the Temple
John 8:12 Jesus, the Light of the World

Catechism of the Catholic Church
48, 422–423, 529, 854, 2199

In this chapter, help your child to
+ recall how God prepared his people for the Savior.
+ discuss Mary's role in the mystery of the Incarnation.
+ tell the story of the first Christmas.
+ tell the story of the Presentation, when Simeon called Jesus the Light of the World and Anna told people about the Savior.
+ tell what the Fourth Commandment requires.
+ recognize that he or she responds to life as Jesus did by doing ordinary things that please God.

Word Your Child Should Know
+ Incarnation

We Love All That Is Holy

FOCUS: In this chapter, you will be helping your child to understand that the Second Commandment tells us to respect God's name and all that is related to God.

God deigned to name himself to the Israelites as Yahweh, "I am who am." (Exodus 3:14) Out of reverence, the Jewish people would not pronounce this sacred name and chose instead names such as Elohim ("God") or Adonai ("the Lord"). We avoid all practices that profane God's name.

With our appreciation for all that is holy, we can uplift a society that has lost its sense of the sacred. We respond to all that is sacred with words and gestures that show our reverence. Just as Moses removed his sandals and bowed before the voice of God (Exodus 3:5–6), so we bow our heads in prayer and listen to the Word of the Lord. We refrain from any profane action toward objects set apart for sacred use.

Scripture in This Chapter
Matthew 21:12–13 Cleansing of the Temple
Philippians 2:9–10 Name of Jesus Exalted

Catechism of the Catholic Church
1667–1670, 2142–2155

In this chapter, help your child to
+ describe how words and actions reflect reverence for the sacred.
+ explain that the Second Commandment obliges us to use God's name with respect.
+ explain that we honor God's name by always saying it respectfully.
+ explain that using God's name with reverence can help us become conscious of God's presence.
+ explain that people, places, and things are holy when they remind us of God and lead us to praise God.

Word Your Child Should Know
+ Temple

Key Terms for Your Information
+ curse—to ask God to harm someone or to destroy something
+ pilgrimage—a journey made by believers to a place where God has shown grace and power
+ swear—to use God's name as proof that we are telling the truth
+ Yahweh—God's name as revealed to Moses

We Are Sent to Love and Serve

FOCUS: In this chapter, you will be helping your child to understand that we go from Mass empowered and sent to bring the love of Jesus to the world.

Saint Catherine of Siena was once asked how we could possibly make a return for God's love, since everything we have comes from him. Catherine responded that we have only one thing we can offer God that is of value to him: we can give our love to people who are as unworthy of it as we are of his love.

We are sent to do just that in the Concluding Rite of the Mass. The priest or deacon dismisses us and sends us to love and serve God and others. He tells us to praise and bless the Lord in all that we do. We go forth to love and serve the Father and one another with the mind and heart of Jesus Christ. Imbued with Christ's presence, we can meet the challenging situations of daily life with greater strength and vitality.

Scripture in This Chapter
Matthew 28:19–20 The Commissioning of the Disciples
Luke 24:44–53 The Appearance to the Disciples in
   Jerusalem
John 13:1–15 The Washing of the Disciples' Feet

Catechism of the Catholic Church
1391–1398

In this chapter, help your child to
+ express an understanding of our mission to be witnesses.
+ describe his or her responsibility to spread the Good News and identify ways to do it.
+ express a desire to help missionaries.
+ express a desire to love others as Jesus does.
+ analyze situations and determine how a person can love and serve Jesus in each.

God Gives Us the Law

FOCUS: In this chapter, you will be helping your child to understand that God protected the Israelites in the desert, made a covenant with them, and gave them laws.

The Israelites' desert pilgrimage was filled with challenges. They doubted the power and wisdom of a God who permitted them to suffer such trials. Gradually, however, as God continued to lead them along the way, their trust grew. They learned that each day God was calling them into a deeper, more loving relationship.

Certain principles govern the relationship between God and God's people, principles through the Mosaic covenant and the Ten Commandments. With the coming of Christ, however, the Ten Commandments took on a new and deeper meaning. Jesus, who is God and man, taught his followers how to live according to the full spirit of these laws. As we become more like Jesus, we bring his love, justice, and peace to others on earth and prepare for eternal happiness with him.

Scripture in This Chapter
Exodus 10–17 Struggles in the Wilderness
Exodus 19–26 A Covenant with the Lord
Exodus 27–34 The Ark of the Covenant

Catechism of the Catholic Church
708, 2056–2063, 2083–2084

In this chapter, help your child to
+ describe the difficulties the Israelites met on their journey through the desert.
+ explain how God cared for the Israelites in the wilderness.
+ explain what the Sinai covenant entailed and how it was sealed.
+ describe the purpose of the Ark of the Covenant.

Words Your Child Should Know
+ Ark of the Covenant   + idolatry

Key Terms for Your Information
+ manna—food that God sent the Israelites during their journey in the desert
+ oasis—a fertile or green area in a dry region
+ quail—migrating birds that flew over the Sinai wilderness and were food for the Israelites
+ Tent of Meeting—the sanctuary or tabernacle that God instructed Moses to build to house the Ark of the Covenant; it was a sign of God's presence from which God spoke to the people

Miracles: Signs Jesus Worked—Jesus the Miracle Worker

FOCUS: In this chapter, you will be helping your child to understand that the power of Jesus over nature, sin and evil, sickness, and death was displayed in his miracles.

The miracles of Jesus, as recorded in Scripture, fit the pattern of his entire life. They are essential parts of his mission and his ministry. He proclaims the kingdom in which God breaks through all barriers. The miracles are signs of a kingdom in which God overturns the present reality. The wondrous deeds of Jesus reveal the power of God working through him. He is master over nature, life, and death. He conquers Satan and all forms of evil.

The miracles manifest the goodness, compassion, and mercy of Jesus. He not only preached the coming of the kingdom and the way to salvation, but he also lived his message by being healer, teacher, and Savior in his miracles. People were healed physically, mentally, and spiritually by the power of his love. All the miracles culminate in the miracle of Jesus' death and Resurrection, his ultimate and complete triumph over evil.

Scripture in This Chapter
Mark 2:1–12 The Healing of a Paralytic
Mark 4:35–41 The Calming of a Storm at Sea
John 2:1–12 The Wedding at Cana

Catechism of the Catholic Church
547–550, 1503–1504

In this chapter, help your child to
✦ explain what a miracle is.
✦ discuss how miracles reveal the identity and mission of Jesus.
✦ discuss Jesus' power over nature, sin and evil, sickness, and death.
✦ explain how Jesus was motivated by compassion to work miracles.
✦ name more of Jesus' miracles.

Word Your Child Should Know
✦ miracle

The Church Grows

FOCUS: In this chapter, you will be helping your child to understand that, led by the efforts of Peter and Paul, the early Church grows and gives witness to Jesus Christ.

In his letter to the Church at Rome, Paul tells us that this initiative comes from God and is not of his own doing. To be an apostle means to be one who is sent. Paul is clear in his words and actions that the Church must not stand still. Instead, the Church must go forth and proclaim the Good News of Jesus to all people. From Paul, we learn that the Church fulfills its mission by spreading and growing. Salvation is a gift that is not to be hoarded but rather spread to all people. Christianity is not an idle religion. By virtue of our Baptism, we are called and sent forth to give witness to Jesus Christ.

Scripture in This Chapter
Acts of the Apostles 9:1–22; 22:2–16; 26:9–18 Accounts of Paul's Conversion
Acts of the Apostles 10 Peter and Cornelius
Acts of the Apostles 15 The Council of Jerusalem
Galatians 1:15–17 Paul's Version of His Conversion

Catechism of the Catholic Church
179, 183, 747, 1486, 1490, 2505–06

In this chapter, help your child to
✦ retell the story of Paul's conversion.
✦ identify Saint Paul's contributions to the Catholic Church.
✦ describe how Peter and Paul came to see that Baptism was also for the Gentiles.
✦ retell the story of Peter and Cornelius.
✦ summarize Paul's travels.
✦ identify the names of several of Paul's letters.

Words Your Child Should Know
✦ Council of Jerusalem   ✦ ecumenical council

Key Terms for Your Information
✦ conversion—a radical changing of direction of one's life away from sin and toward God
✦ Pharisees—a sect in Judaism around the time of Christ that centered on observance of the Law
✦ epistles—letters in the New Testament originally sent to a community or an individual, telling how Christians can apply the message of Jesus to daily life
✦ inculturation—the process of adapting the Gospel to a specific culture without compromising the message of Jesus

Families Share Life and Love

FOCUS: In this chapter, you will be helping your child to understand that the Holy Family shows us how to live in our own family and in our parish family.

Jesus, Mary, and Joseph spent many happy moments with one another. The Holy Family each lived the prayer that began and ended each day in every Jewish home: "Therefore, you shall love the lord, your God, with all your heart, and with all your soul, and with all your strength." (Deuteronomy 6:5)

To live this life of love in our families, we need to be filled with God's spirit. As a Christian family, we open ourselves to the power of God's Spirit when we celebrate the Eucharist. We confess our sins, mindful of the times we fail to show our love to one another. We pray that the love of God that has been poured into our hearts (Romans 5:5) may give us the strength, gentleness, and compassion to embrace all in our love, and to anticipate the needs of others as Jesus, Mary, and Joseph did in their humble home at Nazareth.

Scripture in This Chapter
Luke 2:22–38 The Presentation in the Temple
Luke 2:39–40 Mary and Joseph Raise Jesus.
Luke 2: 51–52 Jesus Is Obedient to Mary and Joseph.

Catechism of the Catholic Church
531–533, 1140–1141, 1154

In this chapter, help your child to
+ describe the simple, loving lifestyle of the Holy Family.
+ realize that family life can be a happy, loving experience.
+ accept responsibility for contributing to family happiness.
+ recognize the importance of participating in the parish family's weekly celebration of Mass.
+ review some Mass responses.

Words Your Child Should Know
+ Holy Family
+ Mass
+ parish

We Meet Jesus in the Sacrament of Reconciliation

FOCUS: In this chapter, you will be helping your child to understand that Jesus forgives us in the Sacrament of Reconciliation when we confess our sins.

The entire Christian life is a process of reconciliation, a call for us to "put on" the mind and heart of Jesus. In the ritual of the Sacrament of Penance and Reconciliation, the penitent expresses a definite desire to live more fully the Christian life and receives the encouragement and strength needed to conform his or her life to the inspirations of the Holy Spirit. Reconciliation is the work of a lifetime.

As we grow in our ability to consider, judge, and arrange our lives in the light of God's holiness, we recognize more clearly how we fail to respond to all that God has done for us. In the Sacrament of Reconciliation, the warmth and tenderness of God's love reaches out to us through the ministry of the Church.

Scripture in This Chapter
Mark 2:1–12 Forgiving the Paralyzed Man
John 20:19–23 Authority to Forgive Sins

Catechism of the Catholic Church
1450–1451, 1454–1460

In this chapter, help your child to
+ explain that he or she may choose how to go to the sacrament.
+ identify the opening rites of the sacrament.
+ describe how to confess sins.
+ explain the meaning of penance.
+ explain that in the Sacrament of Reconciliation, Jesus helps us give up selfishness and form a deeper friendship with him.
+ identify an area in themselves that needs improvement in order to become a better person.

Words Your Child Should Know
+ confession   + penance

Key Terms for Your Information
+ amen—a word of agreement; yes
+ beatification—a step in the process of being canonized a saint
+ pardon—forgiveness for sins
+ confess—to admit sins

Jesus Revealed the Kingdom of God

FOCUS: In this chapter, you will be helping your child to understand that through miracles and parables, Jesus taught us about the Kingdom of God, which we are called to belong to and spread.

Christ used parables, short stories based on familiar life experiences, to teach spiritual lessons. People who accepted him as the Messiah understood the parables, whereas people who rejected his messianic role and his teachings found them unintelligible.

Jesus used parables to teach about his kingdom. When he compared the kingdom to a tiny mustard seed that grows into a huge tree, he was speaking of his kingdom on earth, which would grow and develop. When he spoke of the kingdom reserved for those who have carried their crosses lovingly and patiently, he was referring to the heavenly kingdom.

Scripture in This Chapter
Matthew 3:13–17   The Baptism of Jesus
Matthew 4:1–11   The Temptation of Jesus
Matthew 13:45–46   Parable of the Priceless Pearl
Mark 4:30–32   Parable of the Mustard Seed

Catechism of the Catholic Church
535–536, 538–540, 546

In this chapter, help your child to
+ describe the role of John the Baptist.
+ name ways to help bring about Jesus' kingdom.
+ tell the story of how Jesus overcame temptation.
+ explain how temptations can be overcome.
+ describe miracles of Jesus as signs of the authenticity of his message.
+ become familiar with some of Jesus' parables.

Words Your Child Should Know
+ Kingdom of God
+ Revelation
+ Messiah
+ Satan
+ mission
+ Son of God
+ parable

Key Terms for Your Information
+ demon—a devil; an evil spirit
+ fast—to eat not more than one full meal a day
+ miracle—a work or sign that Jesus performed to reveal God's kingdom

We Keep the Lord's Day Holy

FOCUS: In this chapter, you will be helping your child to understand that the Third Commandment tells us to celebrate the Eucharist, to rest, and to enjoy others' company in honor of God's day, Sunday.

In a tradition handed down from the apostles, the Church celebrates Christ's day of Resurrection, Sunday, as the Lord's Day. It is a special day when, according to God's command, our more-frantic activities should grind to a halt, allowing us to converse with God peacefully, reflect on our lives, renew our covenant of faith and love with our Lord, and rejoice with one another. The Church in *The Constitution of the Sacred Liturgy* (106) has decreed this:

> On this day Christ's faithful are bound to come together into one place. They should listen to the word of God and take part in the Eucharist . . . the Lord's Day is the original feast day, a day of joy.

Catholic Christians have the obligation to gather and celebrate the Eucharist on the Lord's Day to thank God for all his gifts.

Scripture in This Chapter
Genesis 2:1–3   God's Rest After Creation
Exodus 20: 8–10   The Holy Sabbath

Catechism of the Catholic Church
2168–2188

In this chapter, help your child to
+ describe what the Third Commandment is and why God has given it to his people.
+ explain how the Israelites and the early Christians kept the Lord's Day holy.
+ describe Sunday as a day to worship God, rest, and play.
+ explain that we celebrate the Eucharist with the Catholic community on Sunday or Saturday evening and holy days.
+ explain that the Eucharist includes all forms of prayer.

Words Your Child Should Know
+ Sabbath
+ Precepts of the Church

Key Term for Your Information
+ holy days—feast days that we are obliged to celebrate by participating in the Eucharist

Unit 2 Review

FOCUS: In this chapter, you will be helping your child to understand that the Eucharist animates us in the Christian spirit to become witnesses to the world.

When we approach the altar of God, we receive refreshment and nourishment: Jesus himself in the Eucharist, who is the heart and center of Christian life. He fills us with the Spirit, his life, and his grace. United with Jesus in his perfect sacrifice, we offer praise and thanksgiving to the Father. We offer ourselves and our efforts to be like Christ, who emptied himself and gave himself up for us. Strengthened by the Eucharist and the blessing of the Father, the Son, and the Holy Spirit, we are commissioned to fulfill his divine mandate.

By accepting this challenge to minister to others in love, we are doing what Jesus did. We are his witnesses, filled with the Spirit, doing his will, and building his kingdom— a kingdom of peace, love, and justice.

Scripture in This Chapter
John 6:1–15   Multiplication of the Loaves
John 6:34–35   The Bread of Life

Catechism of the Catholic Church
1341–1344

In this chapter, help your child to
+ recognize the prayers and actions of the Eucharist.
+ identify the works of mercy.
+ discuss his or her personal participation at Mass.

We Live the Commandments Today

FOCUS: In this chapter, you will be helping your child to understand that the Ten Commandments tell us to love God and one another.

The Ten Commandments free us from false ideas of loving and being. The true freedom of this law is revealed in Christ who showed us a love that knows no hardship too great to bear. It is a love that was willing to die on a cross. It is a love that rose again to new life. As we love, we discover we are not sharing some*thing*, but some*one*. Through the love of the Father, of the Son, and of the Holy Spirit, we are caught up in an eternity of being loved and of loving others.

Scripture in This Chapter
Exodus 20:1–17   The Ten Commandments
Mark 12:30–31   Jesus Summarizes the Commandments.
Matthew 7:12   The Golden Rule
John 13:34–35   The New Commandment

Catechism of the Catholic Church
2052–2055, 2069, 2072

In this chapter, help your child to
+ explain that the commandments help us express love in practical ways.
+ describe how the commandments guide us to love God and neighbor.
+ explain the liturgical year.
+ propose practical applications of the Golden Rule.

Words Your Child Should Know
+ natural law
+ social justice
+ blasphemy
+ blessing
+ Holy Days of Obligation
+ Ordinary Time
+ perjury

Key Terms for Your Information
+ cursing—calling on God to bring evil or harm to someone or something
+ Golden Rule—rule that requires us to treat others as we would like to be treated
+ oath—solemn statement that one is speaking the truth with God as one's witness
+ ouija board—a board used to supposedly communicate with the spirit world
+ profanity—careless use of God's name
+ swearing—taking an oath; used informally for cursing

Penance and Anointing of the Sick—Jesus the Healer

FOCUS: In this chapter, you will be helping your child to understand that Jesus continues to heal body and spirit in the sacraments.

With every one of Jesus' healings, God's kingdom was manifested. Jesus' mission has been handed on to the Church. The priest heals in Jesus' name, using signs and symbols that Jesus used: the touch of a hand, the pouring of oil, the granting of absolution, the depth of faith and the power of words—healing, freeing, and transforming.

Our own hands can bring about healing by a handshake of peace, a reassuring pat, a gentle caress. Our words can heal by expressing forgiveness, acceptance, advice, encouragement, enthusiasm, and understanding. When the kingdom comes in its fullness, we shall recognize that those who healed were those who loved.

Scripture in This Chapter
Luke 15:3–32 The Lost Sheep, The Lost Coin, The Lost Son

Catechism of the Catholic Church
1420–1421, 1440, 1448, 1499, 1502, 1511–1513, 1524

In this chapter, help your child to
+ understand how the Sacrament of Penance continues Christ's ministry of healing and forgiveness.
+ identify three rites for the Sacrament of Penance.
+ discuss his or her understanding of the need for reconciliation.
+ explain how the Sacrament of the Anointing of the Sick continues Christ's ministry of healing.
+ explain the rite of the Anointing of the Sick.

Key Terms for Your Information
+ absolution—pardon for sin
+ confession—telling sins to a priest
+ contrition—sorrow for failing to love; promise of conversion
+ penance—a prayer, an act of self-denial, or a work of charity that makes up for damage or pain caused by sins and helps to overcome sin
+ Sacrament of Penance and Reconciliation—the sacrament in which Christ offers forgiveness and reconciliation to those who have turned away from God and the community
+ viaticum—the rite in which a dying person receives Holy Communion

A House Built on Rock

FOCUS: In this chapter, you will be helping your child to understand that after the persecutions, the Church, faced with heresy, clarified its beliefs through the councils and through the teachings of the Fathers of the Church.

After the persecutions, how did the Church grow so dramatically? First, the Church is a divine institution with a divine founder. The Church teaches a holy doctrine that inspires holiness in its members. Consequently, it is not subject to merely temporal or human limitations. Second, the quality of the Church's early membership was remarkable. There is something in the human heart that compels most men and women to aspire to heroism and nobility.

Later, when the Church was threatened by internal dissension, the Lord, through his saints, steadied the ship of Peter and guided it safely through the dangerous waters of heresy. Empowered by the Holy Spirit, the Fathers of the Church defended the rich heritage of faith and tradition that had been handed on to them.

Scripture in This Chapter
Psalm 62:3 God Is My Rock.
John 15:20 They Will Persecute You.

Catechism of the Catholic Church
461–478, 770–771, 817, 914–924, 2089

In this chapter, help your child to
+ describe how the Church was persecuted.
+ explain the role of the martyrs in the Church.
+ describe the role of monks and hermits in the Church.
+ identify the contributions of the Fathers of the Church and ecumenical councils.
+ identify saints of the early Church.
+ describe how the New Testament evolved.

Words Your Child Should Know
+ heresy
+ poverty

Key Terms for Your Information
+ ecumenical council—a meeting of all the bishops of the universal Church
+ hermit—a person who lives alone to seek God through prayer, silence, and penance
+ monk—a man who lives a life of prayer and takes vows such as poverty, chastity, and obedience; usually he lives in community with other men

Jesus Calls Apostles

FOCUS: In this chapter, you will be helping your child to understand that Jesus invites everyone to help him.

Human experience through the ages testifies that we fear the call to a different way of life. There is the challenge to answer the divine call and the temptation to resist. There is the fear of being set apart and of losing one's security. Yet there is the conviction that we must follow our call. Jesus, in calling his apostles to follow him, does not hide what his invitation to "great expectations" requires: "Come after me, and I will make you fishers of men." (Mark 1:17)

The call to share in the work of the Lord is given to all who have been graced by Baptism. In the Memorial Prayer of Eucharistic Prayer II, as the priest offers the life-giving bread and the saving cup to the Father, we are reminded of our sublime call:

> We thank you for counting us worthy to stand in your presence and serve you.

Scripture in This Chapter
Mark 1:16–20; 2:13–14 and John 1:35–51 Jesus Calls the Apostles.
Matthew 8:23–27 Jesus Calms the Storm at Sea.

Catechism of the Catholic Church
541, 547–548, 849–856, 934

In this chapter, help your child to
+ know that Jesus had helpers and that we are all called to be one of Jesus' helpers.
+ explain that people in all walks of life work together to bring God's love to our world.
+ understand that all Christians are called to be Jesus' helpers.
+ understand that deacons, priests, and religious share Jesus' work in a special way.
+ discuss the life of Frances Cabrini.

Word Your Child Should Know
+ apostle

Key Terms for Your Information
+ Good News—the message that God loves us
+ missionary—someone who brings the Good News of Jesus to others
+ religious sisters and brothers—women and men who have publicly professed vows of poverty, obedience, and chastity

We Become Better Persons

FOCUS: In this chapter, you will be helping your child to understand that through sorrow for sin and penance, we become better friends of Jesus.

When obstacles block our path, the mere act of clearing them away does not bring us any closer to our goal. Removing the obstacles is but the first task; we must take some steps once the way is clear. The Scriptures emphasize that the sincerity of our repentance can be known only by what we do after forgiveness is granted. In the Sacrament of Reconciliation, after the priest encourages us to improve, he speaks the words of absolution.

The Holy Spirit, constantly working within us, makes us aware of God's loving intention behind the storms and trials of life. Through the Spirit, we realize how selfish attitudes influence our activities. Then we are able to give the Lord first place in our hearts and lives.

Scripture in This Chapter
Psalm 51:1–14 Prayer for Forgiveness
Luke 19:1–10 Zacchaeus' Change of Heart

Catechism of the Catholic Church
1459–1460, 1465, 1491

In this chapter, help your child to
+ describe ways to make up for unloving behavior.
+ explain that penance is how we make up for unloving acts.
+ explain the importance of contrition and the significance of absolution.
+ describe the part of the rite of the Sacrament of Reconciliation that follows the confession of sins.
+ describe the procedure for the Sacrament of Reconciliation

Words Your Child Should Know
+ absolution
+ contrition

Key Terms for Your Information
+ Act of Contrition—prayer of sorrow for sin
+ praise—to declare how great and wonderful God is
+ sorrow—extreme sadness

Jesus Came to Give Life

FOCUS: In this chapter, you will be helping your child to understand that Jesus cured people and brought them back to life as a sign of the new life he brings us.

Jesus showed love and compassion for those who suffered from physical disabilities. He healed people who were lame, gave sight to those who were blind, and even raised the dead to life. In doing so, Jesus not only showed his great love for people, but also was revealing the presence of the Kingdom of God here on earth. Jesus' healings truly announced that the Kingdom of God was at hand.

Today, Jesus continues his works of healing through the sacraments, as divine love continues to be translated into living deeds. The Sacrament of Penance and Reconciliation is the great source of spiritual healing, in which the triumph of Jesus over sin and Satan is truly celebrated. The Eucharist has healing power, as does the Anointing of the Sick. Through the Church, Jesus continues to minister to those who suffer. All of us participate in this ministry to some extent when our acts of thoughtfulness and assistance show Jesus' love to those who suffer.

Scripture in This Chapter
Mark 1:40–45 The Cure of the Man with Leprosy
Luke 7:11–16 Raising of the Widow's Son
Luke 8:40–56 Jairus's Daughter and the Woman with a
    Hemorrhage
Luke 18:35–43 The Cure of the Blind Man

Catechism of the Catholic Church
547–549, 2609, 2616

In this chapter, help your child to
+ know of Jesus' compassion for people who suffer through the story of his healing the man with leprosy.
+ tell the story of Jesus bringing the widow's son back to life.
+ describe the stories of the miracle of Jesus' cure of the blind man and of the hemorrhaging woman.
+ describe the story of Jesus raising a girl from the dead.
+ tell how Jesus' healing miracles announced God's kingdom.

Key Term for Your Information
+ Nain—village in southwest Galilee; the name means "pleasant"

We Grow in Holiness

FOCUS: In this chapter, you will be helping your child to understand that we must not only hear God's Word, but we must also live it.

As followers of Jesus, we are privileged to hear God's saving Word at every Eucharist and to read it ourselves in Scripture. We are free to respond as we wish. We may walk away untouched and unmoved by these words, letting them go in one ear and out the other. Or we may let them take root in our heart and work in us, transforming us into the people we were intended to be—people full of love.

In the parable of the sower, Jesus elaborates on the various responses to the Word. He also points out that those who listen to the Word bear abundant fruit—as much as a hundred times the amount of those who do not listen. If all who heard God's Word reflected on it and applied it to their own lives, what a wonderful world it would be.

Scripture in This Chapter
Mark 4:3–9 Parable of the Sower
Mark 4:14–20 Jesus' Explanation of the Parable

Catechism of the Catholic Church
102–103, 108, 131–133, 546

In this chapter, help your child to
+ discuss the Parable of the Sower.
+ explain that good deeds witness to God's Word.
+ review his or her understanding of the first three commandments by participating in games and activities.
+ explain that he or she can show love for God by keeping the first three commandments.
+ explain the importance of spreading Christ's kingdom.

God's Healing Love

FOCUS: In this chapter, you will be helping your child to understand that conscience helps us exercise our freedom to choose what is good.

Jesus, the perfect Revelation of the Father, manifested the mercy of God by his healing and forgiving love while on earth. Jesus' cures, or healings, were for the spirit as well as for the body. He forgave the paralytic his sins before he cured his illness; he absolved the woman taken in adultery after he saved her body from stoning. His final act of love was to suffer and die on the cross so that we might be healed and saved from sin, and even while he suffered, he forgave those responsible.

Sinners that we are, we have all benefited from Christ's healing love and forgiveness many times in our lives. We in turn should share that healing love with others by forgiving those who in any way have offended us and by asking forgiveness of those we have in any way offended.

Scripture in This Chapter
Luke 5:17–26   The Healing of a Paralytic
1 Peter 1:18–19   Ransomed by the Blood of Christ

Catechism of the Catholic Church
1778–1781, 1783–1785, 1849, 1854–1863

In this chapter, help your child to
+ define conscience as a judgment of the rightness or wrongness of an act.
+ define the term Anointing of the Sick.
+ describe sin and the effects of sin.
+ distinguish between mortal sin and venial sin and their effects.
+ define the term sanctifying grace.
+ evaluate the choices made in problem situations.

Words Your Child Should Know
+ Anointing of the Sick
+ sanctifying grace

Key Terms for Your Information
+ Act of Contrition—prayer recited to express to God one's sorrow for his or her sins
+ contrition—sorrow for one's sins, which can be perfect contrition (sorrow because one offended God) or imperfect contrition (sorrow due to other motives, such as fear of hell)

Learning God's Way

FOCUS: In this chapter, you will be helping your child to understand that, like the Israelites, we are called to grow in our ability to make decisions based on faith.

By our Baptism we have entered into a covenant relationship with the God of all Creation. We have pledged to live according to the mind of Jesus, as enlightened by the Holy Spirit. Our daily lives, with their many decisions, can give evidence of the depth of our faith and the stability of our commitment. We will want to open our lives to God and allow him to work in and through us. Each day we will strive to listen to God as we are challenged to apply the values and principles of Gospel living in our lives.

Do we have informed Christian consciences that prepare us to make Christian decisions, to accept responsibility for our decisions, and to cope with their consequences? If we would meet this challenge, we must devote time to both prayer and study, allowing the Lord himself to form our minds and hearts according to the Gospel values of Jesus.

Scripture in This Chapter
Numbers 13–14   The Israelites Reach Canaan.
Numbers 20:1–13   A Complaining People
Matthew 5:3–12   The Beatitudes

Catechism of the Catholic Church
1778–1794, 2070, 2634–2636

In this chapter, help your child to
+ describe why the Israelites did not enter Canaan immediately.
+ explain that belief demands a certain mode of behavior.
+ identify the need for taking responsibility for the consequences of his or her decisions.
+ identify the function of conscience in decision making.
+ describe how to form a correct conscience.
+ explain how making Christian decisions is a sign of faith.

Word Your Child Should Know
+ intercession

Key Term for Your Information
+ Promised Land—Canaan, the land promised by God to the Israelites; its modern-day name is Israel

The Message of Jesus: Choose Life—Jesus the Teacher

FOCUS: In this chapter, you will be helping your child to understand that keeping Jesus' Great Commandment of love means to respect life.

Christian morality is not merely a list of what is permitted and what is not. Rather, it is an invitation to respond to the love of the one who has called us into being, and, through Jesus, to become all that we are called to be. By our creation and by our Baptism, we have been drawn into and washed over by the love of Jesus. We are enabled to love after the example of Jesus. In loving as Jesus loves, we encounter the mystery of God, who is love.

Christian love nurtures life at all times. It protects the unborn and those who are aged. It heals the wounds of hasty words. It hopes all things and engenders that hope in sin-weary humanity.

Scripture in This Chapter

Matthew 5:21–48 Jesus Teaches a New Understanding of the Law.
Matthew 22:36–40 The Greatest Commandment
Luke 10:29–37 The Good Samaritan

Catechism of the Catholic Church

2268–2287, 2302–2317, 2447–2448

In this chapter, help your child to

+ explain some implications of Jesus' Sermon on the Mount for his or her own life.
+ explain that Jesus accepts us as we are, but challenges us to grow.
+ list ways to protect and nurture the gift of life.
+ define certain sins against life and explain why they are wrong.
+ identify the Spiritual and Corporal Works of Mercy and ways to carry them out.

Words Your Child Should Know

+ abortion
+ ageism
+ euthanasia
+ racism
+ scandal
+ sexism
+ suicide

Key Term for Your Information

+ prejudice—unreasonable dislike of a particular group of people

---

A Light in Darkness: Part I

FOCUS: In this chapter, you will be helping your child to understand that during invasions by northern tribes, strong popes, monks, and holy men and women helped preserve civilization and the faith.

With the end of the persecutions, the Roman Empire, which had been the sworn enemy of Christianity for almost three centuries, became its champion. In the late fifth century, a movement began that was to topple every institution of the empire except the Church. For many years, uncivilized tribes had lived on the borders of the empire. Compelled by their need for food and land and fleeing the vicious Huns, they invaded. Germanic tribes gradually overran the empire, burning, looting, and pillaging. By the early sixth century, they controlled practically all of Europe.

For European Christians, the invasions of Germanic tribes marked the end of the world as they had known it. Scholars, who have dubbed this period the Dark Ages, consider it a low point in Western history. But amid the murk and gloom, a small flame shone bravely and steadily. In those monasteries that had survived the invasions, monks were tending the light of Christian civilization, culture, and learning.

Scripture in This Chapter

Luke 8:16 That Others May See the Light

Catechism of the Catholic Church

817, 873, 920–921, 925–927, 2089

In this chapter, help your child to

+ describe the role of the Church in preserving faith and culture after the Fall of the Roman Empire.
+ explain the work of the monks as missionaries and educators.
+ identify and explain the theological and cardinal virtues.
+ explain how the Church adapted to change.
+ identify great women of the Middle Ages who are models of holiness.
+ propose ways to make Christ's values a part of his or her life.

Word Your Child Should Know

+ virtue

Key Term for Your Information

+ Germanic tribes—uneducated, pagan tribes that invaded Europe during the fifth century and contributed to the Fall of the Roman Empire

Jesus Shows God's Love

FOCUS: In this chapter, you will be helping your child to understand that Jesus, who healed and forgave people, asks us to show his love today.

The sick of body were brought to Jesus or sought him out and were healed. People in spiritual need found Jesus even more concerned about healing them. He himself took the initiative to cure them. His tender compassion was the sign Jesus gave John the Baptist to cause him to recognize that God was visiting his people, that the Lord was truly present among them.

> When John heard in prison of the works of the Messiah, he sent his disciples to him with this question, "Are you the one who is to come, or should we look for another?" Jesus said to them in reply, "Go and tell John what you hear and see: the blind regain their sight, the lame walk, lepers are cleansed, the deaf hear, the dead are raised, and the poor have the good news proclaimed to them."
>
> *Matthew 11:2–5*

Scripture in This Chapter
Mark 2:1–12 The Healing of the Paralyzed Man
Mark 5:21–24,35–43 Jesus Raises the Daughter of Jairus

Catechism of the Catholic Church
1503–1509

In this chapter, help your child to
+ explain that Jesus had compassion for suffering people.
+ show awareness of those who are suffering.
+ desire to alleviate the sufferings of others.
+ describe how Jesus has power over life and death.
+ show thoughtfulness and concern toward those who are suffering.

Key Terms for Your Information
+ leprosy—a contagious skin disease that was once more common; people with leprosy were isolated from the rest of the community

Jesus Calls Us His Friends

FOCUS: In this chapter, you will be helping your child to understand that God's love brings us healing and forgiveness in the Sacrament of Reconciliation.

Christ's saving death has reconciled us to God, but our human sinfulness imposes on us a continual need to order our lives more fully in accord with God's holiness and love. In approaching the Sacrament of Reconciliation, Catholics externalize their internal desire for a deeper relationship with God and proclaim the power of his forgiving love. Although the Eucharist is the central and most meaningful sign of our reconciliation with God and with each other, the Sacrament of Reconciliation brings us face-to-face with our unique struggles against evil and facilitates a freer and fuller response to God. The value of frequent sacramental reconciliation is expressed in the opening prayer for communal celebrations:

> Where sin has divided and scattered,
> may your love make one again;
> where sin has brought weakness,
> may your power heal and strengthen;
> where sin has brought death,
> may your Spirit raise to new life.
>
> *Rite of Reconciliation 99*

Scripture in This Chapter
Luke 10: 38–42 Mary and Martha

Catechism of the Catholic Church
1485, 1489–1490, 1496

In this chapter, help your child to
+ describe through the story of Martha and Mary that friendship with Jesus is shown in prayer and loving service.
+ identify the key concepts related to the Sacrament of Reconciliation.
+ describe God's gifts to us in the Sacrament of Reconciliation.
+ demonstrate an understanding of the Sacrament of Reconciliation as presented in Unit 3.

God's Kingdom Is a Kingdom of Love

FOCUS: In this chapter, you will be helping your child to understand that Jesus taught us to love one another.

The wonders Jesus worked in Galilee and Judea throughout the years of his public life revealed his power and might, his mercy and love, and his profound desire to bring everyone to faith and union with him in his kingdom. By his death on the cross, he defeated evil and brought us fullness of life. The greatest sign of his love was his willingness to suffer and die so that we might come into his kingdom.

Jesus invites us to trust in his Father's care and his ever-faithful love, even when the harsh realities of everyday life obscure his presence in our world. Only by the light of Jesus' life and teachings can we see what we are truly called to be. The more we become aware of how much God loves us, the more we strive to give him what he expects from us.

Scripture in This Chapter
Matthew 5—7 The Sermon on the Mount

Catechism of the Catholic Church
1723–1724, 1889, 2608

In this chapter, help your child to
* describe Jesus' lessons in the Sermon on the Mount.
* name ways to help spread the kingdom by acts of service.
* recall the keywords and ideas presented in Unit 3.
* better express an understanding of Jesus' mission of inaugurating the Kingdom of God.
* demonstrate how well he or she knows the concepts presented in Unit 3.

We Honor and Obey

FOCUS: In this chapter, you will be helping your child to understand that the Fourth Commandment tells us to respect our parents and other people in authority.

In giving us the Fourth Commandment, God shows that he values the family. God stresses the relationship of love and respect that should exist between children and parents. God considers this commandment so important that he promises a special blessing to those who are faithful to it.

The family is the source of life and the primary center of education. Ideally, it should offer a loving environment in which children flourish and mature into adults ready to contribute to the improvement of society. Parents who create a strong family unit through love, patience, self-sacrifice, and self-control provide their children with a sense of responsibility. In an atmosphere of love, children are better able to accept the necessary guidance and direction they need to become mature Christians. The Holy Family should be the inspiration of today's modern family, which seeks love, unity, and permanence.

Scripture in This Chapter
Exodus 20:12 The Fourth Commandment
Mark 12:13–17 Paying Taxes to Caesar

Catechism of the Catholic Church
2197–2200, 2215–2217, 2238–2240

In this chapter, help your child to
* describe what the Fourth Commandment is and why God has given it to us.
* explain that he or she can bring happiness to his or her family by showing honor and respect for parents.
* explain that the Fourth Commandment tells us to respect and obey those in authority.
* describe ways to respect and obey the adults who guide and protect him or her.
* describe ways to be a good citizen of his or her neighborhood, country, and Church.

Word Your Child Should Know
* obedience

Key Term for Your Information
* honor—to show respect and love

Jesus Heals Us in the Sacrament of Reconciliation

FOCUS: In this chapter, you will be helping your child to understand that Jesus forgives us in the Sacrament of Reconciliation when we are sorry for our sins.

God's invitation is the moving force in our relationship with him. And so it was that Zacchaeus was inspired to climb a tree to catch a glimpse of Jesus as he passed by. The idea stemmed from a desire to see what kind of man Jesus was. Thus, the Lord initiated even that first movement toward a radical life conversion that began when Jesus reached out to Zacchaeus. Jesus' invitation was a declaration of love and respect for a tax collector—a person spurned by others. This affirmation by Jesus enabled Zacchaeus to admit that he had done wrong, that he had sinned.

Being loved and forgiven by Jesus gave Zacchaeus a new freedom; he was no longer driven by his desire for money and power. He had found the love of Jesus. He was moved to respond by making reparation for his dishonesty and injustice.

Scripture in This Chapter
Luke 19:1–10 Zacchaeus the Tax Collector
John 20:22–23 Forgiveness of Sins

Catechism of the Catholic Church
1440–1442, 1446, 1448, 1450–1451, 1455, 1461

In this chapter, help your child to
+ recognize the pattern of penance through the story of Zacchaeus.
+ identify the importance of reparation for sin.
+ propose the means to make up for specific sins.
+ define the word *contrition*.
+ identify the steps of confession.
+ define the words *absolution* and *penance*.

Words Your Child Should Know
+ contrition
+ absolution
+ penance

God Forgives Us

FOCUS: In this chapter, you will be helping your child to understand that God forgives us as he did the Israelites in the desert.

Jesus told us, "I came so that they might have life and have it more abundantly" (John 10:10), and he would spare himself nothing until he fulfilled that promise. Jesus, the Son of the eternal Father, was lifted up on the cross so that, seeing his great love, we might believe in him. He thus overcame the power of sin and death and offered freedom of spirit to all who accept him as Lord and Redeemer.

Those who believe in Jesus and all he has done for them are moved to respond in love. They permit nothing to separate them from their Beloved. Sin is confessed, and forgiveness is asked and given. The Lord Jesus reigns supreme in their hearts. They experience life as never before. Jesus was raised on the cross. He has also been raised to a new life of glory, where he sits at the right hand of the Father, in the unity of the Holy Spirit.

Scripture in This Chapter
Numbers 21:4–9 The Bronze Serpent
John 3:14–15 The Son of Man Must Be Lifted Up.

Catechism of the Catholic Church
1093–1094, 1423–1424, 1440, 1468–1469

In this chapter, help your child to
+ summarize the story of the bronze serpent.
+ explain how the bronze serpent prefigured Jesus.
+ name ways in which we can be reconciled.
+ identify ways of celebrating the Sacrament of Penance and Reconciliation.
+ list ways that we hurt others and ways we can help one another.

Words Your Child Should Know
+ grace   + mortal sin
+ venial sin   + virtue

Key Terms for Your Information
+ bronze serpent—an object that God had Moses make and raise up on a pole in order to heal people who had been bitten by a snake; it prefigured Jesus being raised on the cross to save all people
+ perfect contrition—being truly sorry for sin because God is all good and worthy of all our love

The Challenge of the Beatitudes—Jesus the Light of the World

FOCUS: In this chapter, you will be helping your child to understand that in the Beatitudes, Jesus gives us guidelines for a happy life in this world and in the next.

The Beatitudes are at the center of the mystery of the Kingdom of God. Through them, God breaks into our world with a new power, a new message, and new consolations, enabling us to live with a new hope. Christian living means living the Beatitudes. Jesus reverses our expectations by telling us that it is blessed to be poor in spirit, to mourn, to be meek, to hunger and thirst for righteousness, to be merciful, to be clean of heart, to be peacemakers, and to be persecuted for the sake of righteousness.

Jesus demands loving even unto death. His Beatitudes call us to radical self-giving. They run counter to the values of our times. Yet they are the source of true happiness here and in the hereafter. We need to be touched by God's Spirit to translate the Beatitudes into our lives and the lives of others. Then we can pray with sincerity the words that Jesus taught us: "Your will be done. Your kingdom come."

Scripture in This Chapter
Matthew 5:3–10 The Beatitudes
Mark 10:21 The Rich Young Man

Catechism of the Catholic Church
1716–1719

In this chapter, help your child to
+ identify the Beatitudes as guidelines for Christlike living, which can lead to happiness now and in the hereafter.
+ explain each beatitude.
+ explain how Jesus lived the Beatitudes and how he expects his disciples to do so.
+ describe how great is the call to serve.
+ propose solutions to problem situations that are in line with the Beatitudes.
+ discuss what life would be like if her or she lived according to the Beatitudes.

Key Terms for Your Information
+ Beatitudes—a set of guidelines for Christlike living that will make us happy and lead us to eternal life
+ meek—gentle and humble

A Light in Darkness: Part II

FOCUS: In this chapter, you will be helping your child to understand that the Church often served as a beacon of light in the Middle Ages.

During the Middle Ages, conflicts and power struggles within the Church threatened her ability to serve God's people. The Plague, also referred to as the Black Death, killed at least a third of Europe's population. The schism between the Eastern and Western Churches, the Crusades, and the Inquisition brought serious damage to the institution of the Church. Thankfully, in the face of great challenges, holy men and women brought about renewal in the Church and the world. Like them, we too can call upon the Lord, knowing that he will be with us in times of distress.

Scripture in This Chapter
John 17:21 May All Be One.
Matthew 5:14–16 Your Light Must Shine.
Matthew 22:37 The Greatest Commandment

Catechism of the Catholic Church
866–867, 937, 2133–2134

In this chapter, help your child to
+ explain the problems that resulted from the close connection between Church and state during medieval times.
+ describe the Great Schism.
+ identify the good and bad results of the Crusades and the Inquisition.
+ describe how the Church influenced life in medieval times, especially through the Mendicant Orders and Catholic universities.

Words Your Child Should Know
+ excommunication
+ schism
+ Mendicant Order
+ spirituality
+ *Summa Theologiae*

Key Terms for Your Information
+ lay investiture—the practice whereby political leaders, instead of Church leaders, appointed priests and bishops
+ Great Schism—the separation of the Eastern Church from the Western Church in a.d. 1054
+ Crusades—expeditions, or holy wars, to fight the Muslims and regain the Holy Land
+ Inquisition—trials during the Middle Ages to find and punish heretics

Jesus Teaches Us to Love God

FOCUS: In this chapter, you will be helping your child to understand that the greatest commandment is to love God.

Jesus' love for his Father prompted him to pray. Leaving the throngs who followed him, Jesus went apart to converse with God; Jesus knew the gift of his Father. He knew his Father's love and how it alone can satisfy the human heart. He repeated the command given by God to his people through Moses:

> "You shall love the Lord, your God, with all your heart, with all your soul, and with all your mind. This is the greatest and the first commandment."
>
> *Matthew 22:37–38*

Jesus spells out the meaning of this love during the Last Supper:

> "Whoever loves me will keep my word, and my Father will love him, and we will come to him and make our dwelling with him."
>
> *John 14:23*

Each time we are sent forth from Mass, the priest or deacon reminds us of our obligation to respond to the gift we have received:

> Go in peace to love and serve
> the Lord.

Scripture in This Chapter
Mark 12:28–30 The Greatest Commandment
John 15:9 Jesus Calls Us to Remain in His Love.

Catechism of the Catholic Church
1695, 1803, 2055

In this chapter, help your child to
+ identify ways to show love for God.
+ explain how love can be shown by deeds.
+ discuss ways to show love for God by mirroring his goodness in thought, word, and action.
+ pray a simple Morning Offering.
+ explain how the Morning Offering transforms daily acts, joys, and sufferings into offerings of love.

Key Term for Your Information
+ commandment—law given by God

Jesus Promised the Gift of Himself

FOCUS: In this chapter, you will be helping your child to understand that Jesus gives himself to us under the forms of bread and wine.

The mystery of the Holy Eucharist, Christ's presence among us in the Blessed Sacrament, is a great mystery of our faith. In the Eucharist, Jesus Christ gives his very life for our nourishment. The bread and wine signify its spiritually nutritive value.

When we are receptive to the riches Christ offers us in the Eucharist, we become a community bent on glorifying God and serving others in his name. The eucharistic action is an effective symbol of our unity with one another as well as with our God. When Christ gives himself as food in the Eucharist, his life is shared by all who receive him.

Scripture in This Chapter
John 6: 1–15 Miracle of the Loaves and Fishes
John 6: 35–38 The Bread of Life

Catechism of the Catholic Church
1335, 1336, 1359–1361

In this chapter, help your child to
+ describe bread as an important source of life.
+ repeat the story of the multiplication of loaves.
+ describe how Jesus promised us the Holy Eucharist.
+ explain that Jesus comes in Holy Communion to help us follow him by glorifying God and serving others.

Words Your Child Should Know
+ miracle
+ Holy Communion

Key Terms for Your Information
+ Bread of Life—the Eucharist; the bread that becomes Jesus at Mass
+ Holy Communion—Jesus in the form of bread and wine given to us during the Mass
+ Living Bread—the bread that is Jesus at Mass

Jesus Suffered and Died for Us

FOCUS: In this chapter, you will be helping your child to understand that Jesus makes a New Covenant and offers himself to save us.

The passion is the high point of Jesus' mission on earth, the work that is central to all his other works. Crushed by the enormity of the task before him and by the burden of the world's sins, Jesus' human nature at first cried out to be relieved of the suffering he was to undergo. However, as love triumphed, he immediately added that all should be as his Father willed. Love for his Father and love for us was the driving force, the supreme motivation of his entire life. He left us a legacy of love by his words and his deeds:

> This is my commandment: love one another as I love you. No one has greater love than this, to lay down one's life for one's friends. *John 15:12–13*

Scripture in This Chapter

Matthew 27, Mark 15, Luke 23, John 19 Jesus' Passion and Death

Mark 11:1–11 Jesus' Triumphal Entry into Jerusalem

Mark 14 The Agony in the Garden; The Betrayal and Arrest of Jesus

Luke 19:41–44 Jesus' Lament for Jerusalem

Catechism of the Catholic Church

559–560, 610–612, 616, 2742

In this chapter, help your child to

+ identify Mass as the celebration of the New Covenant.
+ describe how through the Eucharist, God brings us into a deeper relationship.
+ give examples of how the divine life received in the Eucharist empowers God's people to love.
+ tell the main parts of the passion narrative.

Word Your Child Should Know

+ Sacrifice of the Mass

Key Terms for Your Information

+ sacramental—words, actions, or objects blessed by the Church that bring us closer to God
+ New Covenant—God's promise to give us eternal life if we live as his children and love one another as Jesus has loved us
+ Gethsemane (Geth SEM uh nee)—the garden where Jesus and the apostles went after the Last Supper

We Respect the Gift of Life

FOCUS: In this chapter, you will be helping your child to understand that the Fifth Commandment tells us to care for ourselves and others because life is precious.

Our God is a God of being who creates life and calls every person to eternal life with him. It is God's blessing that gives and sustains life, and God clearly forbids any act of mortal violence against any person. Each person's life is a unique expression of the diversity of God's creation, and each person enriches and ennobles the human family. The dignity and worth of each person are so great that Jesus solemnly tells us that we are accountable before God for any thought, word, or act that disregards them (Matthew 25:31–46).

Jesus calls us, as his disciples, to root out from our lives all violence and desire for retaliation. In his parable of the Good Samaritan, Jesus tells us that there must be no discrimination in our respect for human life; we are all neighbors. We are most like our heavenly Father when our reconciling and gratuitous love reflects his compassionate, life-giving attitude toward all.

Scripture in This Chapter

+ Exodus 20:13 God's Law Against Killing
+ Luke 10:25–37 The Good Samaritan

Catechism of the Catholic Church

2258, 2262, 2288, 2447

In this chapter, help your child to

+ explain that the Fifth Commandment tells us to respect the gift of life and to care for it.
+ discuss how all human life is sacred because it comes from God.
+ identify ways to help people with special needs.
+ describe Peter Claver's dedication to people who were oppressed.
+ explain how the Fifth Commandment applies to his or her own life.
+ explain that discrimination toward anyone is wrong.

Key Terms for Your Information

+ mercy—pity; compassion; love that helps others; love that forgives
+ murder—deliberately killing a person
+ Samaritans—people who lived in Palestine and were enemies of the Jews
+ suicide—taking one's own life

A Gift of Strength

FOCUS: In this chapter, you will be helping your child to understand that through the Sacrament of the Anointing of the Sick, Jesus can heal us in body and soul.

God wants us to be healthy and whole, physically, spiritually, and emotionally. Healing was an integral part of Jesus' work among us, and the sick approached him with utter confidence in his power. Jesus has called us to continue his work of healing. Although all our expressions of support and concern for those who are sick bring them his love, it is in the Church's ritual anointing and laying on of hands that we celebrate, as a community, the power of Jesus to heal those who are sick and forgive their sins.

The anointing is a personal sharing in the suffering of Christ. Sick people can respond to their suffering in a way that unites them to Jesus in his passion and death. With him, they can say yes to God's plan and trust the Father as he did. This is our prayer for them: that as they suffer in the Lord, they will come to be identified with Christ and be brought to the glory of his Resurrection.

Scripture in This Chapter

Isaiah 12:2 God is My Strength.
Mark 10:46–52 Blind Bartimaeus
James 5:14–15 Anointing of the Sick

Catechism of the Catholic Church

1499, 1505, 1511–1519, 1524

In this chapter, help your child to

+ describe the Christian attitude toward suffering.
+ explain when the Anointing of the Sick may be received.
+ explain the value of the Anointing of the Sick.
+ describe how the rite is celebrated.
+ define the word *viaticum*.

Word Your Child Should Know

+ viaticum

God's Chosen People Enter the Promised Land

FOCUS: In this chapter, you will be helping your child to understand that Joshua led the Israelites into the Promised Land.

God called Moses to lead the people out of Egypt; Joshua was selected to lead them into Canaan. These leaders were people of faith who obeyed the Lord and served his people.

Human beings need leaders. In a state, judges, police, and elected officials help the people to live together in harmony. In the Church, certain offices, such as that of bishop, have been established to help carry on the work of Christ's kingdom. Leaders can trust in divine help in order to serve God's people to the best of their ability.

Scripture in This Chapter

Deuteronomy 31–34 The Death of Moses
Book Of Joshua The Conquering of Canaan
Matthew 25:32–46 The Last Judgment

Catechism of the Catholic Church

1898–1899, 1930, 2234–2236

In this chapter, help your child to

+ identify Moses' and Joshua's leadership qualities.
+ summarize the purpose and responsibilities of authority and appropriate responses to leaders.
+ describe how the Israelites conquered Canaan.
+ identify leaders in the Church.
+ list the cardinal virtues: fortitude, justice, prudence, and temperance.

Words Your Child Should Know

+ Confirmation
+ heaven
+ hell
+ purgatory

Key Terms for Your Information

+ authority—right to command, to require obedience
+ Jericho—first city in the Promised Land to be conquered by Joshua
+ Levites—descendants of Levi; priests of the Israelites
+ Mount Nebo—place from which Moses saw the Promised Land before he died
+ Shiloh—city where the Ark of the Covenant was placed after the Israelites entered the Promised Land
+ Vicar of Christ—the pope, Christ's representative, who is the visible leader of the Church

Jesus' Kingdom of Justice and Truth—Jesus the King

FOCUS: In this chapter, you will be helping your child to understand that Jesus expects us to live in honesty and faith, respecting others and the things of this world.

The Seventh, Eighth, and Tenth Commandments guide us to show love and respect for others by living in justice and truth. They forbid stealing, cheating, lying, envy, and greed. But they set no limits on what we can do for one another through justice and love.

As people of the kingdom, we strive to see that all of our brothers and sisters enjoy the rights God bestowed on them. We confront attitudes and actions that institutionalize injustice. We secure conditions that enable all people to contribute freely and actively to society. We seek to place goods and materials more generously at the service of others.

Scripture in This Chapter
Mark 1:15 The Kingdom Is at Hand.
Luke 19:1–10 Zacchaeus

Catechism of the Catholic Church
2393, 2401–2402, 2407–2408, 2467–2470, 2477–2487

In this chapter, help your child to
+ identify ways to be a person of justice.
+ make decisions based on honesty.
+ relate how truthfulness is necessary for building relationships (Eighth Commandment).
+ identify ways to become a person of truth.
+ review ways we practice truth and justice.
+ explain how reverence for people determines how we make moral choices.

Words Your Child Should Know
+ Catholic Social Teaching   + social sin
+ greed

Key Terms for Your Information
+ covet—to desire what belongs to another
+ envy—feeling deprived or sad over another person's material possessions or success
+ justice—fairness; giving all people what they deserve; respecting the rights of others
+ restitution—returning or paying for a stolen item or repairing or paying for a damaged item

The Church Faces Challenges

FOCUS: In this chapter, you will be helping your child to understand that a worldly Church gave rise to the Protestant Reformation.

Hints of the Church's decline were already evident during the late 1200s, when some religious and lay leaders became preoccupied with power, pleasure, and possessions. The next 250 years witnessed a succession of power plays involving emperors, kings, and popes.

In time, the vicar of Christ himself was viewed more as a Renaissance prince than as a holy, humble shepherd of souls. Through it all, the Holy Spirit remained with the Church of Christ, inspiring men and women to counter the evil around them. They, unlike Luther, opted to find their answers *within*, not *outside*, the Church.

Scripture in This Chapter
Matthew 28:20 Jesus Will Be With Us Always.
Matthew 16:18 The Church Is Built upon Peter.
John 14:16 Jesus Promises the Holy Spirit.

Catechism of the Catholic Church
843–847, 1471–1479

In this chapter, help your child to
+ describe the Great Western Schism and the Black Death as challenges to the Church.
+ describe how the Church was affected by the Renaissance.
+ summarize the causes, events, and impact of the Protestant Reformation.
+ describe the events that led to a separation of the Church of England.
+ identify a few Protestant faith traditions.
+ explain the need to work for Christian unity.

Words Your Child Should Know
+ annulment   + Protestant Reformation
+ indulgences

Key Terms for Your Information
+ Great Western Schism—the period of Church history from 1378 to 1417 when two—then three—men claimed to be the pope at the same time
+ Renaissance—the period from the 14th to the 16th centuries, during which Europe experienced a great revival of ancient Greek and Roman culture
+ excommunication—separation from the Church as a result of not adhering to its doctrine

Jesus Teaches Us to Love Others

FOCUS: In this chapter, you will be helping your child to understand that we love others by helping those in need.

The notion of neighbor embraces everyone. Jesus makes concrete the meaning of Christian love by his example of love in spite of betrayal. He instructed us by his parable of the Good Samaritan and by his declaration that we would be judged on the last day by how we have loved our neighbor. The charter of Christians (Matthew, chapters 5–7) includes Christ's words on how far-reaching our love must be:

> You have heard that it was said, "You shall love your neighbor and hate your enemy." But I say to you, love your enemies, and pray for those who persecute you, that you may be children of your heavenly Father[.]
> *Matthew 5:43–45*

Our Sunday Eucharist celebrates the bond that unites us to God and to all the people of God. How fitting it is that we prepare for the Eucharist by asking for forgiveness for the times we have not loved God and others as we should.

Scripture in This Chapter

Mark 12:28–31 The Greatest Commandment
Mark 12:41–44 The Widow's Mite
Luke 10:29–37 The Parable of the Good Samaritan
John 13:34–35 The New Commandment

Catechism of the Catholic Church

1931, 1932, 1937

In this chapter, help your child to

+ tell the message of the story of the Good Samaritan.
+ recognize that Jesus wants us to respond to any person in need.
+ name different ways to show love for others, especially for his or her immediate family.
+ see others as neighbors and be moved to help.
+ know the story of the widow's mite.

Key Terms for Your Information

+ missions—groups that help others to live, know, and love God
+ sacrifice—to give up something that we like

We Celebrate God's Love

FOCUS: In this chapter, you will be helping your child to understand that at the Eucharist, we offer Jesus and ourselves to the Father.

At each Eucharist, we celebrate Christ's total self-giving. Christ gives himself to us as our Living Bread so that we may live in him as he lives in the Father. The great sacrifice of praise that Christ gave to his Church at the Last Supper enables us to make present the offering of his life for our salvation each time we celebrate Mass.

Jesus' sacrifice reveals to us the depth of the Father's love. Jesus gave us the Mass as our thanksgiving to the Father, who created and redeemed us. We unite ourselves with Christ's passion, death, and Resurrection, which freed us from the power of sin and death.

Scripture in This Chapter

Exodus 1–14 Israel's Deliverance and the Passover
Luke 22:14–20 The Last Supper
John 13:1–15 Washing of the Disciple's Feet

Catechism of the Catholic Church

901, 1164, 1337–1341, 1368

In this chapter, help your child to

+ describe the history of the Passover.
+ explain that Jesus gave us the Eucharist and a new commandment at the Last Supper.
+ describe the gift of the Eucharist as a sign of Christ's love.
+ describe that at Mass, we listen to God's Word and offer ourselves with Jesus to God.
+ identify the Morning Offering.

Words Your Child Should Know

+ Last Supper
+ Passover
+ sacrifice

Key Terms for Your Information

+ Egypt—country in northern Africa that held the Israelites slaves
+ Manna—special bread that God sent the Israelites while they were in the desert
+ martyr—someone who died for Jesus
+ Mass—the celebration established by Jesus at the Last Supper as a remembrance of his death and Resurrection.
+ Moses—leader of God's people who led them to freedom
+ Pharaoh—ruler of Egypt

CHAPTER 16   **GRADE** 3

Jesus Is Risen

FOCUS: In this chapter, you will be helping your child to understand that we believe that Jesus rose from the dead and will bring us to life everlasting.

The Resurrection is the victorious completion of redemption. Jesus showed his mastery over sin and death—over every hostile power. We share in his Resurrection through the waters of Baptism and are raised to the new life of grace. As partakers of his divine life, we are empowered by his strength to overcome every attack of the evil one. We count on being united with him in perfect happiness for all eternity.

Meanwhile, we have already begun to live in union with Jesus here on earth. We are sent, as were his apostles, to communicate the joy and peace of the Resurrection to all people. Joy and peace are fundamental attitudes of those who share the life and mission of Jesus. We can call peace Jesus' password. Wherever his message penetrates hearts, his peace reigns.

Scripture in This Chapter

John 20:19–23 Appearance to the Disciples
Romans 6:9 Death Has No Power Over Jesus.
1 Corinthians 2:9 God's Preparation for Us
Revelation 21:3–4 The New Heaven and the New Earth

Catechism of the Catholic Church

638, 651–655, 1010–1013, 2304

In this chapter, help your child to

+ know that the risen Jesus brought the gift of peace to the world.
+ know that the Resurrection is celebrated every Sunday.
+ understand the Christian meaning of death.
+ acknowledge and accept his or her feelings about death.
+ seek to solve problems by promoting peace.
+ identify the paschal candle as a symbol of the Resurrection.

Key Terms for Your Information

+ Resurrection—a return to life from the dead
+ paschal—having to do with Easter

CHAPTER 16   **GRADE** 4

We Are Faithful to Ourselves and Others

FOCUS: In this chapter, you will be helping your child to understand that the Sixth and Ninth Commandments tell us to be true to ourselves and others.

Because human beings are created in God's own image and likeness, each person has a dignity and sacredness that is already present at conception. Our first obligation, therefore, is to be faithful to our own inherent dignity. If we respect and revere our own bodies, minds, and souls, then we will be able to respect and revere those of others.

The strongest bond cementing a relationship is faithfulness. God is faithful to his people. Christ is faithful to his Church. Husband and wife are faithful to each other. Friend is faithful to friends. When human faithfulness reflects divine fidelity, we know we have discovered "what is the will of God, what is good and pleasing and perfect." (Romans 12:2)

Scripture in This Chapter

Exodus 20: 14,17 Sixth and Ninth Commandments
1 Corinthians 6:18–20 Temples of the Holy Spirit

Catechism of the Catholic Church

1265, 2201–2203, 2334, 2335, 2347, 2518, 2519

In this chapter, help your child to

+ explain that our bodies help us express ourselves as people.
+ identify the importance of respecting his or her body.
+ describe the value of friendship.
+ explain that, in the Sacrament of Matrimony, husbands and wives promise to be faithful to each other.
+ describe his or her dignity as a baptized person.
+ explain what it means to be a temple of the Holy Spirit and act accordingly.

Key Terms for Your Information

+ adultery—giving to someone else the special love promised to one's marriage partner
+ covet—to desire
+ faithful—keeping our promises; being loyal and true
+ modest—showing respect for one's body, especially by wearing proper clothing
+ pure—true to oneself; holy

Unit 3 Review

FOCUS: In this chapter, you will be helping your child to understand that we celebrate God's love in the Sacraments of Healing.

God's love heals all kinds of suffering and evil in the world. Jesus manifested his Father's love when he healed the deaf and the blind, the sick and the lame, and when he cast out devils and forgave sin. Today, he heals those who are sick or strengthens them in their illness through the Sacrament of the Anointing of the Sick. They also receive his comfort and consolation through the ministries of kind and concerned Christians.

Jesus forgives us, just as he forgave Peter and the paralytic, as he forgave all who desired forgiveness. Through his saving death, he has reconciled us to God, but our human sinfulness imposes on us a continual need for God's healing love and strengthening grace. The Sacrament of Penance and Reconciliation brings us God's forgiveness and makes it easier for us to respond to God more freely and fully.

Scripture in This Chapter
Mark 5:21–43　The Raising of Jairus's Daughter

Catechism of the Catholic Church
1520–1523, 1532

In this chapter, help your child to
+ reflect on the key concepts covered in this unit.
+ describe the Sacrament of Penance and the Sacrament of the Anointing of the Sick.
+ identify acts of healing love.
+ demonstrate an understanding of key concepts related to forgiveness and healing in the Sacraments of Healing.
+ have a deeper understanding of Christ's healing love for those who are sick and suffering.

Unit 3 Review

FOCUS: In this chapter, you will be helping your child to understand that the Jewish people remember what God has done for them and they honor God's Word.

Psalm 33 was composed to be sung during celebration of Israel's great feasts. God's love truly does fill the Earth. God's call comes to each of us many times, in different ways. Each call is an election and a promise: an election to a particular part of God's plan of salvation, and a promise of divine help and blessing if we respond trustingly to God's calling. In whatever manner it is given to us, each call contains a note of personal challenge directed to the deepest level of our sense of moral responsibility.

God awaits our response, for though God is the Lord of history, the events of history depend on people's response to God's call. Mindful that God is true to his word, we come before God and pray:

> I wait for you, O LORD;
>   I lift up my soul
> to my God. . . .
> Guide me in your truth and teach me,
>   for you are God my savior. . . .
>   *Psalm 25:1,5*

Catechism of the Catholic Church
132, 201

In this chapter, help your child to
+ review the concepts learned in Unit 3.
+ express gratitude to God for his goodness and the guidance of God's Word.

Key Terms for Your Information
+ mezuzah—a case or box that attaches to a door or doorpost; contains a small scroll of Deuteronomy 6:4–9 and 11:13–21 and the name of God (Shaddai); for the Jewish people, it is a reminder of their faith
+ Simchat Torah—Jewish feast that expresses gratitude for the Torah

The Sacred Heart—Jesus' Kingdom of Love

FOCUS: In this chapter, you will be helping your child to understand that a follower of Jesus regards sex as a sacred gift used to express deep, life-giving love within marriage.

We were made by love for love. Our deepest longing is to love and to be loved. The presence of sin makes selfless love difficult. We do not always recognize real love and go after cheap imitations that leave us still thirsting.

The love between a man and woman permanently committed to each other in marriage is a sign of Jesus' love for the Church. The love of a married couple entails total surrender and complete openness. It culminates in a union touched with ecstasy and gifted with life-giving power. Sex has been called the liturgy of love. Married love is sacred, fruitful, and a gift to the world.

Scripture in This Chapter

Genesis 1:27 We Are Created in God's Image.
Ephesians 5:25–33 Wives and Husbands

Catechism of the Catholic Church

478, 2332–2337, 2341–2342, 2347, 2360, 2380–2381, 2522

In this chapter, help your child to

+ understand that love builds on friendship.
+ express an understanding of the commitment and responsibilities of marriage.
+ understand that sex is a gift from God to be used in marriage to express love and to create new life.
+ understand that sex is a sacred gift from God for married couples (Sixth and Ninth Commandments).
+ be able to use the decision-making process to make moral decisions related to sex.

Word Your Child Should Know

+ adultery

Key Terms for Your Information

+ chastity—the virtue by which we show respect for our God-given power to bring life into the world
+ modesty—the virtue that helps us choose appropriate dress and behavior so as not to call attention to our sex or ourselves
+ sex—the God-given gift by which a married man and woman express and deepen their love and cooperate with God in bringing forth new life
+ sexuality—maleness or femaleness

Reforming the Church

FOCUS: In this chapter, you will be helping your child to understand that the Church undertook its own reform in the Council of Trent.

As the Middle Ages progressed, it was becoming obvious that the Church needed reform and renewal. Martin Luther's attempts to call the Church to reform led to the Protestant Reformation, a painful split in the Christian Church. Finally, at the Council of Trent (1545–1563), the Church undertook its own reform.

After the Reformation, gifted and Spirit-filled individuals worked to implement the reforms initiated by the Council of Trent. Their way of living and serving the Church was not the easy way. These saintly people found creative ways to heal and reconcile the wounded Church. They stimulated a return to the Gospel witness of prayer and service. Like these holy men and women, we are called to spread the message of salvation to all people. Under the guidance of the Holy Spirit, we participate in the Church's missionary activity, which is driven by God's desire that all people find salvation in Jesus. Through these missionary efforts, the Church continues to be renewed and made holy.

Scripture in This Chapter

Luke 21:15 Wisdom in Speaking

Catechism of the Catholic Church

817–821

In this chapter, help your child to

+ explain how the Church undertook its own reform at the Council of Trent.
+ summarize the reforms of the Council of Trent.
+ explain how saints who lived after the Protestant Reformation helped the Church.
+ describe the Catholic understanding of meditation.
+ review events and people in Church history during the first 15 centuries.

Word Your Child Should Know

+ meditation

Key Terms for Your Information

+ Trent—a city in present-day northern Italy
+ mystic—one who experiences union with God and contemplative prayer in an extraordinary manner
+ Examen—the Spanish word for examination, used by Saint Ignatius of Loyola to describe a form of daily meditation

Jesus Calls Himself the Good Shepherd

FOCUS: In this chapter, you will be helping your child to understand that Jesus loves us when we are sorry.

Jesus called himself the Good Shepherd. Perhaps one of the best commentaries on the Good Shepherd comes from Fernando D'Alfonso, a Nevada sheepherder of our time who cared for his flock in much the same way that good shepherds did thousands of years ago. He points out that sheep follow their shepherd wherever he leads. They instinctively trust that the shepherd will guard them, which often requires the shepherd to leave his fold to go in search of stray sheep.

At some time every day, each sheep leaves its place and goes to the shepherd. After a few minutes with the shepherd, the sheep returns to its place refreshed and made content by this personal contact. Jesus not only cares lovingly for his sheep, but he also lays down his life for them.

Scripture in This Chapter
Psalm 23   The Lord Is My Shepherd
Luke 15:1–7   The Parable of the Lost Sheep
John 10:1–21   The Good Shepherd

Catechism of the Catholic Church
1443, 1451–1453, 1490

In this chapter, help your child to
+ know why Jesus calls himself the Good Shepherd.
+ understand that a parable is a story with a hidden meaning.
+ know that Jesus loves sinners.
+ realize that when he or she does wrong, Jesus still loves him or her and will forgive him or her.
+ recognize Psalm 23.

Key Terms for Your Information
+ everlasting life—life in heaven that lasts forever
+ parable—a story with a hidden meaning

Jesus Invites Us

FOCUS: In this chapter, you will be helping your child to understand that at Mass, God's family gathers to worship and give thanks.

The Eucharist is Christ's gift to his Church. Christ calls us together, and it is his saving mystery that is made present in every eucharistic celebration. Christ calls us as a community that gives praise and thanks to the Father at Mass and in the words and deeds of each day.

The Introductory Rites of the Mass prepare us to offer ourselves along with Jesus' sacrifice to the Father. The entrance song of the Introductory Rite of the Mass and the dialogue between the celebrant and the congregation help us form a unified community. As his people, we come together before God and humbly recall our sinfulness. We ask for forgiveness and receive it if we are truly sorry. The Penitential Rite ends on a note of praise to the Lord for his saving, merciful love. On festive days, the ancient hymn of praise, the Gloria, is sung by all.

Scripture in This Chapter
Luke 22:14–20   The Last Supper

Catechism of the Catholic Church
1348

In this chapter, help your child to
+ identify the roles of the community and the different ministries at Mass.
+ describe the importance of participating in the communal prayers, listening, and singing at Mass.
+ recite the response to the priest's greeting.
+ describe the Penitential Rite.
+ describe the Glory to God as a special prayer of praise.
+ explain that the Opening Prayer petitions God on behalf of all people.

Word Your Child Should Know
+ altar

Key Terms for Your Information
+ deacon—an ordained man who assists the priest at Mass
+ Lectionary—book of readings for the Mass
+ Sacramentary—book that contains prayers and directives for the Mass

Jesus Christ Is Lord and King

FOCUS: In this chapter, you will be helping your child to understand that Jesus ascended to heaven, but he will come again in glory to judge the world according to its love.

The risen Christ came from the world of glory to manifest himself to his disciples. After appearing to many, Jesus returned to his Father, as Scripture and Tradition put it, by ascending to heaven from the Mount of Olives. Jesus left his own; he withdrew his visible presence from Mary, the apostles, the disciples, and all in generations to come.

None of his people is forgotten. He has gone to prepare a place for his own, those who believe, hope, and love. He will return and lead them to the heavenly mansion. The final coming of Jesus the Lord and King is the Parousia, at which time all things will be complete. The battle between Satan and God's friends will be over. Christ will reign as Lord and King forever, and all his faithful will share in his glory. Those who love and serve Christ look forward to that time with joy.

Scripture in This Chapter

Psalm 47   God Rules All Nations

Matthew 25:31–46   The Judgment of the Nations (The Sheep and the Goats)

Matthew 28:16–20   The Commissioning of the Disciples

Luke 24:50 and Acts of the Apostles 1:4–8   The Ascension of Jesus

Acts of the Apostles 3:1–10   Cure of a Man Who Could Not Walk

Catechism of the Catholic Church

659, 671, 678, 1038, 2447–2449

In this chapter, help your child to

+ know that Jesus returned to heavenly glory at the Ascension.
+ understand that Jesus told his apostles to witness to him before the whole world.
+ desire to be a witness to Jesus in one's family and in the world.
+ understand Christ's role as judge.
+ know that Christ considers what is done to others as being done to himself.

Words Your Child Should Know

+ Ascension
+ Paschal Mystery
+ witness

We Respect What God Has Given Us

FOCUS: In this chapter, you will be helping your child to understand that the Seventh and Tenth Commandments tell us to respect others' things and be generous and satisfied with what we have.

The Seventh and Tenth Commandments ensure each person's right to own property, receive just compensation for work, and share in earth's natural resources. We must respect the property of others and use what we have responsibly.

By trusting in God, we can overcome evil desires and the tendency to feel too self-sufficient. People who have the necessary material goods, education, cultural opportunities, and recreational facilities may live a fuller life. In the struggle to maintain human dignity, people need work that provides fair compensation and enables them to obtain food, clothing, and shelter.

Scripture in This Chapter

Exodus 20:15,17   Seventh and Tenth Commandments

Luke 6:31   The Golden Rule

Catechism of the Catholic Church

2401–2409, 2536–2540

In this chapter, help your child to

+ explain that all people have a right to what they need.
+ describe why he or she can be content with and grateful for what he or she has.
+ describe ways to respect others' possessions.
+ describe how the just sharing of goods is part of the Seventh Commandment.
+ explain that those who have more than enough should share.

Words Your Child Should Know

+ free will   + moral choice

Key Terms for Your Information

+ envy—sadness or anger about others having what we want
+ respect—to think highly of someone or something and care for that person or thing
+ cheating—taking something through trickery or dishonesty
+ greed—a desire to have more than we have a right to
+ honesty—respect for others' property; refusal to lie or steal

God Calls Us to Be Holy

FOCUS: In this chapter, you will be helping your child to understand that God calls us to holiness through different states of life.

We travel various routes to perfection. Some people are called to marriage or to the single life; others to religious life, secular institutes, or the ordained ministry. However, no vocation can be followed or lived without prayer. We must always be centered on Jesus. Christ seeks us: "Behold, I stand at the door and knock." (Revelation 3:20) If we open our hearts to him and live in his presence, he will give us the joy, peace, and grace of perseverance in our daily struggles.

Our vocation in life is nurtured in our family, the domestic church. In the family, we learn to love, to listen, to share, and to serve. We first learn to worship God, to forgive, and to work together. Our first experience of God and his Church is through the domestic church of our families. The Church prays that all people will attain the perfection to which they are called.

Scripture in This Chapter

1 Samuel 3:1–10 The Call of Samuel
Matthew 19:29 The Reward of Discipleship
Philippians 3:12–14 Saint Paul's Pursuit

Catechism of the Catholic Church

914, 916, 940–943, 1658, 2013, 2015

In this chapter, help your child to

+ recall that all people are called to holiness.
+ identify ways to prepare for his or her vocation.
+ describe how single people can live for God and for the Church.
+ define the terms *religious life* and *vow*.
+ explain how we can choose to serve Christ and his people in any state of life.

Words Your Child Should Know

+ holiness
+ vocation
+ religious life
+ vow

The Period of Judges

FOCUS: In this chapter, you will be helping your child to understand that when the Israelites turned from God and were attacked by enemies, God saved them through the judges.

It seems that we are forever failing and making new resolutions. This is also the story of the lives of families, nations, and cultures. How senseless all of this could seem, had Jesus not taken upon himself our weakness, carried our sinfulness, and experienced our pain. The Resurrection is God's proclamation that failure and defeat shall not be the final answer.

We still carry our weakness. We continue to sin. But because of God, we cannot remain downcast. We are still God's instruments. Our very faith is a declaration that God is faithful. How else could Christianity continue, or love grow, but through the power, the glory, and the love of God?

Scripture in This Chapter

Judges 4, 5 The Story of Deborah
Judges 6–8 An Obedient Judge, Gideon
Judges 13–16 The Strongman, Samson
The Book of Ruth Ruth's Faithfulness

Catechism of the Catholic Church

210, 1432, 2496

In this chapter, help your child to

+ describe the judges' role in Israel's history.
+ understand that mistakes and failures are part of life.
+ summarize the stories of Deborah, Gideon, Samson, and Ruth.
+ describe how to be a good example to others.
+ describe how much the media influence us.

Word Your Child Should Know

+ abstain

Key Terms for Your Information

+ charism—special gift or grace given by God to a person for the good of others
+ judges—temporary leaders of Israel who ruled from Joshua's death until the beginning of the rule by the kings
+ media—Internet, podcasts, TV, newspapers, movies, comic books, magazines, CDs, tapes, videos, DVDs
+ values—goals, ideals, or ideas we believe in or hold as important and worthwhile

Unit 2 Review

FOCUS: In this chapter, you will be helping your child to understand that Jesus teaches us the truth that we can live by.

In Matthew, Jesus' words describe his own teaching of the truth. New life could not be given to the old order merely by patching; that would only weaken it. Jesus raised the whole law to a new plane. He did not destroy the old wineskin, but he brought the new wineskin, the new order of living that preserved all that was good, universal, and life-giving. His was a radical morality, demanding that those who claim to belong to the Father demonstrate it by their mercy and their love.

Unit 2 presented the law of love that prevails in this kingdom. In a world that depends so much on reasonableness, the path of Christ appears to be folly. Love is unreasonable. In a world that depends so much on narrow views of justice, the demands of Christ appear immoderate. Love is merciful. Love is other-centered.

Scripture in This Chapter
Psalm 25 Prayer for Forgiveness and Guidance
Matthew 13:44–46 The Buried Treasure

Catechism of the Catholic Church
459, 638

In this chapter, help your child to
+ explain what it means to live in truth.
+ evaluate how he or she lives the message of Jesus.
+ recall the significant facts and basic concepts introduced in the Unit 2.
+ grow in appreciation of the values of the Kingdom of God.
+ demonstrate an understanding of the key concepts in Unit 2.

In a Changing World

FOCUS: In this chapter, you will be helping your child to understand that the Church responds to a changing world.

About 200 years ago, some events led to significant changes in the Church. Eighteenth-century achievements, especially in the sciences, initiated a philosophical system that exalted reason and set it at odds with faith. As science began to help us understand the universe, some people began to question whether the universe was governed by chance rather than by a transcendent and good God. Some came to think that even if God did create the universe, he was no longer involved with it. They concluded that science could answer all our questions.

As Catholics, we believe we need science to help us understand the nature of the world we live in, the process of how it came to be, and the process of how we and everything in it have developed over time. But we also believe that it is through faith in God that we understand God's loving action in creating and sustaining all things.

Scripture in This Chapter
Psalm 139:13–17 Wonderful Are God's Works.
Matthew 25:35–37 The Judgment of the Nations

Catechism of the Catholic Church
884, 891, 1901–1904, 1938–1942

In this chapter, help your child to
+ describe how new thinking in the 16th century affected people's concept of God.
+ describe how the Church came under attack as a result of the French Revolution.
+ summarize the purpose of the First Vatican Council.
+ explain how the Fourth Commandment calls us to honor legitimate authority.
+ explain the Catholic understanding of the relationship between science and religion.
+ articulate a Catholic interpretation of the first story of Creation in Genesis that finds no contradiction with evolution.

Word Your Child Should Know
+ rationalism

Key Term for Your Information
+ Age of Enlightenment—period in the 18th century when people believed that human reason and science had all the answers

We Come to Our Good Shepherd

FOCUS: In this chapter, you will be helping your child to understand that the Church comes together to ask forgiveness.

The Lord is our shepherd, always caring for his flock, always faithful to his promises. He has revealed himself as ever-present and full of mercy. God has drawn the portrait of his merciful love. God's promise to hear our pleas and respond to them is recorded by the psalmist:

> Whoever clings to me I will deliver;
> whoever knows my name I will set on high.
> All who call upon me I will answer;
> I will be with them in distress;
> I will deliver them and give them honor.
> With length of days I will satisfy them
> and show them my saving power.
> *Psalm 91:14–16*

Micah, a prophet keenly aware of the people's sinful ways, ends his book by recalling to the Lord his faithful and merciful love:

> Who is there like you, the
> God who removes guilt
> and pardons sin for the remnant
> of his inheritance;
> Who does not persist in anger forever,
> but delights rather in clemency?
> *Micah 7:18*

Scripture in This Chapter
Matthew 18:10–14 The Parable of the Lost Sheep
1 Peter 2:24–25 The Stray Return to Jesus.

Catechism of the Catholic Church
1425–1428, 1454, 1468–1469

In this chapter, help your child to
+ become aware of unloving personal acts that offend Jesus, the Good Shepherd.
+ make a simple examination of conscience.
+ learn to express sorrow for offenses.
+ be more aware of what living as a Christian child means.
+ demonstrate an understanding of the concepts in Unit 3.

We Listen and Pray

FOCUS: In this chapter, you will be helping your child to understand that God speaks to us in the Mass readings, and we respond with a prayer of faith and prayers of petition.

The Liturgy of the Word offers us God's self-revelation and invites us to live more completely in God's love. If we open ourselves to God's Word, God cleanses our minds, our hearts, and our lips, thus enabling us to proclaim his Gospel with our lives. We pray for this grace as we make the Sign of the Cross on our forehead, lips, and heart while we say mentally: "The Lord be in my mind, on my lips, and in my heart."

The Liturgy of the Word concludes with our profession of faith followed by our intercessory prayer for the needs of the Church and the world. The General Intercessions or Prayer of the Faithful make it clear that we desire to make Christ's saving love visible in the Church and in the world.

Scripture in This Chapter
Matthew 25:35–40 Works of Mercy
Luke 11:28 True Blessedness

Catechism of the Catholic Church
185–187, 195, 1100–1103, 1154–1155, 1349

In this chapter, help your child to
+ explain the importance of listening to God's Word at Mass.
+ recite the responses from the Liturgy of the Word.
+ describe the Creed as a statement of beliefs that all Catholics hold.
+ explain that in the Prayer of the Faithful, we pray for the Church and world intentions.
+ explain that Jesus wants us to ask for what we need.

Word Your Child Should Know
+ ambo

Key Terms for Your Information
+ believe—to accept something as true
+ Bible—the Word of God
+ Gospel—the life of Jesus as told in the Bible
+ homily—a talk after the Gospel at Mass in which the priest or deacon explains the readings and how to live God's Word
+ Prayer of the Faithful—petitions to God during Mass for the needs of the Church and the world
+ truth—what is real and taught by the Church

Jesus Gives his Spirit to the Church

FOCUS: In this chapter, you will be helping your child to understand that the Holy Spirit helps us live and work as members of the kingdom.

When Pope John Paul II wrote, in *Catechesis in Our Time*, about the Holy Spirit, he made three important affirmations about the role of the Spirit in the Church. First, the Spirit is our teacher within the Church by acting in our minds and hearts to make us understand and love the depths of God's love. Second, the Spirit transforms us into people who are willing to proclaim the Lord Jesus, even to the extent of giving up our lives for him. Third, the charisms and Gifts of the Holy Spirit enlighten and strengthen us so that we can bear witness to Christ within our daily spheres of activity. They help us to build up the Church.

Although there is a variety of gifts, each springs from the Spirit and complements the others. We are all gifted in some way, and we have been given these gifts so that we may help further Christ's kingdom in the world. We pray with the Church that the Holy Spirit will direct our use of every gift and that our lives may bring Christ to others.

Scripture in This Chapter
John 15:26–27; 16:7–14 Jesus Promises to Send the Holy Spirit.

Acts of the Apostles 2:1–4 The Coming of the Holy Spirit

Catechism of the Catholic Church
683, 721–726, 731, 1266

In this chapter, help your child to
+ explain that the Holy Spirit empowers the Church to continue the work of Jesus.
+ recall that the Holy Spirit is received at Baptism.
+ know that Mary always followed the guidance of the Holy Spirit.
+ realize that the Holy Spirit guides every member of the Church.
+ see the action of the Holy Spirit in the life of Kateri Tekakwitha.

Words Your Child Should Know
+ Abba
+ Lord
+ Pentecost

We Respect the Gifts of the Earth

FOCUS: In this chapter, you will be helping your child to understand that we are to use the gifts of the earth carefully and share them.

When we study the Seventh and Tenth Commandments, we should keep in mind the ecological and social issues that confront us today. Earth's natural resources are magnificent gifts from God, which we are meant to share and conserve for future generations. Instead, we often exploit those resources. Some people are beginning to admit negligence in the use of God's gifts and are trying to conserve and renew our resources for future generations. It is to be hoped that world and national attention will continue to focus on environmental protection and the principles of ecology. People and nations must take responsible action to prevent further exploitation of the gifts of nature—exploitation that stems from avarice and leads to materialism.

Awareness of these problems ought to develop increasing moral concern in present and future generations about the use of God's gifts. Those who accept their social responsibilities and trust in God's help will reap their reward.

Scripture in This Chapter
Genesis 1:27–30 Dominion Over Creation
Luke 16:19–31 The Rich Man and Lazarus

Catechism of the Catholic Church
2402–2405, 2407, 2415, 2443–2444

In this chapter, help your child to
+ explain the need to use and share Earth's gifts responsibly.
+ explain that earth's gifts belong to all.
+ explain that Jesus expects us to share.
+ explain that Jesus helped poor and hungry people.
+ describe his or her responsibility to help people in need.

Christian Marriage Leads to Family Holiness

FOCUS: In this chapter, you will be helping your child to understand that through the Sacrament of Matrimony, couples help each other be holy and found a family.

Lifelong fidelity in marriage is possible because of the grace won for us by Christ. Yet we cannot necessarily achieve it easily. Fidelity requires sacrifice. This mutual sacrifice is akin to martyrdom, and the only valid reason for accepting martyrdom is love. Both partners must make their love grow. This will happen most certainly when a marriage is firmly based on love of God and a desire to fulfill his will. Praying together leads the couple to discussion of joys and sorrow, and a willingness to deal with both. Together the couple will grow in holiness.

Strong trust and love for each other and for God enable a couple to welcome children joyfully when God bestows them. Seeing these children as the incarnation of their love for each other, and of God's love for them all, couples will surround each child with love. The children, in turn, will love and respect God and others and bring joy to their parents and glory to God.

Scripture in This Chapter
Genesis 1:27–28　God Made Man in His Image

Catechism of the Catholic Church
1604–1605, 1614, 1621–1632, 1641–1648, 1652, 1654

In this chapter, help your child to
+ describe the rite of the Sacrament of Matrimony.
+ appreciate the permanence of marriage.
+ define the word matrimony.
+ explain how the Sacrament of Matrimony helps families.
+ explain why the family is called the domestic church.

Word Your Child Should Know
+ Matrimony

Key Term for Your Information
+ nuptial blessing—blessing the priest gives a bride and groom

The Kings of Israel

FOCUS: In this chapter, you will be helping your child to understand that Samuel anointed Saul, and later David, as kings of Israel.

When God chose Saul to lead the Chosen People, he was anointed by Samuel and the Spirit of the Lord came upon him. However, when Saul later turned from the Lord, God told Samuel to anoint a new king. Samuel then anointed David. From that day forward, the Spirit of the Lord was with him. Saul's experience shows that the gift of God's presence is conditional. Saul remained God's anointed, but his reign as king became very troubled because he rejected God's guidance.

The Lord is near to all who call on him, and God will never reject anyone who comes to him. But we must also be mindful that empowerment comes from following God's guidance.

Scripture in This Chapter
1 Samuel 1–4:7　Samuel Hears God's Call.
1 Samuel 8　The Request for a King
1 Samuel 10—16; 2 Samuel 5　Saul's Reign

Catechism of the Catholic Church
695, 1293–1296, 2013, 2528

In this chapter, help your child to
+ describe how a kingdom was established in Israel.
+ identify and describe the roles of Samuel, Saul, and David in Israel's history.
+ describe the symbolism of anointing.
+ identify when and why people are anointed.
+ describe how God guides us through Scripture.

Words Your Child Should Know
+ anoint
+ Christ
+ Messiah

Key Terms for Your Information
+ chrism—blessed mixture of olive or vegetable oil and balsam or perfume used during Baptism, Confirmation, and Holy Orders
+ consecration—act of setting apart as holy or for God's service
+ David—second and greatest king of Israel, who united the tribes of Israel into one great nation
+ ritual—the words and actions used in a religious ceremony
+ Saul—first king of Israel, who was anointed by Samuel

Living Faith in Jesus— Jesus the Prophet

FOCUS: In this chapter, you will be helping your child to understand that through faith and virtue, our life of grace grows, and we become more like Jesus.

God dwells within each of us. We call this divine indwelling *grace*. This gift cannot be measured, but it can be deepened and strengthened. It can transform us. Yet it can also be rejected. Although God always takes the initiative, we, by the gift of freedom, can be open to God or close our hearts.

With so much at stake, with so many invitations to divine love, our greatest journey in life becomes the journey of the spirit. Love is the continual turning to catch the gaze of divine love, the continual yearning to be so fired with God's love that our whole being will be sparked with the Holy Spirit and will enkindle that same love and life in everyone we meet.

Scripture in This Chapter
John 3:1–21 Nicodemus
John 4:4–30 The Samaritan Woman

Catechism of the Catholic Church
1805–1809, 1813–1815, 1817–1818, 1822–1824

In this chapter, help your child to
+ explain that God initiates all life and grace, but that he or she is free to accept or reject it.
+ explain grace as a free gift of God, a share in divine life, and friendship with God.
+ name and explain the Theological Virtues and the cardinal virtues.
+ express a growing understanding of the spiritual life.
+ understand the demands of Christian love.

Words Your Child Should Know
+ cardinal virtues
+ prudence
+ fortitude
+ temperance
+ justice
+ Theological Virtues

Key Terms for Your Information
+ grace—the free gift of God's life in us; friendship with God that strengthens us and makes us holy; the prompting of the Spirit to do good
+ sanctifying grace—God dwelling within us
+ Sanhedrin—the Supreme Council of the Jews
+ spiritual life—friendship with God

Signs of the Times

FOCUS: In this chapter, you will be helping your child to understand that the Church responded to the Industrial Revolution with concern for those who are poor and oppressed.

The Industrial Revolution was the result of inventions that changed the social and economic order of the world. Pope Leo XIII anguished over the exploitation of people as cheap labor for factories. In 1891, he wrote the first major social encyclical, *Rerum Novarum*, about the working class. His declaration that the Church—no longer a powerful earthly force—would, as a spiritual leader, work for the eternal welfare of humanity and oppose any system threatening that welfare. Later popes followed Leo's example.

During the past 200 years, the world has endured numerous wars and hardships. During these traumatic times, the Church has changed to more fully minister to pressing needs. It has issued documents covering a wide range of topics and has held two ecumenical councils. The political, economic, and moral concerns of all people are the Church's concerns as well.

Scripture in This Chapter
Luke 10:29–37 The Good Samaritan

Catechism of the Catholic Church
1895, 1921, 1925, 1943–1944, 1947, 2250, 2254, 2451–2452, 2458, 2461

In this chapter, help your child to
+ summarize the spiritual leadership of the popes of the 18th to 20th centuries, especially in regard to social justice.
+ identify and describe the seven themes of Catholic Social Teaching.
+ describe the new ways of thinking and acting that the Second Vatican Council introduced to the Church.
+ demonstrate an understanding of the key concepts in this chapter.

Word Your Child Should Know
+ encyclical

Key Terms for Your Information
+ *Rerum Novarum*—the first social encyclical, written by Pope Leo XIII in defense of the worker
+ collegiality—shared decision-making among the pope and bishops

Jesus Gives the Gift of Himself

FOCUS: In this chapter, you will be helping your child to understand that Jesus offered himself for us at the Last Supper and on the cross.

The cross, the expression of Jesus' love, is traced on our foreheads in Baptism. Through the cross, we share in the mystery of Christ's Resurrection. We are chosen and empowered to relive Christ's passage from death to life. Jesus gave us his life that we might be born anew.

At Mass, we offer the same gift that Jesus offered to his Father the night before Jesus died. As we join the gift of our life to the offering of our Lord's life, we die to sinfulness and experience new life. We leave the church with the blessing of the cross traced once again over us. We carry to the world the gift of our own lives transformed by the outpouring of Christ's redemptive love.

Scripture in This Chapter
Mark 11:1–11 Jesus' Triumphal Entry into Jerusalem
Matthew 26:26–29; Luke 22:14–20 The Last Supper
Matthew 27, Mark 15, Luke 23, John 19 Jesus' Death

Catechism of the Catholic Church
559–560, 610–611, 613–614, 616–617

In this chapter, help your child to
- describe how Jesus was honored as a king on Palm (Passion) Sunday.
- explain that we celebrate Jesus' triumphal entry into Jerusalem each year.
- describe the "Holy, Holy, Holy" as an expression of our desire to let Jesus be king of our hearts.
- explain that at the Last Supper, Jesus offered his life to his Father.
- explain that through his apostles and priests, Jesus gives himself to us in Communion.

Key Terms for Your Information
- Blessed Sacrament—the Eucharist
- Bread of Life—Jesus Christ in the form of bread
- chalice—the cup that holds the wine at the Eucharist
- Holy Communion—Jesus Christ's gift of himself in the form of bread and wine so we can share his life
- Holy Thursday—the day Jesus gave us the Eucharist
- Hosanna—acclamation of praise with which people greeted Jesus when he entered Jerusalem
- Passover—Jewish feast in remembrance of God's saving love in his freeing his people from slavery in Egypt

We Prepare Our Gifts

FOCUS: In this chapter, you will be helping your child to understand that at the Eucharist, we offer ourselves to God and give praise and thanks.

During Mass, we present bread and wine, fruit of the earth and the work of human hands, as signs of ourselves with all our gifts and limitations. Through these gifts, we show our desire to praise and thank God for being so good to us. Our imperfect gifts become a perfect offering when, during the Eucharistic Prayer, we offer the Body and Blood of Christ to the Father.

We prepare for that offering by recalling the mystery of our salvation: that the Father's love sent the Son, who gave his life for us, and that, risen from the dead, he sent his Holy Spirit to help us glorify his name in each prayer, work, joy, and suffering of our days. The rite of the Preparation of the Gifts ends with a prayer asking the Father to bless and accept the gifts we offer.

Scripture in This Chapter
1 Corinthians 12:7–11 Diversity of Spiritual Gifts
James 3:14–17 True Wisdom

Catechism of the Catholic Church
1333–1334, 1350–1352, 1357

In this chapter, help your child to
- describe the symbolism of the presented gifts.
- describe the Mass as a banquet to praise and thank the Father.
- explain the purpose of the prayers of the Preface.
- identify wheat and grapes with bread and wine through making a picture.
- discuss the symbols of bread and wine.
- describe the vestments and articles the priest uses at Mass.

Key Terms for Your Information
- banquet—a special meal
- Eucharist—the Mass; the word means "thanksgiving"
- Preparation of the Gifts—the part of the Mass when the altar is prepared and the gifts are brought up
- Vestment—special clothing that the priest wears during Mass

We Belong to the Kingdom

FOCUS: In this chapter, you will be helping your child to understand that the members of the Communion of Saints are one in Christ. They honor Mary, his Mother, as Queen of Heaven and Earth.

Jesus Christ is our glorious king. He lifts us into the life of God, into the fullness of our being. He works in us and through us to effect the Christian transformation of the world. Although Christ's universal dominion will not reach its perfection until the end of time, many are already united with him and with one another in the Communion of Saints. Jesus is truly Lord, yet we can choose to follow other leaders. Throughout our lives, Jesus invites us to accept his reign, but he will never force us.

All that God has done until now justifies our faith in our final union with him. On his word, we believe that we will one day be with God in eternal happiness and glory. For this we were created, for this we hope and pray, for this we live and love.

Scripture in This Chapter

Acts of the Apostles 1:12–14   The First Community in Jerusalem

1 Corinthians 13:4–8   The Way of Love

Catechism of the Catholic Church

954–959, 966, 969

In this chapter, help your child to

✦ define the Communion of Saints as the union of the saints in heaven, the souls in purgatory, and the Church on earth.

✦ understand how the members of the Communion of Saints help one another.

✦ know that Mary was taken body and soul into heaven.

✦ name titles of Mary and ways that we show we honor her.

✦ recall the main concepts learned during this unit.

Words Your Child Should Know

✦ Communion of Saints

✦ purgatory

✦ Assumption

Key Terms for Your Information

✦ Aztecs—indigenous people of Mexico

✦ intercede—to speak on behalf of someone

✦ litany—a prayer made up of phrases or titles to which a response is repeated

---

We Speak the Truth with Love

FOCUS: In this chapter, you will be helping your child to understand that the eighth commandment tells us to speak the truth and keep promises and secrets.

> Our God is a God of truth. He is a "faithful God who keeps his merciful covenant down to the thousandth generation toward those who . . . keep his commandments."   (Deuteronomy 7:9)

The love and peace that mark true Christian living cannot exist without the trust that is built up by honesty in our dealings with one another. Christ came into the world "to testify to the truth." (John 18:37)

When he stood before Pilate, the Roman governor challenged him, "Then you are a king?" (John 18:37) Jesus was aware that only those with minds open to the truth would not be threatened by his answer. Yet, quietly and calmly, without force or display of power, he stated the nature of his kingship. His accusers could not bear being confronted with his truth, and so Jesus was condemned to death. He "bore our sins in his body upon the cross, so that, free from sin, we might live for righteousness." (1 Peter 2:24)

Scripture in This Chapter

Exodus 20:16   The Eighth Commandment

1 Corinthians 13:1–6   Loving Speech

Catechism of the Catholic Church

2464–2468, 2475–2492

In this chapter, help your child to

✦ describe how truthfulness fosters love and trust.

✦ describe the courage of Thomas More in dying for the truth.

✦ discuss Saint Paul's treatise on love.

✦ explain how silence can show love.

✦ explain that we find the strength to be truthful in prayer and the sacraments, and through good habits.

Key Terms for Your Information

✦ false witness—a lie, especially one that accuses an innocent person

✦ truth—whatever is real

Holy Orders Is a Sacrament of Service

FOCUS: In this chapter, you will be helping your child to understand that through the Sacrament of Holy Orders, bishops, priests, and deacons are called to minister in the name of Christ and of the Church.

Holy Orders is a shared sacrament received in a lesser degree by deacons, in a greater degree by priests, and in its fullness by bishops. Priests work to build up and strengthen the Christian community. A priest must always be ready to minister to needs, both spiritual and physical. As a pastor, he must often be a temporal administrator as well as a spiritual minister. We should also pray for our priests and for new vocations to the ministry of Holy Orders, that Christ's work may continue.

Scripture in This Chapter

Mark 16:15 Go and Proclaim the Gospel.

Catechism of the Catholic Church

1536, 1547, 1551–1571, 1573–1579, 1581, 1582

In this chapter, help your child to

+ describe the Sacrament of Holy Orders.
+ explain that the priesthood is Christ's way of continuing his priestly work.
+ describe the general duties of the priesthood.
+ explain the role of the deacon in the Church.
+ describe the responsibilities of a bishop.

Words Your Child Should Know

+ clergy
+ laity
+ diocese
+ ordination
+ Holy Orders

Key Terms for Your Information

+ chasuble—a full vestment a priest wears over the other vestments
+ common priesthood—the share in the priesthood of Christ that all Christians have through their Baptism
+ crosier—staff of a bishop, a symbol of his role as chief shepherd
+ miter—high, pointed hat of a bishop
+ ordain—to bring another into an order of people who share in the priesthood of Jesus
+ ordained priesthood—the share in the priesthood of Christ that men receive through Holy Orders
+ stole—a long, narrow vestment like a scarf

David and Solomon

FOCUS: In this chapter, you will be helping your child to understand that David, the greatest king, sinned and repented. Solomon, despite his gift of wisdom, turned to idols and caused the division of the kingdom.

King David decided that the Lord should have a permanent dwelling place. Through the prophet Nathan, God told David that he would not be the one to build it (it was built by David's son, Solomon) and reminded David that God's real dwelling place was among the people, not in a building. God promised to strengthen the royal house (lineage) of David and make it last forever.

God's response to David teaches us three things: first, that God is generous, for God promised David much more than David offered him; second, that God is not bound to places or material things, but abides with and in his people; and third, that God promised the Messiah, the fulfillment of which would be Jesus Christ, the "Son of David," whose kingdom is forever.

Scripture in This Chapter

1 Samuel 16:1–12 David Is Anointed.
2 Samuel 5–8,11–12 King David
1 Kings 1–3 King Solomon
Psalm 51 A Clean Heart

Catechism of the Catholic Church

583, 709, 1093, 2579–2580, 2586–2589

In this chapter, help your child to

+ summarize David's leadership as king.
+ describe the strengths, achievements, and weaknesses of Solomon.
+ explain the significance of the Temple.
+ identify the purposes of certain psalms.

Words Your Child Should Know

+ Judaism
+ Temple

Key Terms for Your Information

+ Holy of Holies—the inner sanctuary of the Temple
+ penitent—a person who is sorry for doing wrong
+ proverb—wise saying; short statement that expresses truth
+ repent—to be sorry, to make up for the wrong done, and to resolve not to do wrong again
+ repentance—sorrow for sin and determination to make up for it and to avoid doing it again

Opposition to Jesus—Jesus the Suffering Servant

FOCUS: In this chapter, you will be helping your child to understand that Jesus' suffering led to eternal life and glory for him and for us.

Faith is a radical trusting in Jesus, who saves because he is always faithful. Faith fortifies the believer with the strength and courage to look at the ambiguity of life and see beyond to the great, incomprehensible God. It helps us come to know who Jesus is and discover how we can be one with the Father through him and in the Holy Spirit. Without this faith, death can look like the final end, the ultimate terror. But Jesus changed the nature of death when he accepted his own death as an act of love and was raised from the dead by the Father.

The death of Jesus was anticipated by his raising Lazarus from the dead. Jesus returned physical life to his friend, but Lazarus would die again. However, in this sign, an even greater restoration—Jesus' Resurrection—was foreshadowed. Although death is still feared, through Jesus' promises, we receive the strength to hope for an eternal life in glory where every tear will be wiped away.

Scripture in This Chapter
Matthew 17: 1–8   The Transfiguration of Jesus
John 11:1–53   The Raising of Lazarus

Catechism of the Catholic Church
554–556, 585–586, 591, 618, 1680–1682

In this chapter, help your child to
+ explain Jesus' courage in the face of opposition.
+ describe a Christian attitude toward death.
+ list events in Christ's life on a timeline.
+ name and describe the three parts of the Catholic funeral rite.
+ explain how the Catholic funeral rite celebrates the Christian view of death.

Key Term for Your Information
+ Transfiguration—the glorified appearance of Jesus witnessed by Peter, James, and John

The Church in North America

FOCUS: In this chapter, you will be helping your child to understand that the Church in North America flourished when freedom of religion was granted.

The Catholic Church in North America was founded by missionary explorers before a.d. 1600. It struggled to grow in the English colonies, whose members disliked "papists," or Catholics. It began to flourish when the Constitution of the United States guaranteed religious freedom. But the United States was still a young mission country in 1789, when John Carroll was appointed its first bishop. From the Civil War to the 1900s, the Church in America was concerned mostly with caring for the Catholic immigrants who poured into this country. The Church supported the building of schools, parishes, hospitals, orphanages, and homes for those who were aged and homeless. Little by little, the Church rooted itself in this continent.

Scripture in This Chapter
Luke 9:1–6   Jesus Sends the Apostles.
Luke 1:26–38   Mary Says Yes.

Catechism of the Catholic Church
2104–2109

In this chapter, help your child to
+ explain how missionaries and pioneers practiced and spread faith in America.
+ identify some of the firsts for the Church in the United States.
+ describe some of the Church's struggles in North America.
+ explain that he or she is called to contribute to the growth and life of the Church in America.
+ recall people and events from the history of the Church in America.

Word Your Child Should Know
+ Immaculate Conception

Key Terms for Your Information
+ North American Martyrs—Jesuit missionaries martyred during their work with the Native Americans in the Great Lakes region
+ Catholic Worker movement—organization founded by Dorothy Day and Peter Maurin that addresses social issues
+ United States Conference of Catholic Bishops (USCCB)—organization of bishops that carries out the social teachings of the Church

Jesus Is Risen

FOCUS: In this chapter, you will be helping your child to understand that Jesus rose from the dead and so we will also rise.

Looking down on a city at night from a plane or high building, one sees what appears to be a fairyland of lights. The beauty of an otherwise ordinary city is enhanced. The shift in perspective can totally change how we've seen something day in and day out. In like manner, how we see things shifts as we explore different aspects of those things. Expanding our perspectives can be a challenging but worthwhile endeavor.

Belief in the Resurrection moves us from a limited, earthbound outlook to a radically different, eternity-oriented view of the pilgrimage of life. It keeps Christians from losing heart over the mysterious interweaving of misunderstanding, betrayal, loneliness, and all the other faces of suffering. We acknowledge the Lordship of the risen Christ, we accept his ways as our ways, and we ask that he bring to perfection in us his spirit of life.

Scripture in This Chapter

John 20   The Resurrection
Luke 24:13–35   The Road to Emmaus

Catechism of the Catholic Church

638, 641, 644, 1443–1444, 1468

In this chapter, help your child to

* recognize Easter as the celebration of Jesus' rising from the dead with new life.
* relate that Jesus' friends saw and talked with him after his Resurrection.
* recall the many ways the risen Jesus comes to us.
* understand what peace is and value it.
* know that Jesus wants us to have peace and to share it with others.
* deepen his or her appreciation for Jesus' gift of peace.

Words Your Child Should Know

* Easter
* Eucharist
* Resurrection

Key Terms for Your Information

* Alleluia—term of joy that means "Praise God"
* Emmaus (eh MAY us)—town near Jerusalem where Jesus revealed himself to two disciples after his Resurrection

Jesus Offers Himself

FOCUS: In this chapter, you will be helping your child to understand that at the words of the priest, bread and wine become Jesus, who offers himself to the Father.

The word *sacrifice* comes from two Latin words, *sacrum facere,* which mean "to make holy." Any gift that we give to God is called a sacrifice. When we consider the Mass a sacrifice, we understand it as the offering of a gift to God. This giving of a gift expresses our desire to be united to the Father in love.

The gift we offer at Mass is the same gift that Jesus offered to his Father on the night before Jesus died and as he was dying on the cross. Whenever we join the priest in doing what Jesus did at the Last Supper, we offer the perfect sacrifice, the gift of the Lord's life, given so that God may live in us and unite us to himself and to one another. Jesus' life is God's life, given to us in the Holy Eucharist. During the Eucharistic Prayer of the Mass, Christ becomes present among us and for us.

Scripture in This Chapter

John 19:1–23   Passion and Death of Jesus

Catechism of the Catholic Church

1106, 1353–1354, 1361, 1375

In this chapter, help your child to

* explain the meaning of the first part of the Eucharistic Prayer.
* describe that the Mass is Jesus' perfect sacrifice to the Father.
* explain that after the consecration, we pray to the Father.
* describe the Great Amen as assent to the offering of Jesus and ourselves.
* create a clay model of the bread and cup used at Mass.

Word Your Child Should Know

* Body and Blood of Christ

Key Terms for Your Information

* consecrate—to change bread and wine into the Body and Blood of Christ at Mass
* Eucharistic Prayer—the central part of the Mass, during which bread and wine become Jesus and he offers himself to the Father
* Great Amen—our response of assent or agreement to the sacrifice of Jesus during the Eucharist
* host—the sacred bread
* sacrifice—a gift offered to God

God Shares the Wondrous Life of Grace

FOCUS: In this chapter, you will be helping your child to understand that even after sin, God shares divine life with us through the sacraments.

Grace is forever changing us. God touches our innermost being, transforming us without interfering with our freedom. A sign of God's presence within us is our restless dissatisfaction with anything less than the transformation of our whole selves for the love of God and our neighbor.

In this lies the value of grace: that the spirit of God dwells within us. God can transform our anxieties and tensions into prayer and enduring hope. God refreshes, delights, and gladdens our souls, leading us to grow in love, longing to see his face. We can never reach perfection until we are transfigured into the image of our love, Jesus himself.

Scripture in This Chapter
Genesis 3:1–19 The Fall
John 3:1–21 The Story of Nicodemus
1 Corinthians 2:9 Saint Paul Describes Heaven.

Catechism of the Catholic Church
27, 404–405, 1024, 1257, 1266, 2566

In this chapter, help your child to
+ recall how Adam and Eve rejected the gift of God's grace.
+ see how through grace, we can live in God's love and be happy with God now and forever in heaven.
+ know that Baptism removes original sin and gives us God's life of grace.
+ understand the significance of the signs of water and the words used in Baptism.
+ become more aware of symbolism as used by the Church.

Key Terms for Your Information
+ Baptism—the sacrament in which we receive grace, are cleansed from original sin and our sins, and become children of God and members of the Church
+ divine—godlike
+ eternity—forever
+ grace—God's life
+ heaven—being with God in the next life
+ original sin—the first sin; the state in which every human being is born—because of the first sin of Adam and Eve—without grace and with a tendency toward selfishness and sin

We Live God's Laws

FOCUS: In this chapter, you will be helping your child to understand that we show our commitment to God and to others by following his laws.

God's laws are the basic rules for Christian social living. They govern our moral duties and obligations to God, others, nature, and ourselves. They protect and keep sacred our human rights and liberty. They provide the foundation for all human society, whether civil, religious, or familial. These laws tell us that God wants liberty and justice to triumph, peace and harmony to prosper, love and concern to flourish, human dignity to be revered, and himself to be worshiped as Lord of all.

Christians of conviction and commitment are much needed in today's world. Preparing children to become such Christians is our duty and privilege as parents. Children will learn much from our teaching but more from our example. The *General Directory for Catechesis* affirms this: "The best way to feed this apostolic awareness is by identifying with the figure of Jesus Christ . . . by seeking to acquire the zeal which Jesus had for the Kingdom." (239)

Scripture in This Chapter
Psalm 119 Blessings of the Law
Hebrews 10:16 God's Laws on Our Hearts

Catechism of the Catholic Church
2070–2074

In this chapter, help your child to
+ explain that actions have consequences.
+ apply the Ten Commandments to situations.
+ describe the Ten Commandments as a means of expressing love for God.
+ demonstrate their understanding of the main concepts of Unit 4.
+ express concretely their understanding of the Ten Commandments.

Unit 4 Review

FOCUS: In this chapter, you will be helping your child to understand that God calls us to holiness through living out our vocations.

As Christians, we keep in mind our heavenly goal and follow God's continuing call to holiness of life. With God's grace, we follow his Son, Jesus, day after day in the sure hope of seeing God face-to-face. Through Christ Jesus, we have the ability to respond, to lift up our hearts, to fall down in adoration, to offer sacrifice, and to serve God's people.

God has shown his great love and power through his Son, Jesus, and made available to us all the spiritual treasures we need to reach holiness of life. When we respond to God's call to enter upon a way of life, we trust that God will channel his graces to us. We respond with love, acceptance, and joy, knowing that we are brought to holiness by God's mighty love and power.

Scripture in This Chapter

Psalm 25   A Prayer for Guidance
Luke 1:26–38   The Annunciation

Catechism of the Catholic Church

825

In this chapter, help your child to

+ relate that people in each vocation can contribute to make a better world.
+ reflect on the key concepts covered in this unit.
+ explain how to prepare for his or her vocation and be ready to respond to God's call
+ demonstrate an understanding of key concepts relating to the Sacraments at the Service of Communion.

Unit 4 Review

FOCUS: In this chapter, you will be helping your child to understand that through good leaders and bad, God is faithful to the people.

Relying on the call and promises of God, the Israelites fled Egypt in search of a homeland. This Promised Land of their dreams awaited them, but before it could become their home, they would face battles, confusion, infidelities, and sorrows. Israel would grow from a family to a number of tribes and eventually to a nation and kingdom. Yet this kingdom, led by anointed kings and resplendent in palaces and warriors, would not be the fulfillment of the Lord's promises.

The human heart, when finally rooted in Christ, takes possession of a new kingdom. Here, all promises are fulfilled. Here, hope fades into possession of all that is longed for. For those who believe and trust, the Kingdom of God is within—unshakable, tried by fire, and greatly loved.

Catechism of the Catholic Church

128, 205

In this chapter, help your child to

+ review the main facts about people in salvation history.
+ review concepts from Unit 4.

The Eucharist—Jesus the Bread of Life

FOCUS: In this chapter, you will be helping your child to understand that the Eucharist nourishes us with the Body and Blood of Jesus uniting us with him and one another.

In the Eucharist, Jesus is sacramentally present. He makes present his sacrifice on the cross and the victory of his Resurrection. We join our lives with his in an offering to the Father. In faith and in love, we approach the table of the Lord to be nourished by the Body and Blood of Christ. Jesus unites all who partake of the one bread and the one cup, forming us into one body, for the Eucharist is both the sign and source of our unity in Christ. We go forth from the Eucharist in peace to love and serve the Father and one another.

Scripture in This Chapter
Mark 6:30–44 Jesus Feeds the Five Thousand.
John 15:4–7 The Vine and the Branches

Catechism of the Catholic Church
610–611, 1324–1326, 1341–1344, 1402–1405

In this chapter, help your child to
+ explain that the Eucharist is a memorial meal through which Jesus nourishes individuals and the community.
+ explain the structure and prayers of the Eucharist.
+ discuss how in receiving the Eucharist, he or she becomes one with Christ and with others.
+ explain the parts of the Mass.

Word Your Child Should Know
+ transubstantiation

Key Terms for Your Information
+ covenant—an agreement between God and human beings
+ Eucharist—the sacrament in which Jesus becomes present under the appearances of bread and wine.
+ Passover—the Jewish feast commemorating God's saving action of leading the Israelites from slavery in Egypt to the Promised Land
+ Liturgy of the Eucharist—the second part of the Eucharist, in which we receive Jesus under the appearance of bread and wine.
+ Liturgy of the Word—the first part of the Eucharist, in which we hear and respond to the Word of God
+ Sacramentary—the official book of prayers and directives for the celebration of the Eucharist

The Way of Holiness

FOCUS: In this chapter, you will be helping your child to understand that in answering our call to holiness, we are helped by virtue and hindered by vice.

In the early chapters of the Acts of the Apostles, Luke portrays for us the ideal of such commitment. The earliest followers of the Way risked everything out of loyalty to Christ. Their love for one another was so obvious that it eventually became the hallmark of the Church. For 20 centuries now, Jesus Christ has required the same proofs of discipleship: "I give you a new commandment: love one another. As I have loved you, so you also should love one another." (John 13:34)

Empowered by the Spirit, we, the Church today, try to respond in love to God. Like our forebears in the faith, we find in the Eucharist and in personal communion with Christ, the strength to weed out from our lives all that hinders our transformation into him. Only when pride has been replaced by humble ministry to Christ can we know the freedom of being true children of God.

Scripture in This Chapter
1 John 4:8 God Is Love.
John 14:6 Jesus Is the Way.
John 13:34 A New Commandment

Catechism of the Catholic Church
1768, 1805–1813, 2013–2014

In this chapter, help your child to
+ identify ways to use his or her gifts in ways that show love and gratitude to God.
+ identify the capital sins and the opposing virtues.
+ explain how vices and virtues are manifested in daily life.
+ identify the virtues listed and lived in the New Testament.
+ identify practical ways to grow in virtue.

Word Your Child Should Know
+ capital sins

Key Term for Your Information
+ covenant—a sacred agreement between God and people

Jesus Sends Us the Spirit

FOCUS: In this chapter, you will be helping your child to understand that the Holy Spirit came to the Church on Pentecost to guide and strengthen us.

Christ promised to fill the hearts of his people with the Spirit before he ascended into heaven. On Pentecost, fire and wind—two powerful symbols signifying light and love, life and strength—accompanied the Spirit's coming. The Holy Spirit filled the apostles and disciples with Jesus' gifts and made them a light to the nations and a breath of new creation.

The Church asks the Spirit to work through us to bring Christ to the world today. Through the love of God poured into our hearts by the Holy Spirit, we can endure any hardship, welcome all who come to us, and proclaim the kingdom of God.

Scripture in This Chapter

Matthew 28:16–20 The Commissioning of the Disciples
Acts 1:6–12 Jesus' Ascension
Acts 1:13–2:47 The First Christian Community and the Coming of the Holy Spirit

Catechism of the Catholic Church

659, 731–732, 1266, 1813, 2623

In this chapter, help your child to

+ tell the story of Christ's visible departure and entry into heavenly glory.
+ associate our celebration of the feast of Pentecost with the first coming of the Holy Spirit.
+ name ways that the Holy Spirit is present in his or her own life.
+ describe the Theological Virtues.
+ identify how the virtues operate in daily life.

Word Your Child Should Know

+ Holy Spirit

Key Terms for Your Information

+ Ascension—Jesus' return to heaven
+ faith—virtue that helps us to believe in God
+ Holy Spirit—the Person of the Trinity whom Jesus sent to help his Church
+ hope—virtue that helps us trust that God will help us reach heaven
+ love—virtue that helps us love God and all others
+ Pentecost—the coming of the Holy Spirit to the Church
+ virtues—powers to do good

We Receive the Bread of Life

FOCUS: In this chapter, you will be helping your child to understand that Jesus comes to us in Communion and unites us with himself and with one another.

Saint Augustine, in an Easter sermon to newly baptized Christians, expresses how the mystery of the Body and Blood of Christ is both a sign and an effect of our unity.

> You should know what you have received, what you will receive, what you should receive daily. The bread that you see on the altar, when it has been sanctified by the word of God, is the Body of Christ. . . . If you have received it rightly, you are what you have received.
>
> *Sermon 227*

We cannot consciously partake of the one bread, be nourished by the Body of Christ, without striving more earnestly to become one in the Spirit.

Scripture in This Chapter

Matthew 8:5–13 Cure of the Roman Soldier's Servant
1 Corinthians 10:16–17 Participation in the Body and Blood of Christ

Catechism of the Catholic Church

1355, 1384–1388

In this chapter, help your child to

+ explain that the prayers of the Communion rite make us aware of our union with Christ.
+ explain how to prepare for Communion.
+ distinguish between eating food and eating the Bread of Life.
+ describe how close Jesus is to us in Holy Communion.

Word Your Child Should Know

+ holy

Key Terms for Your Information

+ extraordinary minister of Holy Communion—person appointed to assist in distributing Communion
+ fasting—refraining from food and drink, except water, in preparation for receiving Communion
+ Lamb of God—the prayer before Communion in which we ask for mercy and peace
+ Sign of Peace—a gesture of love and forgiveness that we extend to others during Mass
+ unworthy—not ready for such an honor

The Holy Spirit Lives Within Us

FOCUS: In this chapter, you will be helping your child to understand that the Holy Spirit within us helps us to follow Jesus by doing good and avoiding evil.

Although we strive to imitate Jesus, no one can be exactly like him, not even the Blessed Virgin, because no one can become God. Moreover, no two people reflect the holiness of Jesus in the same degree or even in the same way. These differences in divine grace are the result of God's marvelous providence, which deals differently with each person.

The more faithful we are in responding to this grace, the more perfectly we imitate the Savior. Thus, we each reflect in a varied manner and to a different extent the qualities of Jesus, which are really the attributes of God. With God's grace, we can overcome the obstacles of our fallen natures and follow the direction of the Holy Spirit.

Scripture in This Chapter

Mark 10:17–21   The Rich Young Man
2 Corinthians 3:18   The Spirit Makes Us More Like Jesus.
Galatians 5:16–26   The Spirit Helps Us Avoid Evil

Catechism of the Catholic Church

562, 2003, 2846–2849

In this chapter, help your child to

- explain that following Jesus is the way to eternal happiness with God in heaven.
- name ways to follow Jesus even when it involves suffering.
- explain how the Holy Spirit helps us live as God's children.
- explain how unhappiness results from yielding to selfishness.
- recall the terms accident, temptation, and sin.

Word Your Child Should Know

- personal sin

Key Terms for Your Information

- accident—a harmful event that is not done deliberately
- Holy Spirit—the third Person of the Trinity who was sent by Jesus and the Father to help us; the Spirit within us who inspires us to do good
- sin—choosing to do what is wrong; failing to love God and others
- temptation—something that makes us feel like choosing to do what is wrong

Happy Are the Poor in Spirit

FOCUS: In this chapter, you will be helping your child to understand that Jesus teaches us to be satisfied with having what we need.

As followers of Christ, we realize that true happiness does not consist in possessing many earthly things. We should live in a spirit of detachment from material possessions in order to focus on what is really important: the kingdom of heaven and union with God.

This does not mean that we should be impractical or careless in regard to the possession and use of material things, nor does it mean using poverty as a form of social protest against society. On the contrary, being poor in spirit means we care for and appreciate the things of the world insofar as they are the work of God, who provides them for our needs. As God's creatures, we respect these gifts and lovingly use them according to God's plan. We can be aware of the true value of earthly things and their proper use, without becoming dependent on or attached to them.

Scripture in This Chapter

Psalm 119:2   Happiness in the Lord
Matthew 5:3–12   The Beatitudes

Catechism of the Catholic Church

1716, 1724, 2544–2547

In this chapter, help your child to

- explain that Jesus gave us the Beatitudes to help us find true happiness.
- describe how Saint Francis showed dependence on God.
- explain the need to be concerned about the world's resources.
- describe how to do with less in order to share with those who are needy.
- explain that being poor in spirit means to depend on God.

Words Your Child Should Know

- Beatitudes
- Sermon on the Mount

Key Terms for Your Information

- lowly—meek; gentle
- poor in spirit—satisfied with and grateful for what one has
- clean in heart—holy; aiming to please God
- canticle—a song of praise

Life Is Precious

FOCUS: In this chapter, you will be helping your child to understand that life is a precious gift from God that must be cherished and protected.

Throughout his life, Jesus showed his concern for the health of the body as he went about curing disease, restoring sight or hearing, and even working miracles to provide food and drink for the people. God's love for us calls for nothing less than a total response of love. We are to share that love with each person we encounter in our daily lives. Jesus told his Father "I made known to them your name and I will make it known, that the love with which you loved me may be in them and I in them." (John 17:26)

Jesus pointed out in his Sermon on the Mount that his love is evident in us when we show to others a reconciling and gratuitous love that reflects his life-giving attitude toward all. His presence in us and with us gives us power to bestow the gift of kindness where the forces of evil and suffering threaten to engulf or destroy human life.

Scripture in This Chapter
Psalm 23 The Lord Is My Shepherd.
Luke 23:33–34 Forgive Them.
John 6:1–15 Multiplication of the Loaves

Catechism of the Catholic Church
2258–2262, 2268–2291, 2306

In this chapter, help your child to
* explain why all life, especially human life, is precious.
* explain how Jesus is the Good Shepherd.
* describe what the Fifth Commandment says and how it applies to all life.
* define the terms *abortion* and *suicide.*
* distinguish between healthy and unhealthy expressions of anger.
* identify ways to deal with anger.

Words Your Child Should Know
* abortion
* suicide

Elijah and Amos Speak for the Lord

FOCUS: In this chapter, you will be helping your child to understand that prophets such as Elijah and Amos spoke for God, calling people to worship God alone and to practice justice.

In Scripture, justice and righteousness are seen as two sides of a coin. Justice is a way of acting. Righteousness is a quality of the one who acts. Justice informs a decision that gives others their due; righteousness speaks of the gentleness, generosity, and kindness that characterize the just person.

Justice seems precise and static, as indicated by the scales that symbolize it. Righteousness, on the other hand, surges "like an unfailing stream." (Amos 5:24) Justice gives form to righteousness as the bed of a stream gives form to its waters, while righteousness gives life and beauty to justice.

Scripture in This Chapter
1 Kings 18, 21; 2 Kings 2 The story of Elijah
The Book of Amos A Prophet of Justice

Catechism of the Catholic Church
61, 64, 218, 2420–2423, 2581–2584

In this chapter, help your child to
* define *prophet* and the role of the prophet in Israel.
* describe the messages of Elijah and Amos.
* identify strategies for fighting injustice.
* explain how Israel failed to respond to God.
* compare the evils in society during Amos's time to the evils of today.
* explain what the term *social justice* means.

Words Your Child Should Know
* prophet   * Spiritual Works of Mercy

Key Terms for Your Information
* Corporal Works of Mercy—acts that meet others' physical needs
* justice—virtue that enables us to give everyone his or her rightful due; fair treatment of everyone
* major prophets—Isaiah, Jeremiah, and Ezekiel
* minor prophets—the 12 prophets whose books are shorter than those of the major prophets
* social justice—a state in which people lead truly human lives by calling society to better serve the good of all
* works of mercy—good deeds done out of love based on Christ's teaching in Matthew 25:35–36

Jesus' Final Hours—Jesus the Lamb of God

FOCUS: In this chapter, you will be helping your child to understand that Jesus' suffering and death won eternal life for us.

Suffering leads to growth; death leads to life. Nature reflects this pattern in the planted seed becoming a flower and the cocooned caterpillar being transformed into a butterfly. Human experience reflects this pattern in the common sufferings and separations, and the small deaths that come into every human life such as moving to an unfamiliar city or losing a job. This pattern shines through the mystery of the cross, the mystery of God's love transforming evil, hatred, and pain into goodness, love, and joy.

Jesus also showed that God responds to hatred and suffering, not with blind revenge or almighty power, but with healing. If our God responds in this way, can our response be any different? As God's people, we learn acceptance in love, acting freely, obediently, trustingly, and humbly. In Christ, we see the result of following in his footsteps, where death leads to eternal life.

Scripture in This Chapter
Matthew 26:39 Jesus in the Garden of Gethsemane
Luke 23:39–43 Jesus on the Cross

Catechism of the Catholic Church
612, 616–618, 632, 678–682, 1023, 1030, 1033, 1040

In this chapter, help your child to
+ describe the physical and mental suffering that Christ endured to redeem us.
+ review events of Christ's passion.
+ analyze decisions to see whether he or she reaches out to others or satisfies personal desires.
+ evaluate the groups he or she belongs to and how he or she influences his or her following of Christ.

Words Your Child Should Know
+ Last Judgment   + particular judgment

Key Terms for Your Information
+ Parousia (pah-ROO-see-uh)—the Second Coming of Christ in glory when God's plan of salvation will be revealed
+ passion—the events from the Last Supper to Jesus' death on the cross; suffering
+ purgatory—the purification after death that transforms people not yet perfect in love for heaven

The Way of Faith

FOCUS: In this chapter, you will be helping your child to understand that God is to be loved above everyone and everything and that God's name is to be honored.

Out of love, the Lord gave us the first three commandments to bind us to himself. The other seven commandments guide us to further happiness through love of others. In every age, sadly, some people worship their own gods: power, pleasure, and possessions. They are doomed to emptiness, for the human heart is far larger than all these idols.

Scripture in This Chapter
Exodus 20:2–7 The First and Second Commandments
Matthew 22:37 The Great Commandment

Catechism of the Catholic Church
2083, 2132, 2142–2155

In this chapter, help your child to
+ explain the importance of responding to God in faith, prayer, and reverence.
+ describe the types of prayer according to purpose.
+ describe what it means to respect God's name.
+ identify sins related to the Second Commandment.

Words Your Child Should Know
+ sacrilege   + vow
+ sacrifice

Key Terms for Your Information
+ astrology—the belief that the sun, moon, planets, and stars control our lives
+ atheism—the rejection of God's existence
+ blasphemy—words that insult the goodness of God
+ cult—a system of misguided religious beliefs that center around a strong religious leader
+ cursing—calling on God to bring evil or harm to someone or something
+ idol—anything considered more important than God
+ oath—calling on God to witness to the truth
+ perjury—lying under oath
+ presumption—thinking that one can save oneself or that God will save one even without repentance
+ profanity—careless, casual, and inappropriate use of God's name
+ satanism—the worship of the devil
+ spiritualism—the belief that the souls of the dead or spirits of the other world can be contacted
+ vulgar language—offensive and "dirty" words

Jesus Is with Us in His Church

FOCUS: In this chapter, you will be helping your child to understand that the Holy Spirit guides and cares for the Church through its leaders.

In Baptism, Jesus has made us children of God and members of his Church, the family of God's people. He remains with us through the Holy Spirit and unites us with himself and with one another. From its very beginning, the Church has been a community united in the Lord, sharing beliefs, experiences, and even material goods.

Saint Thomas Aquinas compares the role of the community to the life-giving role of a mother. Just as babies in their mothers' wombs are sustained by their mother's nourishment, young baptized Christians depend on the Christian community for the development of the gifts they receive in Baptism. The faith, hope, and love given with the grace of Baptism need a positive, nurturing environment if they are to grow. The Church accepts, loves, supports, forgives, encourages, and educates each person. As a Christian family, we are strengthened as we gather around the table of the Lord.

Scripture in This Chapter
John 21:1–19 Jesus and Peter

Catechism of the Catholic Church
818, 836–838, 880–882, 1267–1270

In this chapter, help your child to
+ explain how Baptism has made us members of the Church.
+ express a sense of belonging to the Church.
+ explain the holiness of the Church and acknowledge a responsibility to contribute to it and make it holier.
+ describe how the Holy Father leads and serves the people of God as Jesus' visible representative.
+ identify themselves as members of the Catholic Church.

Words Your Child Should Know
+ Catholic
+ pope

Key Terms for Your Information
+ Catholic Church—the family of Christians who have the pope and bishops as their leaders
+ Church—God's family
+ Holy Father—another name for the pope
+ pope—the leader of the Church

We Share God's Love with Others

FOCUS: In this chapter, you will be helping your child to understand that we live the Mass by loving and serving the Lord and one another.

Saint Catherine of Siena was once asked how we could adequately express our love for God, since everything we have comes from God. Catherine answered that we have only one thing we can offer God that is of value to God: we can give our love to people who are as unworthy as we are of God's love.

At the conclusion of the Mass, the priest or deacon dismisses us, sending us to live a life of love and service for God and for others, praising and blessing the Lord in all that we do. This attitude of thanksgiving is our effort to bring the mind and heart of Jesus Christ to our daily duties. Every celebration of the Eucharist imbues us with Christ's presence, which we reflect by showing greater strength and vitality in situations that challenge us to express his love to others.

Scripture in This Chapter
Mark 14:22–24 The Last Supper

Catechism of the Catholic Church
1391, 1394–1397, 1416

In this chapter, help your child to
+ explain that Mass ends with Jesus' call to love and serve him.
+ explain that God can help us make the best of difficult circumstances.
+ suggest ways to overcome obstacles to loving and serving the Lord.
+ review Chapters 15 through 22 on the Mass and Holy Communion.
+ demonstrate his or her understanding of the concepts presented in Unit 4.

Words Your Child Should Know
+ Blessed Sacrament
+ tabernacle

God Blesses Contrite Hearts

FOCUS: In this chapter, you will be helping your child to understand that God forgives us when we are sorry for our sins.

The woman at Simon's house knelt at Jesus' feet. Zacchaeus climbed a tree to catch sight of Jesus. Peter looked at him as Jesus left the judgment hall. Each of these encounters with the Lord was a turning point for the person involved. These people had their sinfulness revealed to them, and they received God's forgiving love. Their joyful gratitude found expression in a new and deeper relationship with the Lord as they realized that, in spite of their sinfulness, he loved them and desired their love in return. Trusting in his help, they exposed themselves to the brightness of his light and the warmth of his love. They allowed his grace to call forth their best, but they never forgot that their individual capabilities were a gift from God. No matter what they did for the Lord, it was merely a humble response to his great love for them.

Scripture in This Chapter

Luke 7:36–50 Jesus and the Woman at Simon's House
Luke 15:4–7 The Shepherd and His Lost Sheep
Luke 18:10–14 The Two Men in the Temple
Luke 19:1–10 Jesus and Zacchaeus
Luke 22:31–62 Jesus Forgave Peter.

Catechism of the Catholic Church

588–589, 1429, 1439, 1484

In this chapter, help your child to

+ describe God's forgiving love as expressed in the story of Jesus forgiving Peter.
+ demonstrate a desire to turn to the Lord with contrite hearts to receive his forgiveness.
+ recall some stories from the Bible about sorrow for sin and forgiveness.
+ identify his or her need of the Holy Spirit to know and be sorry for sins.
+ review how to make a daily examination of conscience and realize its importance

Words Your Child Should Know

+ conscience
+ examination of conscience

God's Sorrowing and Meek People Receive a Special Promise

FOCUS: Jesus teaches us that the sorrowing will be comforted and the meek will inherit the earth.

Those who live the Christian life in its fullness experience within themselves an inexhaustible supply of strength. Because of their utter confidence in the Lord, our Blessed Mother and the saints faced the trials and sufferings in their lives with the love, joy, peace, and patience that are the fruits of the Spirit (Galatians 5:22).

We all have shortcomings that can keep us from enjoying these Fruits of the Spirit. Saint Francis de Sales confessed he had to struggle throughout his life to master his impatient disposition, yet he eventually became known for his amiable serenity in extremely difficult situations.

Francis urges us to invoke God's assistance by praying "Lord, have mercy on me" whenever we are tempted to respond to someone with irritability or impatience. Then he suggests a method for acquiring a gentle nature so that we might receive the heritage God promised to the meek and the humble of heart.

Scripture in This Chapter

Matthew 26:39 Doing the Father's Will
Luke 19:41–44 Lament for Jerusalem

Catechism of the Catholic Church

164, 1521, 1820, 2262

In this chapter, help your child to

+ explain how Saint Francis de Sales overcame his temper to become a model of gentleness.
+ describe ways to respond to provoking situations with gentleness.
+ review what he or she has learned about the first three beatitudes.
+ describe how some of the saints lived these beatitudes.
+ describe the first three beatitudes.

Word Your Child Should Know

+ salvation

Key Terms for Your Information

+ humble—meek; gentle; not proud or boastful
+ meek—patient; gentle

Christians Are Faithful in Love

FOCUS: In this chapter, you will be helping your child to understand that God wants us to respect the gift of sex and wants married people to be faithful.

Human dignity and sacredness, already present at conception, are rooted in the fact that each human being is created by God in his image and likeness.

Our first obligation, therefore, is to be faithful to our own inherent dignity. If we respect and reverence our own bodies, minds, and souls, we are able to respect and reverence those of others.

One of the strongest bonds cementing any relationship is faithfulness. God is faithful to his people. Christ is faithful to his Church. Husband and wife are faithful to each other. Friend is faithful to friend.

Scripture in This Chapter

Matthew 5:8 Blessed are the Clean of Heart.
1 Corinthians 3:16 You are the Temple of God.

Catechism of the Catholic Church

2337–2345, 2349, 2354, 2364–2365, 2380

In this chapter, help your child to

+ explain why we show a special reverence for the gift of sex.
+ explain the meaning and purpose of the Sixth and Ninth Commandments.
+ describe how being chaste requires grace, self-control, and courage.
+ identify and know how to respond to situations that endanger chastity.
+ explain how making the right decision in small matters aids us to do so in great ones.

Words Your Child Should Know

+ chastity
+ covet

Key Terms for Your Information

+ adultery—the sin a married person commits when he or she is not faithful to the love promised at marriage
+ sexuality—our state of maleness or femaleness

Isaiah Proclaims the Promised Messiah

FOCUS: In this chapter, you will be helping your child to understand that Isaiah called the people to be faithful and spoke of a suffering servant to come.

The prophet is a person of vision who sees how the present leads to the future. The prophet sees beyond a world in turmoil to the glory of a future age. The prophet dwells in the here and now but also abides outside of time, for the prophet speaks the God's eternal Word.

We are all called to be prophets, speaking God's Word in our time. We are to care passionately for the "state of affairs," while trusting in God to be God. To see the great light leading us onward, we must tear down all barriers that cast shadows: hardness of heart, self-pity, pride, selfishness, and refusal to forget yesterday's pain.

Scripture in This Chapter

The Book of Isaiah The Prophet Proclaims the Promised Messiah.
Matthew 7:21–23 Do the Father's Will.

Catechism of the Catholic Church

208, 711–714

In this chapter, help your child to

+ describe Isaiah's call, his work, and the Book of Isaiah.
+ identify ways to respond to situations with trust in God.
+ identify Jesus as the suffering servant of whom Isaiah spoke.
+ trace important events in salvation history.
+ identify key passages from Isaiah.

Words Your Child Should Know

+ Amen
+ holy

Key Terms for Your Information

+ Assyria—powerful nation that conquered Israel and exacted a tribute from Judah
+ Isaiah—prophet of Judah who foretold characteristics of the Messiah; he warned that Israel would be conquered but God would preserve a remnant of the people
+ Second Isaiah—chapters 40 through 55 of the Book of Isaiah, written by a disciple of Isaiah
+ seraphim—the highest order in the hierarchy of angels (mentioned in Isaiah 6:2); seraphim are God's attendants, and they also proclaim his glory
+ Third Isaiah—chapters 56 through 66

CHAPTER 22　　**GRADE 7**

The Victory of Jesus—Jesus the Risen Lord

FOCUS: In this chapter, you will be helping your child to understand that Jesus rose from the dead, ascended to the Father, and is still with us.

The Resurrection is God's guarantee that those who trust the Father and follow his plan through the mystery to the end, as Jesus did, will have victory. In the upper room, Jesus appears and shows his wounds. He says, in essence, "My friends, look what they tried to do to keep me away from you. But they could not do it. Because love is stronger than death." A band of frightened disciples had an experience of the risen Christ that radically changed them. Christ had broken the power of death. They could share his power; through Baptism, they would share eternal life with him. The deepest of all desires is the desire for life, and Jesus fulfills this desire forever.

The Church is a saved and saving community. Whenever a Christian stands up for truth, fights an unjust status quo, or speaks up for a neighbor despite opposition, he or she is joined by others who proclaim the Gospel of the risen Christ.

Scripture in This Chapter
Luke 24:1–11 The Resurrection of Jesus
1 Corinthians 15:54–55 Christ Is Victorious Over Death.

Catechism of the Catholic Church
648–655, 662–664, 904–905

In this chapter, help your child to
+ describe the significance of the Resurrection and the appearances of the risen Lord.
+ identify ways the risen Jesus is present.
+ discuss what sacramentals are.
+ describe the significance of the Ascension.
+ respond to Christ's call to be a witness to the world.

Words Your Child Should Know
+ apostle
+ Ascension

Key Term for Your Information
+ sacramentals—objects, words, and actions that are sacred signs given by the Church and which can make us holy by the prayers of the Church and by the way we use them

CHAPTER 22　　**GRADE 8**

The Way of Worship

FOCUS: In this chapter, you will be helping your child to understand that Sunday is to be a day for worship and rest.

The best witness we can give to God's place in our lives is our worship. Worship begins in the heart. We love God and want to respond to God's goodness. As members of the Church, we worship by participating in the Eucharistic Liturgy for each Sunday. We join together as a community of Christ's faithful followers to praise the Father in and through Jesus. Through his Church, Christ calls us to deeper friendship with himself and offers us salvation. We experience his nearness, and we are transformed, nourished, and impelled to recognize God's presence in the entire Christian community, especially in our families. Sunday is the high point of the week for the Christian community. We set aside one day to re-create and renew ourselves by enjoying the beauty in the world around us and by revering the people with whom we live.

Scripture in This Chapter
Exodus 20:8 The Third Commandment
Psalm 95 Bow Down in Worship.

Catechism of the Catholic Church
2168–2188

In this chapter, help your child to
+ describe the Eucharist as the center of Christian life.
+ identify ways to celebrate Sunday with his or her family and parish community.
+ explain the Church's liturgical calendar.
+ identify the Holy Days of Obligation.
+ identify the terms and procedures for liturgy preparation.

Words Your Child Should Know
+ Holy Day of Obligation
+ Lord's Day
+ Sabbath
+ liturgical year

Key Term for Your Information
+ ritual—an established, ordered procedure for celebrating a religious ceremony

Mary Is the Mother of the Church

FOCUS: In this chapter, you will be helping your child to understand that we honor and imitate Mary, God's Mother and ours.

God has given each of us many gifts that show us his profound, incomprehensible love for us. The greatest gift is, of course, Jesus, whose words and actions tell us the depth of God's loving plan—that we are called to be one with him and with one another. Jesus gave us one last gift when he was dying on the cross—Mary, his Mother, to be our Mother. Just as Mary brought Jesus into the world, she helps to form us into good Christians who bring the love of Jesus to others.

After Mary was assumed into heaven, she was crowned Queen of Heaven and Earth. Every May we ask her to be the queen of our hearts, and we turn to her to learn how we can experience the love of the Lord in the joys and sorrows of daily life.

Scripture in this Chapter
Luke 1:26–38 The Annunciation
John 19:25–27 Mary and John at the Cross

Catechism of the Catholic Church
966–967, 971–972

In this chapter, help your child to
- understand that Mary was taken body and soul into heaven.
- pray with confidence to Mary, our Mother and queen.
- describe Mary as a model for Christians.
- recognize that the Church honors Mary.

Key Terms for Your Information
- Assumption—Mary's being taken up body and soul into heaven
- Ave Maria—Latin for "Hail Mary"
- immaculate—free from sin

We Are One in the Church

FOCUS: In this chapter, you will be helping your child to understand that we who are united in the Body of Christ, the Church, try to bring others to Jesus.

Christ, the head of the Church, is the image of the invisible God (Colossians 1:15). All of us who are members of the Church must be formed in the likeness of Christ, our head. For this purpose, Christ continually provides for our growth in the Spirit through the Holy Eucharist, the heart and center of Christian life. The Eucharist, like a life-giving sap, nourishes us by giving us the spiritual joy and fruit of a life hidden with Christ in God (Colossians 3:3).

Through sacramental union with God, we obtain the strength we need to control our passions, purify ourselves of daily venial faults, and avoid grave sins.

The Eucharist defines our Christian way of life: giving self for others. Through the gift of himself in the Eucharist, Jesus shares with us his selfless love. He empowers us to give glory to the Father by our lives.

Scripture in This Chapter
John 10:14–16 One Flock, One Shepherd

Catechism of the Catholic Church
771, 782, 789, 795, 813

In this chapter, help your child to
- explain that they belong to the Body of Christ, the Church.
- describe the Eucharist as a means to living the Christian commitment.
- review how all Church members are called to share God's love as Jesus did.
- describe how Church leaders, priests, deacons, religious, married people and single people serve the Church.
- discuss how Holy Communion gives us strength to be like Jesus.
- describe some characteristics of a Catholic Christian.

Word Your Child Should Know
- deacon

Key Terms for Your Information
- Body of Christ—the Church
- religious brothers and sisters—men and women who live a special way of life, devote themselves to serving God and the Church, and do not marry

God Forgives Us

FOCUS: In this chapter, you will be helping your child to understand that we are reconciled to God and the Church in the Sacrament of Penance and Reconciliation.

In the parable of the lost son, it was the realization of his father's love that gave the son the courage to confess his sin and to acknowledge his unworthiness. The father's response reveals the joy Jesus spoke of when he said that there would be more joy in heaven over one sinner who repents than over ninety-nine others, who had no need of repentance (Luke 15:7).

In the Sacrament of Reconciliation, the Church proclaims, by word and sign, God's forgiving love. We confess our sins and come before the Lord, whose healing forgiveness opens up a new and deeper relationship of love. As we grieve over the evil we have done, God's gracious compassion makes us more attentive to the invitations of grace.

Scripture in This Chapter
Luke 15:11–24 The Parable of the Lost Son

Catechism of the Catholic Church
1448–1449, 1468–1469

In this chapter, help your child to
* describe how the parable of the lost son and the forgiving father tells of God's mercy.
* describe how God forgives us and helps us overcome sin in the Sacrament of Reconciliation.
* name the steps for celebrating the Sacrament of Reconciliation.
* review the procedure for sacramental reconciliation.
* review what was learned about the Sacrament of Penance and Reconciliation.

Key Terms for Your Information
* absolution—the forgiveness we receive from God through the priest in the Sacrament of Penance and Reconciliation
* confession—the act of telling our sins to a priest in the Sacrament of Penance and Reconciliation. The sacrament itself is sometimes referred to as "Confession."
* penance—the turning away from sin with a desire to change our life and more closely live the way God wants us to live. This is also the name of the action that the priest asks us to take or the prayers that he asks us to pray after he absolves us in the Sacrament of Penance and Reconciliation

God's People Long to Be Clean of Heart and Holy

FOCUS: In this chapter, you will be helping your child to understand that Jesus teaches us to be clean of heart and to hunger and thirst for holiness.

Holiness is the presence of God's grace in the soul. It enables us to desire God and his kingdom. As we grow in holiness, we gain in the purity that is the true beauty of the soul. Purity of heart, then, is a positive thing; it consists of union with the source of purity, God himself.

As we attempt to climb the Lord's mountain, we have before us the example of the Blessed Virgin Mary and the saints. Underlying their actions were a profound acceptance of and union with the will of God. These gave purity to their intentions and were the root of all they did.

We too are called to holiness. We must examine our own actions and see whether the motive behind them is pure—seeking only God. If so, we will be able to see God in this world even in the people, things, and circumstances of our daily lives.

Scripture in This Chapter
Matthew 5:6 Hunger and Thirst for Justice
Matthew 5:8 The Clean of Heart
John 4:31–34 Doing God's Will

Catechism of the Catholic Church
1821, 2013, 2518–2519, 2543

In this chapter, help your child to
* define purity of heart as selfless love for God and for others.
* describe what holiness is from the example of the lives of Jesus and Mary.
* identify how Saint Thérèse desired holiness.
* describe what it means to be holy.

CHAPTER 23 **GRADE 5**

Christians Respect What Belongs to Others

FOCUS: In this chapter, you will be helping your child to understand that Christians are obliged to promote justice by respecting the property of others and sharing their own possessions.

Wishing to share God's gracious love, we open our eyes to the needs of others and use our own gifts to help fill those needs. Saint John repeats Christ's teaching that we must express charity in deeds of love:

> If someone who has worldly means sees a brother in need and refuses him compassion, how can the love of God remain in him? Children, let us love not in word or speech but in deed and truth. [Now] this is how we shall know that we belong to the truth and reassure our hearts before him[.]
> *1 John 3:17–19*

All people need food, clothing, and shelter. Those provided with a good education as well as cultural and recreational opportunities will live richer and fuller lives. The spirit of justice and Christian charity leads us to share material goods with others, to respect their property, and to be honest in our dealings with them.

Scripture in This Chapter
Luke 12:16–21 The Parable of the Rich Fool
Luke 16:19–31 The Parable of the Rich Man and Lazarus

Catechism of the Catholic Church
2401–2412, 2415–2418, 2432–2434, 2443–2448

In this chapter, help your child to
+ explain how the Seventh and Tenth Commandments promote respect for property.
+ analyze good and bad behavior with respect to the Seventh and Tenth Commandments.
+ recognize justice and injustice.
+ acknowledge his or her responsibility to share money and goods with others.
+ tell the story of the life of Saint Lawrence.
+ propose a practical way to work for justice personally.

Key Terms for Your Information
+ justice—giving everyone what he or she deserves
+ restitution—the act of making up for the loss of or damage to another's property

---

CHAPTER 23 **GRADE 6**

Prophets Proclaim God's Everlasting Love

FOCUS: In this chapter, you will be helping your child to understand that Jeremiah suffered for calling people to justice, while Ezekiel prophesied during the Exile in Babylon.

The Chosen People needed to experience captivity and exile before they would be ready to entrust their lives to the Lord. In the midst of their affliction, however, God called them back and made a New Covenant with them.

The New Covenant would not be written on stone; instead, it would be given in the heart. It would fashion a new people, a people inclined to seek God—and to obey God's commands. The Lord's mercy and faithfulness would restore the humbled people and bring them into a new and deeper relationship with God.

Scripture in This Chapter
2 Kings 22–25, Jeremiah 1,7,18,29–33,38; 31:31–34 The Story of Jeremiah, His Rejection, and God's Promise
Ezekiel 1,18 Ezekiel Speaks to Those in Exile.
Ezekiel 34,36,37 Ezekiel's Vision

Catechism of the Catholic Church
64, 218–221, 709–710, 1431

In this chapter, help your child to
+ summarize the messages of Jeremiah and Ezekiel.
+ describe the New Covenant and the Exile.
+ explain that God brings good out of disappointment and failure.
+ explain his or her duty to work for justice.

Words Your Child Should Know
+ Exile
+ synagogue
+ Jews

Key Terms for Your Information
+ Babylon—the capital of Babylonia, where the people of Jerusalem were exiled in 587 b.c.
+ Book of Lamentations—book of Scripture that contains the prophecies of Jeremiah
+ Ezra—priest who guided the people after they returned to the Promised Land
+ Josiah—king of Judah, who worked for reform
+ Nehemiah—governor who began political reforms after the Jews' return from captivity
+ potter—someone who forms figurines and vessels out of clay

Alive with the Spirit—Jesus the Head of the Church

FOCUS: In this chapter, you will be helping your child to understand that the Holy Spirit came to the Church, making the members courageous witnesses and forming a community of love.

When the Spirit came at Pentecost, accompanied by wind, fire, and songs of praise, a new era began. The power of love and faith was liberated, bathing the world in a hope that neither trial nor persecution could dim. In the outpouring of that Spirit, the Church as the community of believers was born and its mission launched. The disciples were empowered with a mission: to proclaim Christ to the world.

The Spirit brought life and grace to a world that needed to be whole again. We, the Church, hunger to be one body—one visible community in the Lord, witnessing together. We devote all we are to our one Lord. In one faith, we anchor our trust in him. By one Baptism, we are plunged into a new life in him. And we become one family, bonded together forever, children of one God.

Scripture in This Chapter

Matthew 28:19–20 Make Disciples of All People.
Acts of the Apostles 2:1–41 The Coming of the Spirit

Catechism of the Catholic Church

685–686, 731–733, 737, 747

In this chapter, help your child to

* describe the account of Pentecost in Scripture.
* explain how with the coming of the Spirit at Pentecost, the disciples were strengthened for mission and the Christian community was formed.
* describe the characteristics of the early Christian community.
* identify better the role of the Spirit in the Church.
* evaluate his or her commitment and response to his or her local Christian community.

Word Your Child Should Know

* Fruits of the Holy Spirit

Key Term for Your Information

* Pentecost—the coming of the Holy Spirit upon Mary, the apostles, and disciples, empowering them to proclaim the Good News as courageous witnesses and to form a community of love, the Church

The Way of the Family

FOCUS: In this chapter, you will be helping your child to understand that God commands us to obey lawful authority and to respect human life (Fourth and Fifth Commandments).

Explicitly, the Fourth Commandment says that parents should be honored. Implicitly, it says that the family, the setting for parental and filial love, should be exalted. With the social development of the human race, the Fourth Commandment also came to mean that we are required to obey parents and to submit to lawful authority. Intelligent obedience demands surrender of the will.

The Fourth and Fifth Commandments are linked. The Fourth Commandment exalts those who transmit life and blesses the obedient with fuller life. The Fifth Commandment protects the gift of life itself: "You shall not kill." (Deuteronomy 5:17) Because human life is priceless, Christ came to earth as its champion. He raised the quality of life by curing diseases and defending the victims of injustice. On several occasions, he even restored life to the dead. Jesus showed his love for children, the little ones who are too helpless to defend themselves or save their own lives.

Scripture in This Chapter

* Exodus 20:12–13 The Fourth and Fifth Commandments
* Luke 10:29–37 The Good Samaritan
* Acts of the Apostles 5:29 We Must Obey God.

Catechism of the Catholic Church

2196–2246, 2258–2317

In this chapter, help your child to

* explain that lawful authority comes from God.
* identify strategies for expressing his or her opinions to authority respectfully.
* describe ways to grow in respect, love, and gratitude for parents, others in authority, and those who are elderly.
* identify actions that are harmful to life.
* describe ways to show more obedience, reverence, and love in his or her family.

Word Your Child Should Know

* obedience

Key Term for Your Information

* scandal—leading other people to sin by bad example

The Holy Spirit Helps the Church

FOCUS: In this chapter, you will be helping your child to understand that we share the Good News in the Gospels by our lives.

In John's Gospel, Jesus calls himself the light of the world and assures us that anyone who follows him will not be walking in the dark, but will have the light of life (John 8:12). At the Last Supper, Jesus promised to send the Holy Spirit to those he had called out of darkness into his wonderful light (1 Peter 2:9). The work of the Spirit who leads us to see things as they really are is described in the Acts of the Apostles.

When Peter and the apostles became aware of the presence of the Spirit of the risen Jesus within them, they proclaimed it to all of Jerusalem. Great changes occurred as the people realized Christ's life-giving presence among them, and they became witnesses to Christ and his love. Christians filled with the Spirit today proclaim the same message Peter announced on the first Pentecost Sunday.

Scripture in This Chapter
Matthew 5:14–16 Let Your Light Shine.
Mark 16:14–20 The Mission of the Eleven
Acts of the Apostles 2 The First Pentecost

Catechism of the Catholic Church
84, 125–127, 849–856

In this chapter, help your child to
+ explain and name the Gospels.
+ identify ways to show respect for the Gospels out of reverence for Jesus, who speaks through them.
+ tell how the first Christians lived under the inspiration of the Holy Spirit.
+ describe the meaning of mission and our call to it.
+ demonstrate what was learned about the Holy Spirit and the call to help Jesus spread the Good News of God's kingdom.

Word Your Child Should Know
+ Gospel

Key Words for Your Information
+ association—an organized group of people; a club
+ missions—work that people do to spread the Good News
+ sacrifice—to offer up things to help someone
+ scroll—long rolled sheet of paper on which Bible books were written

Mary, Mother of the Church, Cares for Us

FOCUS: In this chapter, you will be helping your child to understand that we love and imitate Mary, the Mother of God and our Mother.

No human love can match the love between Jesus and Mary. At Cana, Mary saw the need of the bridal couple. Her motherly heart, moved with compassion, brought their need to the attention of her Son, with complete confidence that he would help them. As Mother of the Church, Mary continues to intercede on our behalf.

In the United States bishops' pastoral letter on our Blessed Mother, we read:

> Through her life on earth, and now through her union with the risen Christ, the Mother of Jesus is the supreme example of loving association with the Savior in his mission of redeeming mankind . . . Pope Paul put it this way: "Since Mary is rightly to be regarded as the way by which we are led to Christ, the person who encounters Mary cannot help but encounter Christ likewise."

Behold Your Mother 66, 67

Scripture in This Chapter
John 2:1–10 The Wedding at Cana
John 19:25–27 Mary, Our Mother

Catechism of the Catholic Church
721–726, 963, 2617–2619

In this chapter, help your child to
+ repeat the story of the wedding feast at Cana.
+ describe Mary's role as intercessor.
+ explain that we can turn to Mary for help.
+ describe the outstanding virtues of Mary.
+ describe ways to show devotion to Mary.

God's Family Celebrates the Eucharist

FOCUS: In this chapter, you will be helping your child to understand that we are reconciled to God and the Church in the Sacrament of Penance and Reconciliation.

At the Last Supper, Jesus gave us the Sacrament of the Eucharist by which we remember his death and Resurrection, are united with him in Holy Communion, and enjoy his sacramental presence among us. Through this sacrament, we have the risen Jesus with us today, healing, teaching, and giving us his peace. In the encyclical *Mystery of Faith*, Pope Paul VI wrote that the eucharistic mystery stands at the heart and center of the liturgy, since it is the font of Christian life (2).

Scripture in This Chapter

Matthew 7:12; 21; 24–27 The Golden Rule, The True
  Disciple, A House Built on Rock
Matthew 13:33 The Parable of the Yeast
Luke 6:43–45 A Tree Known by Its Fruit

Catechism of the Catholic Church

610, 1323, 1337–1340, 1349

In this chapter, help your child to

+ describe the eucharistic sacrifice as a sacred meal.
+ identify the Eucharist with Jesus' real presence.
+ describe Benediction.
+ explain the importance of following Jesus' words.
+ explain what a parable is.

Words Your Child Should Know

+ Benediction
+ blessing
+ Epistle
+ homily
+ Lectionary
+ Liturgy of the Word

Key Terms for Your Information

+ benediction—special prayer service in which we honor Jesus and receive his blessing
+ Lectionary—book of readings for Mass
+ lector—the person who does the reading at Mass
+ Liturgy of the Word—the first main part of the Mass, in which we hear God's Word
+ monstrance—metal container that holds the sacred host for exposition
+ parable—a story Jesus told that has a message for us about God and the kingdom
+ pyx—a container in which the Eucharist is carried to those who are homebound

God's People Bring Mercy and Peace to Others

FOCUS: In this chapter, you will be helping your child to understand that Jesus tells us to show mercy and to work for peace.

Just as a touchstone produces a streak revealing the purity of a gold or silver object, so the compassionate help offered to anyone in need reveals the genuineness and depth of our proclaimed love of God. When we allow ourselves to be led by the Holy Spirit, our love embraces all God's children.

> If anyone says, "I love God," but hates his brother, he is a liar; for whoever does not love a brother whom he has seen cannot love God whom he has not seen. This is the commandment we have from him: whoever loves God must also love his brother. *1 John 4:20–21*

Those who truly hear the Lord and walk his path come to experience the blessings of his truth and justice. We pray that God, who has revealed that peacemakers will be called his children, may help us to work without ceasing for that justice, which will bring God's true and lasting peace.

Scripture in This Chapter

Matthew 5:7 Blessed Are the Merciful.
Matthew 5:9 Happy Are the Peacemakers.
Luke 6:27–28 Love of Enemies

Catechism of the Catholic Church

2304–2306, 2317, 2447

In this chapter, help your child to

+ explain that Jesus taught us that being merciful includes loving our enemies.
+ explain what peace is and that Jesus came to bring it to our world.
+ list ways he or she can bring peace to others.
+ describe the evils of war.
+ identify their responsibility for working for peace and justice.
+ review what he or she has learned about the Beatitudes.

Words Your Child Should Know

+ Corporal Works of Mercy
+ Spiritual Works of Mercy

Christians Speak the Truth with Love

FOCUS: In this chapter, you will be helping your child to understand that truth and kind words build up the Christian community.

Our God is a trustworthy God, "the faithful God who keeps his merciful covenant down to the thousandth generation." (Deuteronomy 7:9) God's people are called to be truthful, sincere, and trustworthy. The love and peace that mark true Christian living cannot exist without the trust that is built up by honesty in our dealings with one another. Christ came into the world "to testify to the truth." (John 18:37)

Every violation of the truth breaks down trust and causes friction among members of the Christian community. Good Christians see Christ in others and refrain from rash judgments and critical remarks. They live in harmony and peace. God has promised to remain with us and help us to live in communion of mind and heart with him and with others. God has asked us, in return, to be true to him and to keep his Word.

Scripture in This Chapter
1 Corinthians 3:9　We Are God's Co-Workers.
1 Corinthians 13:4–6　Love Is Patient and Kind.
Ephesians 4:32　Be Kind to One Another.

Catechism of the Catholic Church
2464, 2467–2470, 2475–2487, 2538–2540

In this chapter, help your child to
+ explain what the Eighth Commandment tells us to do and to avoid.
+ identify times when he or she might be tempted to lie.
+ realize how words can build up or destroy.
+ list Christian responses to situations.
+ resolve to be kind in word and action.

The Savior Is Jesus, the Son of God

FOCUS: In this chapter, you will be helping your child to understand that John the Baptist prepared for the Messiah, Jesus Christ, who fulfilled the Scriptures.

God sent John the Baptist to prepare the way of the Lord. Luke's Gospel tells us that the angel Gabriel called Mary *favored one*—full of grace. Mary was so filled with God that she surpassed all others. Mary was the first to hear the Good News of the Incarnation. Her prompt reply showed her obedience: "I am the handmaid of the Lord. May it be done to me according to your word." (Luke 1:38)

Scripture in This Chapter
Matthew 3:1–7; 11:2–15; 14:1–12　The Baptist's Story
Luke 1:5–25,57–80　The Birth of John the Baptist
Luke 1:26–38,39–56　The Annunciation and Visitation
Luke 2:1–7,21　Jesus Is Born.

Catechism of the Catholic Church
488, 523, 717–720

In this chapter, help your child to
+ describe the role of the Maccabees.
+ summarize the story of John the Baptist.
+ recall the story of the Annunciation and Visitation.
+ describe Jesus as the fulfillment of the prophecies and as the Messiah.
+ use a time line to review events in salvation history.

Word Your Child Should Know
+ Magnificat

Key Terms for Your Information
+ canticle—song
+ Essenes—religious group in or near Qumran who lived an ascetic lifestyle
+ Hanukkah—Jewish feast that commemorates the Maccabees' overthrow of the Syrians and the rededication of the Temple
+ incarnate—given bodily form
+ Incarnation—mystery of God's taking on a human nature
+ Maccabees—family of five sons who led the Jewish rebellion of 167 B.C. against the Syrians and won independence for Palestine that lasted until 63 B.C.
+ Qumran (KUM rahn)—area close to the Dead Sea in Palestine where the Essene scrolls were found
+ Zechariah—priest whose son John the Baptist's birth was foretold to him by an angel

Matrimony and Holy Orders—Jesus Emmanuel

FOCUS: In this chapter, you will be helping your child to understand that Jesus calls each of us to be holy in a special vocation.

Each individual has the potential to become holy through a love for God that motivates everything in life. Enlightened, supported, and sustained by grace, each one of us can walk with assurance and peace on the journey through life into eternal blessedness. The path we take may be different from that of our friends, but the goal is the same: holiness.

It is important for each person to discover his or her vocation toward which God's graces and gifts have been directed. We then pray to find the path the Lord has chosen for us so that we can love God most completely.

Scripture in This Chapter

Leviticus 19:18 Love One Another.
1 Thessalonians 4:3 Holiness in Sexual Conduct

Catechism of the Catholic Church

914–916, 1536, 1548, 1570, 1603, 1618, 1644, 1656–1658

In this chapter, help your child to

+ describe how God calls all Christians to holiness and each person to a special way of life.
+ discuss the beauty of Christian marriage and family life.
+ identify the mission of bishops, priests, and deacons.
+ identify how religious serve the Church.
+ discuss the vows of chastity, poverty, and obedience.

Key Terms for Your Information

+ chastity—vow of religious to be unmarried and chaste for the sake of the kingdom
+ fidelity—faithfulness, loyalty
+ laity—strictly speaking, all those who are not ordained; commonly means people who are neither ordained nor religious sisters and brothers
+ obedience—vow of religious to listen to God particularly as he speaks through superiors
+ poverty—vow of religious to live a simple lifestyle and to give up control of material possessions
+ secular institute—a society of laymen and laywomen who are consecrated by private vows but who retain their careers and social activities and do not live in community

The Way of Human Dignity

FOCUS: In this chapter, you will be helping your child to understand that sex is to be respected and used only when it is a sign of the permanent commitment of marriage (Sixth and Ninth Commandments).

God has given us human sexuality, which is integral to the whole human person. Sex is the only human power whose exercise is both sanctified sacramentally and protected by divine law. God provided for the unity of marriage and made man and woman co-creators of life with him. The sexual union of husband and wife is so precious that any abuse of sex is sinful.

Christ elevated the Sixth and Ninth Commandments to the realm of love. Adultery frustrates the purposes of marriage: the generating and raising of children and the preserving of love between husband and wife. Chastity enables us to appreciate human sexuality and to control sexual desires by conforming them to right reason and Christian faith.

Scripture in This Chapter

+ Exodus 20:14,17 The Sixth and Ninth Commandments
+ Matthew 5:27–28 Jesus Speaks on Adultery.
+ John 15:12 The New Commandment
+ John 15:13–14 Sacrifice Is a Part of Love.

Catechism of the Catholic Church

2331–2391, 2514–2527

In this chapter, help your child to

+ explain that sexuality is an integral part of the whole person.
+ explain that the power of the gift of sex is to be directed toward union (love) and procreation (life).
+ describe chastity as a virtue of unselfish love for Christ and for others.
+ identify ways to make good moral decisions.

Words Your Child Should Know

+ chastity
+ Matrimony

Key Terms for Your Information

+ adultery—a sexual relationship between a married person and someone other than the husband or wife
+ fornication—sexual intercourse before marriage
+ homosexual activity—sexual activity with those of the same sex
+ masturbation—self-stimulation to arouse sexual pleasure to the point of orgasm

We Give Glory to God

FOCUS: In this chapter, you will be helping your child to understand that the Holy Spirit helps us to give glory to God in words and in deeds.

Heaven and earth are truly full of God's glory. Saint Peter says that giving glory to God is the goal of human fulfillment, and he also indicates how we can arrive at it:

> He who called you is holy, be holy yourselves in every aspect of your conduct, for it is written, "Be holy because I [am] holy." *(1 Peter 1:15–16)*

If we would live human life in its fullness, we must open ourselves to the creative action of the Spirit within us. An openness to this Spirit enables us to respond joyfully, giving back to God each gift he has given to us, letting God have joy in us. We recall and awaken within ourselves the realization that in God alone is our true human satisfaction and fulfillment.

Scripture in This Chapter

Psalm 148 All Creation Gives Glory to God.
Colossians 3:12 We Give Glory to God.

Catechism of the Catholic Church

293–294, 422–424, 460, 736, 2641

In this chapter, help your child to

* understand the Doxology and know how to pray it.
* identify ways to give glory to God through prayers, words, and actions.
* identify ways to bring God's love to others.
* review what was learned about Jesus' presence in our world today.
* demonstrate an awareness of Jesus' presence in our lives.

Key Terms for Your Information

* Blessed Trinity—God the Father, God the Son, and God the Holy Spirit
* glorify—to give glory, praise, or honor
* glory—honor

The Church Celebrates God's Love

FOCUS: In this chapter, you will be helping your child to understand that the Church's mission in the world is to show Christ's love to all.

The saints were conscious of the gifts God had given them and used those gifts for God's glory. Everyone and everything spoke to the saints of the Father's love and care. While no one ever totally grasps the immensity of God's love, the happiest people in the world are those who strive to return that love by giving glory to God in everything they do. Christ Jesus has clothed us with power from on high (Luke 24:49) and has appointed us to bring his message of peace and self-giving love to all we meet. When we allow our lives to be filled with the power of his Resurrection, we live by his Spirit and experience the gift of his promise to be with us always.

Jesus formed the small group of disciples into his body, the Church, and instructed them to live as God's people. Under the leadership of Peter, the first pope, the disciples were to live the truth in love and spread it with the help of the Holy Spirit (2 Timothy 1:14). All Christians were to use their talents to build up the Body of Christ. At Mass, we unite the sacrifice of our lives with Christ's sacrifice. We praise God for his love and care and ask that we may witness Christ by our words and works.

Scripture in This Chapter

Ephesians 4:5,11–16 Unity in the Body and Diversity of Gifts

Catechism of the Catholic Church

772–776

In this chapter, help your child to

* explain what it means to be a member of the Church.
* describe the Church and its mission.
* demonstrate an understanding of the main concepts in this unit.
* review how to show Jesus' love.
* explain that we do not vacation from being Christian during the summer months.

The Eucharist Is a Gift

FOCUS: In this chapter, you will be helping your child to understand that at Mass, we celebrate Jesus' offering of himself to the Father and receive him in the Eucharist.

Unity is the fulfillment Jesus desires for all of us, and it is his constant prayer. The Sacrament of the Holy Eucharist unites believers with Christ in his perfect offering of praise, thanksgiving, propitiation, and supplication to God on behalf of all people. The faithful who receive Holy Communion are nourished by Christ's Body and Blood and are intimately united with Christ and the Christian community. In this deep eucharistic mystery, the risen Christ remains sacramentally present among us, welcoming with love all who come in faith to receive this precious gift.

Pope Paul VI, in his encyclical *Mystery of Faith* (67–70), stresses the benefits of intimate colloquies with our Lord in the Blessed Sacrament, and says that anyone who has a special devotion to the sacred Eucharist will experience and fully understand how precious a life hidden with Christ in God is.

Scripture in This Chapter
John 17:18–23 Jesus' Prayer for Unity
1 Corinthians 10:17 One Body in Christ

Catechism of the Catholic Church
1350, 1362–1368, 1396

In this chapter, help your child to
+ identify a gift as an expression of love.
+ explain how everyday activities can be united with Jesus' perfect gift and offered to the Father.
+ explain that in the Eucharist, Jesus draws us closer to himself and to one another.
+ review the Sacraments of Baptism, Reconciliation, and the Eucharist.
+ show his or her understanding of the concepts in Unit 5.

Word Your Child Should Know
+ Liturgy of the Eucharist

Key Terms for Your Information
+ communion—oneness with another person
+ Liturgy of the Eucharist—the second main part of the Mass in which Jesus gives himself to the Father, we offer Jesus and ourselves with him, and Jesus comes to us in Communion

---

God's People Are Happy

FOCUS: In this chapter, you will be helping your child to understand that followers of Jesus suffer for what is right.

We are constantly encouraged by Christ's promise of happiness now and for all eternity. We look to the saints who have gone before us, and we admire the zeal and fidelity with which they have followed Christ. They have made their lives holy by doing the will of our loving Father. They are the heroes and heroines of faith, who, having endured the cross, now live with God in heaven as witnesses of the truth. All Christians are called to imitate them and to become living witnesses of the faith by living in Christ.

The very content of catechesis, God's Word, is lived by us, celebrated in our liturgy, and reflected to the world for all to observe (Constitution on the Sacred Liturgy 9). If we truly love Christ, there will be no limits to what we will do for him.

Scripture in This Chapter
Matthew 5:10 A Heavenly Reward for the Persecuted
Luke 21:16–17 Suffering for Christ's Sake

Catechism of the Catholic Church
1716–1719, 1808–1809

In this chapter, help your child to
+ describe how Jesus, Mary, and Saint Joan of Arc suffered for what was right.
+ explain that Christians pray for the courage to do what is right, even if it involves suffering.
+ review what has been learned about the Beatitudes.
+ express in prayer his or her desire to live a particular beatitude.
+ demonstrate an understanding of the key concepts presented in Unit 5.
+ celebrate the Beatitudes in a prayer service.
+ describe how he or she can bring happiness to others by living the Beatitudes.

Word Your Child Should Know
+ martyr

Unit 5 Review

FOCUS: In this chapter, you will be helping your child to understand that Christians are called to show love and respect to all.

God's laws govern our moral obligations to God, the Church, others, nature, and ourselves. They protect our human rights and liberty. They provide the foundation for all human society, whether civil, religious, or familial. It is important that we recognize God's goodness in giving us these laws and that we are aware of their value. God will judge us on our willingness to give of ourselves tirelessly to those in need. God has gifted each of us with time, talents, and some earthly goods. Jesus asks that his followers be alert to see when they have something someone else needs and be generous in sharing—even to the point of laying down their lives.

Following the example of the saints, we will come to see Jesus in each person whom we are privileged to serve. Whatever the person's sex, age, or race, we will minister to his or her bodily and spiritual needs with love.

Scripture in This Chapter
Matthew 25:31–46 The Judgment of the Nations
John 13:35 Love One Another.

Catechism of the Catholic Church
1039, 2447

In this chapter, help your child to
+ reflect on the key concepts covered in this unit.
+ evaluate how he or she puts the concepts in this unit into practice.
+ apply his or her understanding of the commandments to life situations
+ demonstrate an understanding of the concepts related to the Fifth through Tenth Commandments.
+ develop a personal plan for keeping God's law.

Unit 5 Review

FOCUS: In this chapter, you will be helping your child to understand that the prophets renew the people in their faithfulness to God.

The prophets of Israel were first people called by God to proclaim God's Word. They were people who saw things from the divine perspective. They were the ones through whom God spoke of things to come. They were people recognized by their contemporaries as men and women of God.

God calls only a few to be prophets. May they respond generously, and may we listen to their message. All of us, however, are called through Baptism to share in the ministry of Christ, who is priest, prophet, and king. May we be attentive to his voice, and speak out when God gives us the vision to see things that are not according to God's will. May we be true men and women of God whose lives, marked by justice and righteousness, give credence to God's Word, which we are compelled to proclaim.

Catechism of the Catholic Church
64, 218, 522

In this chapter, help your child to
+ recall the prophets studied and the theme of each prophet's teaching.
+ work cooperatively in groups to make banners representing the prophets.
+ express appreciation for the prophets and their messages.
+ review the prophets and their messages for God's people.
+ demonstrate an understanding of the key concepts of this unit.

Unit 3 Review

FOCUS: In this chapter, you will be helping your child to understand that Jesus frees us from sin and leads us to life in God.

Those who believe in Jesus receive God's life-giving Spirit and become children of God. They allow their lives to be strengthened and guided by the gifts of this Advocate. They put their gifts at the service of others. Like the early apostles, they must go out and bear witness, bringing all to know the richness of eternal life.

The Holy Spirit is the Giver of Life. The dynamic power of the Spirit transforms the lives of Christians and ministers of the Church, enabling them to use their charisms and ministries for the building up of the Church. The Spirit unites us and creates community in the Church so that we may love and serve one another generously. The Spirit frees us to seek unity until all form one body, the Church. In the Spirit, Jesus keeps his promise to be with us until the end of the world.

Scripture in This Chapter

John 3:1–5,16 We Are Born of Water and Spirit. In Jesus, We are Given Eternal Life.

John 4:47–53 Jesus Heals the Official's Son.

Catechism of the Catholic Church

505, 520, 521

In this chapter, help your child to

+ recall the significant facts and basic concepts introduced in Unit 3.
+ assess their spiritual growth and plan for the future.
+ evaluate his or her growth in knowledge and understanding of our faith.
+ review the main concepts learned about Jesus this year.

Key Term for Your Information

+ pilgrim—one who makes a journey for a holy purpose

The Way of Justice and Truth

FOCUS: In this chapter, you will be helping your child to understand that the human rights to own property and to know the truth are to be respected (Seventh, Eighth, and Tenth Commandments).

The Seventh and the Tenth commandments confirm the inalienable right of every human being to the goods of the earth, especially to food, clothing, and shelter. The former forbids stealing another's possessions; the latter forbids even the wrongful desire for another's goods. Although ownership is morally permissible, we have a duty to share possessions with those in need. In thankfulness for God's creation, we act as caring and sharing guardians of the earth.

Our right to the truth is protected by the Eighth Commandment. Christ declared that he came to "testify to the truth." (John 18:37) Jesus linked truth with his mission of correcting injustices. Truth and justice are inseparable from love of God and love of neighbor.

Scripture in This Chapter

Exodus 20:15–17 The Seventh, Eighth, and Tenth Commandments

Matthew 25:31–40 The Last Judgment

John 14:1–7 Jesus Is the Truth.

Catechism of the Catholic Church

2401–2449, 2464–2503, 2534–2550

In this chapter, help your child to

+ describe justice as respecting human rights.
+ describe how certain sins are contrary to justice.
+ explain why the truth is important in society.
+ describe his or her responsibility to live in truth.
+ identify ways to keep the Eighth Commandment.
+ review the main concepts learned this year.

Words Your Child Should Know

+ calumny   + detraction

Key Terms for Your Information

+ avarice—an excessive desire for wealth; greed
+ hypocrisy—the act of pretending to be good or to have virtues that one does not possess
+ integrity—wholeness of character; uprightness
+ mental reservation—speech that intends a meaning different from the spoken words when there is a good reason for concealing the truth
+ restitution—the act of repairing, returning, or paying for a damaged or stolen article

Special Seasons and Feasts

The Year in Our Church

Lent
Ordinary Time
Holy Week
Ash Wednesday
Christmas
Epiphany
Easter Sunday
Easter
Christmas
Advent
Winter Spring
Fall Summer
First Sunday of Advent
Feast of All Saints
Pentecost
Ordinary Time

Liturgical Calendar

The liturgical calendar highlights the feast days and seasons of the Church year. Various colors symbolize the different seasons.

Feast of All Saints

FOCUS: In this chapter, you will be helping your child to understand that on All Saints Day, we honor all of the saints who now live with God in heaven.

Sunlight shining through crystal is transformed by the sunlight's penetration of the glass. The rich variety of colors that is refracted delights and fascinates us. Every individual is chosen by God to reflect with prismatic brilliance the divine qualities uniquely embodied in a totally personal response to God's gifts and self-revelation. Yet all the good in each person really comes from God. People who have revealed to the world the light of Christ that has penetrated their very being and who have reached the heavenly kingdom are called saints. They have allowed the Lord's light to shine through in their words and actions.

Each person's particular and personal appreciation of God prompts a unique response that reflects his or her understanding of divine love. However varied the individual expressions are, they all reveal divine goodness and love. Divine light is diffused through the saints as they stand before the Lord, totally open to his love.

Catechism of the Catholic Church
954–957, 2030

In this chapter, help your child to
- define a saint as a person who loved God on earth and now lives with God in heaven.
- understand that God calls everyone to be a saint.
- pray the Litany of the Saints.

Key Terms for Your Information
- All Saints Day—the holy day celebrated on November 1 on which we honor all those who now live with God in heaven
- patron saint—a saint who cares for and prays for a person or group in a particular way
- saint—a person who loved God on earth and now lives with God in heaven

Feast of All Saints

FOCUS: In this chapter, you will be helping your child to understand that on All Saints Day, we honor the saints and celebrate our communion with all of the saints in heaven.

The rich variety of colors we behold when sunlight shines through a prism delights and fascinates us. In like manner, people through whom the light of Christ shines display to the world around them the many facets of God's great love. Such people who have allowed the Lord's light to shine out in their words and actions throughout their lives and who have reached the heavenly kingdom are called saints.

Each individual's relationship with God prompts a unique response that reflects his or her understanding of divine love. However varied these personal expressions are, they all reveal divine goodness. Divine light is diffused through the saints as they stand before the Lord, totally open to his love.

Catechism of the Catholic Church
946–959, 1717, 2030, 2156

In this chapter, help your child to
- define the Communion of Saints as our family of faith.
- celebrate the Communion of Saints on All Saints Day.

Key Terms for Your Information
- All Saints Day—the holy day celebrated on November 1 on which we honor all those who now live with God in heaven
- Communion of Saints—the union of the saints in heaven, the souls in purgatory, and the Church on earth; the family of the Church, including those still living and those who have died
- saint—a person who loved God on earth and now lives with God in heaven

All Saints and All Souls

FOCUS: In this chapter, you will be helping your child to understand that in the Communion of Saints, we are united with those who have died—the souls in purgatory and the saints in heaven.

Since the Resurrection of Christ, a living communion has existed among those still journeying on earth, those who are already in heaven's glory and those who are yet being purified after their death (purgatory). We call this the Communion of Saints. Because of our loving union in Christ, there is a spiritual sharing, an exchange of love among the members of the Church, both living and dead.

As a Church, we dedicate November to remembering our faithful departed. Even as we pray for our deceased loved ones, so should we also ask for them to pray for us. Whether they are in heaven or in purgatory, we trust that they will intercede for us. Because they are his beloved sons and daughters in Christ, the Father will answer their prayers.

Scripture in This Lesson

Philippians 3:20–21 The Transformative Power of Christ

Catechism of the Catholic Church

956, 1030–1032

In this chapter, help your child to

- identify All Saints Day and All Souls Day as special days for honoring those who have died.
- describe the Communion of Saints as a continuing relationship with those who have died.
- pray for those who have died and ask them to intercede for us.

Key Terms for Your Information

- Communion of Saints—the union of the saints in heaven, the souls in purgatory, and the Church on earth
- saint—a person who loved God on earth and now lives with God in heaven
- purgatory—the state after death in which holy souls are made free from the effects of sin before entering heaven
- All Saints Day—the holy day celebrated on November 1 on which we honor all those who now live with God in heaven
- All Souls Day—on November 2, we pray for the souls in purgatory who are being prepared for heaven

Feast of All Saints

FOCUS: In this chapter, you will be helping your child to understand that the saints lived the Beatitudes and now share eternal happiness with God in heaven.

Sunlight shining through crystal is transformed by its penetration of the glass. The rich variety of colors that is refracted delights and fascinates us. Every individual is chosen by God to reflect with prismatic brilliance the divine qualities uniquely embodied in a totally personal response to God's gifts and self-revelation. Yet all the good in each person really comes from God. People who have revealed to the world the light of Christ that has penetrated their very being and who have reached the heavenly kingdom are called saints. They have allowed the Lord's light to shine through in their words and actions.

Each person's particular and personal appreciation of God prompts a unique response that reflects his or her understanding of divine love. However varied the individual expressions are, they all reveal divine goodness and love. Divine light is diffused through the saints as they stand before the Lord, totally open to his love.

Catechism of the Catholic Church

954–957, 2030

In this chapter, help your child to

- identify the Beatitudes as guides for holiness and happiness.
- describe how the saints have lived the Beatitudes.
- determine how the Beatitudes might be lived today.

Key Terms for Your Information

- All Saints Day—the holy day celebrated on November 1 on which we honor all those who now live with God in heaven
- saint—a person who loved God on earth and now lives with God in heaven

Feast of All Saints

FOCUS: In this chapter, you will be helping your child to understand that we honor the saints and strive to imitate them.

People who have allowed the Lord's light to shine out in their words and actions throughout their lives and who have reached the heavenly kingdom are called saints. Each individual's relationship with God prompts a unique response that reflects his or her understanding of divine love. However varied these personal expressions are, they all reveal divine goodness. Divine light is diffused through the saints as they stand before the Lord, totally open to his love.

As we honor the saints, we pray in the words of the Opening Prayer of the Common of Holy Men and Women to follow their example:

> Ever-living God,
> the signs of your love are manifest
> in the honor you give your saints.
> May their prayers and their example encourage us
> to follow your Son more faithfully.

Scripture in This Lesson
Matthew 5:3–10 The Beatitudes

Catechism of the Catholic Church
946–959, 1717, 2030, 2156

In this chapter, help your child to
+ identify each saint's life as a unique expression of God's goodness and love.
+ explain that the saints' lives show how they used their talents for God's greater honor and glory.
+ identify ways that we can follow the examples of holiness found in the lives of the saints.

Key Terms for Your Information
+ saint—a person who loved God on earth and now lives with God in heaven
+ All Saints Day—a holy day celebrated on November 1 on which we honor all those who now live with God in heaven

Feast of All Saints

FOCUS: In this chapter, you will be helping your child to understand that in the Communion of Saints, we are united with those who have died, both the souls in purgatory and the saints in heaven.

As those we know and love are called home to our heavenly Father, it can be consoling to realize that our bonds with them have not been irrevocably broken. Because of our loving union in Christ, there is a spiritual sharing, an exchange of love among the members of the Church, both living and dead. We call this the Communion of Saints. Our ability to help others spiritually comes from the life of grace we receive as members of that body, which is truly united to Christ its Head. It is God who possesses and dispenses the merits of prayers and good works among the members of the Church.

As a Church, we dedicate November to remembering our faithful departed. We pray for all those awaiting entrance into heaven, and ask that God give them the merits and prayers of other members of the Communion of Saints and welcome them into his presence.

Catechism of the Catholic Church
956, 1030–1032

In this chapter, help your child to
+ discuss why some people go to purgatory when they die.
+ examine the relationships existing among the members of the Communion of Saints.
+ pray for those who have died and ask the saints and the souls in purgatory to intercede for us.

Feast of All Saints

FOCUS: In this chapter, you will be helping your child to understand that in the lives of the saints, we find examples of ways to imitate Christ.

The rich variety of colors we behold when sunlight shines through a prism delights and fascinates us. In like manner, people through whom the light of Christ shines display to the world around them the many facets of God's great love. Such people who have allowed the Lord's light to shine out in their words and actions throughout their lives and who have reached the heavenly kingdom are called saints.

Each individual's relationship with God prompts a unique response that reflects his or her understanding of divine love. However varied these personal expressions are, they all reveal divine goodness. Divine light is diffused through the saints as they stand before the Lord, totally open to his love.

Catechism of the Catholic Church

946–959, 1717, 2030, 2156

In this chapter, help your child to

* demonstrate how the saints lived the spirit of the Beatitudes.
* identify the feast of All Saints as a day to honor all of the saints.
* consider ways to emulate the saints today.

Key Terms for Your Information

* saint—a person who loved God on earth and now lives with God in heaven
* All Saints Day—the holy day celebrated on November 1 on which we honor all those who now live with God in heaven

Feast of All Saints

FOCUS: In this chapter, you will be helping your child to understand that in the Communion of Saints, we are united in Christ

How wonderful is the union of all those baptized in Christ! Since the Resurrection of Christ, a living communion has existed among those still journeying on earth, our brothers and sisters who are already in heaven's glory, and those who are yet being purified after their death (purgatory). We call this union the Communion of Saints. Because of our loving union in Christ, there is a spiritual sharing, an exchange of love among the members of the Church, both living and dead. Our ability to help others spiritually comes from the life of grace we receive as members of that body, which is truly united to Christ its Head.

As a Church, we dedicate November to remembering our faithful departed. Even as we pray for our deceased loved ones, so should we also ask for them to pray for us. Whether they are in heaven or in purgatory, we trust that they will intercede for us. Because they are his beloved sons and daughters in Christ, the Father will answer their prayers.

Catechism of the Catholic Church

956, 1030–1032

In this chapter, help your child to

* describe the hope of God's promise of eternal life.
* identify our union with the Communion of Saints.
* reflect upon All Saints Day and All Souls Day as feasts of hope.

Advent

FOCUS: In this chapter, you will be helping your child to understand that during Advent, we celebrate the coming of Jesus.

Advent is a time of longing for the light of Christ's goodness to warm our hearts with his love. It is a time of waiting for salvation from our God, a time of living in God's presence and letting ourselves be filled with God. We come before God. We lift up our hearts to God. We ask God to come to us and teach us his ways of loving mercy.

Advent means "coming." We prepare our hearts to celebrate Christ's birth, his coming as our Savior. Our celebration of the Advent season also sharpens our vision of God's daily comings in the mystery of life. We still wait for what is to come, the fulfillment of the Kingdom of God where all walk in the way of truth and justice. We clear away whatever is separating us from God's saving activity among us.

Catechism of the Catholic Church
522–524, 1095

In this chapter, help your child to
+ identify Advent as a special time to prepare to celebrate Christ's birth at Christmas.
+ explain the significance of each part of the Advent wreath.
+ describe how Jesus comes to us each day.

Key Terms for Your Information
+ Advent—the season of the Church year during which we prepare to celebrate Christ's coming among us as our Savior
+ Christmas—celebration of Jesus' birth

Advent

FOCUS: In this chapter, you will be helping your child to understand that during Advent, we devote ourselves to making our lives a straight path to God.

Advent is a time of longing for the light of Christ's goodness to warm our hearts with his love. It is a time of waiting for salvation from our God, a time of living in God's presence and letting ourselves be filled with God. During Advent, we come before God. We lift up our hearts to him. We ask God to come to us and teach us his ways of loving mercy.

The word *Advent* means "coming." Our celebration of the Advent season sharpens our vision so that we may see God's daily presence in our lives. We still wait for what is to come, the fulfillment of the kingdom of heaven, when the hopes of our lives on earth will be satisfied. Each day, with anticipation, we heed John the Baptist's cry, echoing the prophet Isaiah:

> Prepare the way of the Lord,
> make straight his paths.
> *Luke 3:4*

Scripture in This Lesson
Luke 1:68–79 The Canticle of Zechariah

Catechism of the Catholic Church
522–524, 1095

In this chapter, help your child to
+ explain how John the Baptist is a model for how we prepare to celebrate the coming of Jesus.
+ prepare for Christ's coming through prayer, penance, and good deeds.

Key Terms for Your Information
+ Advent—the four weeks before Christmas when we prepare for Jesus' coming
+ Advent wreath—an evergreen wreath, with four candles, that reminds us to prepare for Jesus' coming
+ Annunciation—the announcement to Mary by the angel Gabriel that God had chosen her to be the Mother of Jesus
+ Emmanuel—name for Jesus that means "God with us"
+ prophet—a person chosen by God to speak God's message
+ Visitation—Mary's journey to help her relative Elizabeth during her pregnancy.

Advent

FOCUS: In this chapter, you will be helping your child to understand that the Jesse tree reminds us to prepare during Advent for the coming of the Savior.

Advent is a time of preparation for Christmas, a time of living in God's presence and letting ourselves be filled with him. We come before God, and we lift up our hearts to him. We ask God to teach us his ways of loving mercy, as we pray:

> I wait for you, O Lord;
> I lift up my soul
> to my God.
> Guide me in your truth and teach me,
> for you are God my savior.
> For you I wait all the long day,
> because of your goodness, Lord.
> *Psalm 25: 1, 5*

Our celebration of the Advent season sharpens our vision to see the ways God comes to us in our daily lives. We still wait for what is to come: the fulfillment of the Kingdom of God, where all will walk in the way of truth and justice. We clear away whatever is blinding us to God's saving action.

Scripture in This Lesson

Genesis 3:1–13; 6:14–21; 15:1–6; 45:3–15 The Fall of Man, Preparation for the Flood, God's Covenant, The Story of Joseph

Deuteronomy 5:16–21 Moses and the Ten Commandments

2 Samuel 7:8–17 God's Promises to David

Matthew 1:18–24 Joseph's Dream

Luke 1:26–38 The Annunciation

Catechism of the Catholic Church

64, 522–524, 1095

In this chapter, help your child to

* identify Advent as a time to prepare for the celebration of Christmas.
* explain that the Jesse tree is a sign of the coming of Jesus and a reminder of the people who waited for him to come.
* prepare for Christ's coming through daily prayer and good deeds.

Key Term for Your Information

* Jesse tree—the family tree of Jesus; it contains symbols for key people of the Old Testament

Advent

FOCUS: In this chapter, you will be helping your child to understand that during Advent, we prepare for the coming of Jesus.

The coming of God's Son for our salvation is a great and wonderful mystery of our faith. During Advent, there are really three comings to which we can turn our hearts and minds. We ponder the historical coming of Jesus as we read the Gospel of Luke (1:26–56; 2:1–20), which tells of the fulfillment of God's promise to send a Savior.

In Advent, we experience Christ's personal coming into each of our lives on Christmas Day—and every day—through the Eucharist, the sacraments, and prayer. These three comings of Christ are part of the great mystery of the Incarnation. Christ is Emmanuel, God-with-us. During this Advent season, we reflect on this mystery, and reform and renew our lives in hope. The season of Advent is a time of joyful anticipation. Only our Lord's personal coming to us ensures true happiness. Our union with Jesus is most intimate in eucharistic communion, in which we are one with him and in him.

Catechism of the Catholic Church

522–524, 1095

In this chapter, help your child to

* explain what it means to make a straight highway for the Lord.
* identify Advent as a time of prayerful longing for Christ and living in his love.
* keep Christ in Christmas by means of Advent practices.
* identify praying the Joyful Mysteries of the Rosary as a way to prepare to welcome Jesus during Advent.
* honor Mary as the Mother of Jesus.

Advent

FOCUS: In this chapter, you will be helping your child to understand that in Advent, we prepare for the coming of Jesus.

The coming of God's Son is a great and wonderful mystery of our faith. During Advent, we ponder and prepare our hearts for three ways that Christ comes to us. We ponder his advent in history. The Gospel of Luke (1:26–56; 2:1–20) shows the birth of God's Son, Jesus, to be the fulfillment of God's promise to send the world a Savior. We experience Christ's personal advent into each of our lives on Christmas Day—and every day in the Eucharist.

The three comings of Christ—in history, in grace, and in glory—are related to one another as one great mystery of the Incarnation. Christ is Emmanuel, God-with-us. It is during the Advent season that we reflect on this mystery, and we reform our lives and renew our hope. Realizing that the time of waiting should be a time of preparing, we make straight the way of the Lord in joy.

Scripture in This Lesson

Luke 1:26–45 Announcement of the Birth of Jesus
Luke 3:2–18 The Preaching of John the Baptist

Catechism of the Catholic Church

523, 524, 1095

In this chapter, help your child to

+ identify the coming of Christ in history, in grace, and in glory.
+ prepare for Christ's coming during Advent.
+ describe how Mary and John the Baptist responded to the will of the Father by preparing the way for Jesus.
+ identify ways to imitate John the Baptist and the Blessed Virgin Mary in their willingness to do God's will.
+ describe Advent as a time of increased longing for the Savior.
+ express desire for Emmanuel in prayer.

Advent

FOCUS: In this chapter, you will be helping your child to understand that during Advent, we recall the people and events of the Old Testament that prepared the way for the Messiah.

During Advent, we recognize Christ as "the light [that] shines in the darkness,/and the darkness has not overcome it." (John 1:5)

In history, Christ came as a rising sun in a sin-darkened world. He dispelled the darkness of ignorance and sin and the shadows of doubt, despair, and death. He was "the true light, which enlightens everyone" (John 1:9). He comes into our lives as Lord of Light to brighten our existence with his presence, to illuminate our spirits with his grace, and to lead us in our journey to the Father. His final coming in majesty will be resplendent with the light of glory. He will come to take us to the heavenly Jerusalem, revealed as

> the city [that] had no need of sun or moon to shine on it, for the glory of God gave it light, and its lamp was the Lamb.
>
> *Revelation 21:23*

Catechism of the Catholic Church

122, 524, 1095

In this chapter, help your child to

+ describe the significance of the season of Advent.
+ identify people who received God's promise and events that prepared for the Messiah from the Book of Genesis.
+ describe symbols for the Jesse Tree from the stories of Jesus' birth.
+ celebrate in prayer the people and events that prepared the way for the Redeemer.
+ prepare for Christ by praying and striving to overcome the darkness of selfishness, thoughtlessness, and ingratitude.

Advent

FOCUS: In this chapter, you will be helping your child to understand that in Advent, we remember the coming of Jesus in history, and we prepare and wait for his coming in mystery and in majesty.

Bombarded by the media to prepare for Christmas by shopping and entertaining, how can we keep things in perspective and rediscover the message of peace and love that underlies the season? The Church offers the season of Advent, the four weeks preceding Christmas. Advent prepares us not only for Christmas but also for all the ways that Christ comes to us in our life.

During Advent, our attention focuses on the total mystery of Christ: the same yesterday, today, and forever. We remember his historical coming. As proclaimed in the Gospel of Luke, we recall the fulfillment of God's promise in the birth of his Son, Jesus. We experience the grace of his personal coming into our lives on Christmas Day and every day in the Eucharist, the sacraments, prayer, people, and events. And we long for his final coming in glory.

Scripture in This Lesson
Matthew 25:31–46   When the Son of Man Comes in glory, He Will Judge the Nations.
Mark 14:62   Jesus Prophecies the Day of Judgment

Catechism of the Catholic Church
524, 1095

In this chapter, help your child to
+ explain the significance of the three comings of Christ.
+ identify the themes of Remember, Prepare, and Wait in Hope as characteristics of the Advent season.
+ prepare for Christ through prayer and the practice of Christian attitudes.
+ tell the story of the Annunciation.
+ honor Mary as the Mother of Jesus.
+ identify ways to imitate Mary's openness to God.

Key Terms for Your Information
+ Advent—the liturgical season in which the Church remembers Christ's coming in history, prepares for his daily coming in mystery, and waits in hope for his coming in majesty
+ Parousia (pah-ROO-see-uh)—the second, or final, coming of Christ in glory

Advent

FOCUS: In this chapter, you will be helping your child to understand that Jesus came in history, comes in mystery, and will come in majesty.

During Advent, the Church first draws our attention to Christ's last coming and then to his birth in time. This is the pattern of the Advent Masses and the Liturgy of the Hours. Most frequently, the poetic genius of Isaiah, the great Prophet of the Incarnation, recaptures for us the prayerful, expectant mood of those long, pre-Christian centuries.

As Advent nears its climax, the Church gives us the beautiful "O" Antiphons, brief prayers that address Christ by one of his messianic titles and invite him to come to the earth anew. In them are compressed all humanity's hopes and dreams. Perhaps the "O" Antiphon for December 21 sums up best what Advent—and our longing for Christ's salvation—is all about:

> O Radiant Dawn, splendor of eternal light, sun of justice: come, shine on those who dwell in darkness and the shadow of death.
>
> *Lectionary* (202) and *Evening Prayer* (Antiphon: Canticle of Mary), December 21

Scripture in This Lesson
Matthew 1:22–33   They Shall Call Him Emmanuel.

Catechism of the Catholic Church
524, 1095

In this chapter, help your child to
+ identify qualities taught by Jesus that answer humanity's needs.
+ recognize that in Christ, we find the fulfillment of all of our needs.
+ pray the "O" Antiphons.
+ make and use an Advent calendar.
+ experience anticipation for the Redeemer.
+ describe how John the Baptist responded to the will of the Father by preparing the way for Jesus.
+ identify the Sacrament of Reconciliation as a way to prepare for Jesus during Advent.

Key Terms for Your Information
+ "O" Antiphons—short prayers addressed to Jesus under various titles and prayed from December 17 to December 23
+ Emmanuel—a biblical title for the promised Messiah that means "God-with-us"

Christmas

FOCUS: In this chapter, you will be helping your child to understand that on Christmas, we celebrate the birth of Jesus, our Savior.

Although many people had longed for the Savior, most were unaware that he had made his quiet entry into the world. But the shepherds and Magi responded to the significance of the event and welcomed the Lord. The shepherds hurried to find the Savior and "returned, glorifying and praising God for all they had heard and seen." (Luke 2:20) The Magi, filled with delight, followed the star's guiding light until they found the child. "Then they opened their treasures, and offered him gifts of gold, frankincense, and myrrh." (Matthew 2:11)

It is this same reality, "God-with-us," that we celebrate when we gather for the Eucharist and profess our faith in the Creed:

> For us and for our salvation,
> He came down from heaven;
> by the power of the Holy Spirit,
> He was born of the Virgin Mary,
> and became man.

Our God has come to be with us. Today, he is still Emmanuel, "God-with-us," waiting for us to welcome his presence and saving help.

Scripture in This Lesson

Luke 2:1–7 The Birth of Jesus
Luke 2:8–16 Jesus' Birth Is Announced to the Shepherds

Catechism of the Catholic Church

525–526

In this chapter, help your child to

+ tell the story of Jesus' birth.
+ participate in a Christmas prayer celebration.

Christmas

FOCUS: In this chapter, you will be helping your child to understand that throughout the Christmas season, we worship Jesus our Savior.

Although many people had longed for the Savior, most were unaware that he had made his quiet entry into the world. But the shepherds and Magi responded to the significance of the event and welcomed the Lord. The shepherds hurried to find the Savior and "returned, glorifying and praising God for all they had heard and seen." (Luke 2:20) The Magi, filled with delight, followed the star's guiding light until they found the child. "Then they opened their treasures, and offered him gifts of gold, frankincense, and myrrh." (Matthew 2:11)

It is this same reality, "God-with-us," that we celebrate when we gather for the Eucharist and profess our faith in the Creed. Our God has come to be with us. Today, he is still Emmanuel, "God-with-us," waiting for us to welcome his presence and saving help.

Scripture in This Lesson

Luke 1:26–38 The Annunciation
Luke 2:1–18 The Birth of Jesus and the Visit of the Shepherds
Matthew 2:1–12 The Visit of the Magi

Catechism of the Catholic Church

525–526

In this chapter, help your child to

+ tell the story of Jesus' birth.
+ identify ways that we can respond in love to the love shown by God our Father, who gave us his Son, Jesus, as a gift.
+ tell the story of Epiphany.
+ explain that God calls us to lead others to Jesus through our words and deeds.

Key Terms for Your Information

+ Magi—Wise Men from the East
+ frankincense—particles that give off a sweet-smelling smoke when they are burned
+ myrrh—a spice used for burial in ancient times

Christmas

FOCUS: In this chapter, you will be helping your child to understand that Jesus, God's gift of love, wants us to love him in return.

Although many people had longed for the Savior, most were unaware that he had made his quiet entry into the world. Only a few shepherds were on hand to welcome the Lord at his birth. They hurried to find their Savior and "returned, glorifying and praising God for all they had heard and seen." (Luke 2:20) In the Opening Prayer of the Mass at dawn on Christmas Day, we say:

> Almighty God and Father of light,
> a Child is born for us and a Son is given to us.
> Your eternal Word leaped down from heaven
> in the silent watches of the night,
> and now your Church is filled with wonder
> at the nearness of her God.
> Open our hearts to receive his life
> and increase our vision with the rising of dawn,
> that our lives may be filled with his glory and his peace.

God is with us today, waiting for us to welcome his presence and saving help.

Catechism of the Catholic Church
525–526

In this chapter, help your child to
+ describe God's love in giving his Son, Jesus, to be the Savior of the world.
+ identify the gift of himself or herself as the best gift that he or she can give to Jesus.
+ share the Good News of Jesus' birth by offering gifts of love to family members.

Christmas

FOCUS: In this chapter, you will be helping your child to understand that during the Christmas season, we welcome Christ, our Light, into our hearts.

Although many people had longed for the Savior, most were unaware that he had made his quiet entry into the world. But the shepherds and Magi responded to the significance of the event and welcomed the Lord. The shepherds hurried to find the Savior and "returned, glorifying and praising God for all they had heard and seen." (Luke 2:20) The Magi, filled with delight, followed the star's guiding light until they found the child. "Then they opened their treasures, and offered him gifts of gold, frankincense, and myrrh." (Matthew 2:11)

The Savior is the light that was coming into the world. The Light of Christ expels the darkness of sin and death and inspires us to participate in the dawning of the New Creation. Christmas is our participation in God's triumphant defiance of sin and death. Our God has come to be with us. We welcome the Light of Christ into our hearts on Christmas Day and every day.

Catechism of the Catholic Church
525–526

In this chapter, help your child to
+ identify ways that he or she might welcome Jesus our Light into his or her heart during the Christmas season.

Key Term for Your Information
+ testimony—giving witness to what a person knows to be true

Christmas

FOCUS: In this chapter, you will be helping your child to understand that the true meaning of Christmas is found in pondering the mystery of the Incarnation and welcoming Jesus into our hearts.

Although many people had longed for the Savior, most were totally unaware that he had made his quiet entry into the world. But the shepherds and Magi responded to the significance of the event and welcomed the Lord. The shepherds hurried to find the Savior and "returned, glorifying and praising God for all they had heard and seen." (Luke 2:20) The Magi, filled with delight, followed the star's guiding light until they found the child. "Then they opened their treasures, and offered him gifts of gold, frankincense, and myrrh." (Matthew 2:11)

It is this same reality, "God-with-us," that we celebrate when we gather for the Eucharist and profess our faith in the Creed:

> For us and for our salvation,
> He came down from heaven;
> by the power of the Holy Spirit,
> He was born of the Virgin Mary,
> and became man.

Our God has come to be with us. Today, he is still Emmanuel, "God-with-us," waiting for us to welcome his presence and saving help.

Scripture in This Lesson
Matthew 1:1 –25 The Birth of Jesus
Matthew 2:1–12 The Visit of the Magi
Luke 2:1–20 The Birth of Jesus

Catechism of the Catholic Church
525–526

In this chapter, help your child to
+ describe how the custom of a crib scene originated with Saint Francis.
+ identify the sources for the stories of Jesus' birth.
+ identify good deeds to do every day to celebrate Christmas.

Christmas

FOCUS: In this chapter, you will be helping your child to understand that the Holy Family is our model for holy and happy families.

Among the feasts celebrated during the Christmas season is the feast of the Holy Family, which is celebrated on the Sunday after Christmas (or December 30 if Christmas itself falls on a Sunday). Thus, the Incarnation leads us to reflect upon the family life of Jesus and to learn its lesson for our own families. Jesus, Mary, and Joseph lived the prayer that began and ended each day in every Jewish home: "[Y]ou shall love the Lord, your God, with all your heart, and with all your soul, and with all your strength." (Deuteronomy 6:5)

To live this life of love in our families, we need to be filled with the Spirit. We pray that the love of God that "has been poured out into our hearts" (Romans 5:5) may give us the strength, gentleness, and compassion to embrace all in our love and to anticipate the needs of others as Jesus, Mary, and Joseph did in their humble home in Nazareth.

Catechism of the Catholic Church
531–533

In this chapter, help your child to
+ identify the few facts about the Holy Family that are contained in the Bible.
+ describe how all families are different, and begin to recognize and appreciate his or her own family's unique gifts.
+ use the Christmas season to reflect on how he or she might add to the happiness and holiness of his or her family.

Christmas

FOCUS: In this chapter, you will be helping your child to understand that during the Christmas season, we celebrate the Incarnation, God's love made visible in Jesus.

We all know the story of the first Christmas—of Mary and Joseph searching for a place to stay in Bethlehem, of Jesus being born and laid in a manger, of his birth being announced by angels and indicated by a special star. His love shows itself in his becoming like us in our weakness, and in suffering all the limitations of being human. The real depth of his love, though, was manifested in the mission he came to accomplish—to suffer and die for our sins so that we might be free.

As baptized Catholics, we seek to carry the spirit of Christmas throughout the year. Sometimes we succeed; sometimes we fall short. Through the Sacrament of Reconciliation, we can receive the grace of forgiveness and conversion. Through the mystery of the Incarnation, we participate in making God's love visible in our world, imperfectly, but truly. May Christ always find us making God's love visible.

Scripture in This Lesson
Matthew 1:18–25 The Birth of Jesus
John 1:14 The Word Became Flesh.

Catechism of the Catholic Church
525–526

In this chapter, help your child to
+ discuss the mystery of the Incarnation as proclaimed through the Gospel readings for Christmas.
+ consider the significance of the Incarnation to our lives as Christians.

Epiphany

FOCUS: In this chapter, you will be helping your child to understand that the Magi found Jesus and worshiped him.

A saying that is printed on posters and banners depicting the adoration of the Magi declares: "Wise Men still seek him." Little is known about the Wise Men from the East whose steps to Bethlehem were guided by a star. Legend has identified them as kings and placed their number at three, possibly because three gifts are mentioned in the scriptural account. The spirit of Saint Matthew, the only evangelist to record the worship of the Magi, is still the focus of the Church's celebration today. The Epiphany marks the manifestation of Christ to the world.

The priest prays over our gifts of bread and wine on the feast of the Epiphany:

> Lord, accept the offerings of your Church,
> not gold, frankincense and myrrh,
> but the sacrifice and food they symbolize:
> Jesus Christ, who is Lord for ever and ever.
> *Prayer over the Gifts*
> *Feast of the Epiphany*

Scripture in This Lesson
Matthew 1:18–25 The Birth of Jesus
Matthew 2:1–12 The Visit of the Magi
Luke 2:1–20 The Visit of the Shepherds

Catechism of the Catholic Church
528

In this chapter, help your child to
+ identify the details of the Magi's journey and worship of Jesus found in the Gospel of Matthew.
+ name the significance of the feast of the Epiphany.

Lent

FOCUS: In this chapter, you will be helping your child to understand that during Lent, we renew our hearts and minds in order to prepare to celebrate new life at Easter.

The Christian way of life is a special one. During the Lenten season, the Church community as a whole looks at the new life Jesus offers all who commit themselves to share in his Paschal Mystery. The entire Lenten season is devoted to acts of Christian living that increase our participation in Christ's saving death and Resurrection. Christ's saving death, which took place in history, was completed and made perfect in his Resurrection. His sufferings, his death, his Resurrection, and his ascension form the Paschal Mystery. Our participation in this mystery is one means by which we honor God.

Christ calls each of us to share in the mystery of his cross, to accept every suffering, every persecution, and even death itself for his sake (Matthew 24:9–13). Each year, during the season of Lent, we recall how Christ's saving love has brought us this far on our journey to God.

Scripture in This Lesson
1 John 3:16,18 Jesus' Action Showed Us Love.

Catechism of the Catholic Church
624–628, 1067–1068

In this chapter, help your child to
* state that Jesus passed through death to begin his glorified life.
* explain that we must pass through death to live with God in heaven.
* acknowledge the reality that all people must die.
* describe Lent as a time to grow more like Jesus.
* identify ways in which we might change during Lent.

Key Term for Your Information
* Easter—the celebration of the raising of Jesus Christ from the dead

Lent

FOCUS: In this chapter, you will be helping your child to understand that during Lent, we think of Jesus' sacrifice of love and try to perfect our love through prayer and sacrifice.

Lent is a time to reflect on the Lord's love poured out sacrificially to give us the only gift that endures forever: union with himself. Lent is a time to be touched by this love. It is a time to study our Lord and to follow his ways. Lent is a time when we follow Christ through his Paschal Mystery— his passion, death, Resurrection, and Ascension. The Lenten season is devoted to acts of Christian living that increase our participation in Christ's saving death and Resurrection.

Christ's sufferings show us how we can follow in his footsteps and pass from death to life. He calls each of us to share in the mystery of his cross, to accept every suffering, every persecution, and even death itself for his sake. Each year, as we recall how Christ's saving love has brought us this far on our journey to God, we accept the cross as the means through which we will enter into the fullness of the resurrected life with him.

Catechism of the Catholic Church
613-614, 616, 1067, 1168–1171

In this chapter, help your child to
* describe ways that people show love for one another by making sacrifices.
* identify Jesus' sacrifice on the cross as the greatest sacrifice ever offered.
* describe Lent as a time to prepare for Easter by following Christ's way of sacrificial love.
* develop a plan to make Lent a time of special prayer and sacrifice.
* identify Lent as a time to follow Jesus on the Way of the Cross.
* pray the Stations of the Cross.

Key Term for Your Information
* sacrifice—a gift given to God to give him thanks

Lent

FOCUS: In this chapter, you will be helping your child to understand that Lent is a time to prepare for the celebration of the Paschal Mystery.

Lent is an annual reminder that we are called to imitate Christ in prayer, sacrifice, and service to our fellow human beings. It is a season of intensified effort to live out the Paschal Mystery with Jesus Christ, to identify with him in the work of salvation. As we reflect prayerfully on the Savior's passion and death during these 40 days, let us joyously renew our baptismal commitment with all those who are about to enter the saving mysteries of Christ for the first time.

With them, let us embrace anew the sublime mystery of life in Jesus Christ:

> We were indeed buried with him through baptism into death, so that, just as Christ was raised from the dead by the glory of the Father, we too might live in newness of life.
> or if we have grown into union with him through a death like his, we shall also be united with him in the Resurrection.
>
> *Romans 6:4–5*

Scripture in This Lesson
Joel 2:12–13 Return to the Lord for He Is Merciful and Kind.

Catechism of the Catholic Church
1067–1068, 1095, 1168

In this chapter, help your child to
+ describe Lent as a time for renewing our baptismal commitment.
+ explain Lenten practices that help us to change our hearts.
+ identify ways to use each day of Lent to prepare for Easter.
+ describe Lent as a season of Penance.
+ tell how we celebrate the Sacrament of Reconciliation.

Lent

FOCUS: In this chapter, you will be helping your child to understand that during Lent, we prepare our hearts so that we may celebrate Easter more fully.

The Christian way of life is a special one. During the Lenten season, the Church community as a whole looks at the new life Jesus offers all who commit themselves to share in his Paschal Mystery. The entire Lenten season is devoted to acts of Christian living that increase our participation in Christ's saving death and Resurrection. Christ's saving death, which took place in history, was completed and made perfect in his Resurrection. His sufferings, his death, his Resurrection, and his ascension form the Paschal Mystery. Our participation in this mystery is one means by which we honor God.

Christ calls each of us to share in the mystery of his cross, to accept every suffering, every persecution, and even death itself for his sake (Matthew 24:9–13). Each year, during the season of Lent, we recall how Christ's saving love has brought us this far on our journey to God.

Catechism of the Catholic Church
613–617, 1067–1068, 1168–1171

In this chapter, help your child to
+ describe Ash Wednesday as the beginning of our observance of Lent.
+ explain the significance of the distribution of ashes on Ash Wednesday.
+ describe Baptism as our immersion into the Paschal Mystery of Christ.
+ identify Lent as a time of prayer, fasting, and almsgiving in preparation for the joy of Easter.

Key Terms for Your Information
+ almsgiving—sharing with those in need
+ Alpha and Omega—another name for Christ; the beginning and the end; the first and last letters of the Greek alphabet
+ fasting—limiting the amount we eat for a period of time, to express sorrow for sin and to make ourselves more aware of God's action in our lives
+ Paschal Mystery—the work of salvation accomplished by Jesus Christ through his passion, death, and Resurrection

Lent

FOCUS: In this chapter, you will be helping your child to understand that during each Lent, we recall with love and gratitude that Jesus died and rose for our salvation.

The Christian way of life is a special one. During the Lenten season, the Church community as a whole looks at the new life Jesus offers all who commit themselves to share in his Paschal Mystery. The entire Lenten season is devoted to acts of Christian living that increase our participation in Christ's saving death and Resurrection. Christ's saving death, which took place in history, was completed and made perfect in his Resurrection. His sufferings, his death, his Resurrection, and his ascension form the Paschal Mystery. Our participation in this mystery is one means by which we honor God.

Christ calls each of us to share in the mystery of his cross, to accept every suffering, every persecution, and even death itself for his sake (Matthew 24:9–13). Each year, during the season of Lent, we recall how Christ's saving love has brought us this far on our journey to God.

Scripture in This Lesson

Luke 4:1–13   The Temptation of Jesus
John 12:24   A Seed Must Die to Produce Fruit.

Catechism of the Catholic Church

1163, 1168

In this chapter, help your child to

+ describe Ash Wednesday as the beginning of our observance of Lent.
+ explain how the distribution of ashes on Ash Wednesday calls us to renew the promises made at our Baptism.
+ discuss the meaning of Lent.
+ propose ways he or she can enter into Christ's Paschal Mystery by prayer, abstinence, and almsgiving.
+ identify the Sacrament of Reconciliation as a means to a deeper relationship with Christ.

Key Terms for Your Information

+ fasting—limiting the amount we eat for a period of time to express sorrow for sin and to make ourselves more aware of God's action in our lives
+ abstain—to deny oneself food, drink, or other pleasures, such as meat on Ash Wednesday and Fridays during Lent
+ almsgiving—giving money or goods to aid people in need Lent

Lent

FOCUS: In this chapter, you will be helping your child to understand that Lent is a time to grow in Christ's life through prayer, fasting, and almsgiving.

Lent is a time to reflect on the Lord's love poured out sacrificially to give us the only gift that endures forever: union with himself. Lent is a time to be touched by this love. It is a time to study our Lord and to follow his ways. Lent is a time when we follow Christ through his Paschal Mystery—his passion, death, and Resurrection. The Lenten season is devoted to acts of Christian living that increase our participation in Christ's saving death and Resurrection.

Christ's sufferings show us how we can follow in his footsteps and pass from death to life. He calls each of us to share in the mystery of his cross, to accept every suffering, every persecution, and even death itself for his sake. Each year, as we recall how Christ's saving love has brought us this far on our journey to God, we accept the cross as the means through which we will enter into the fullness of the resurrected life with him.

Catechism of the Catholic Church

1156, 2565, 2663, 2701

In this chapter, help your child to

+ describe Ash Wednesday as the beginning of our observance of Lent.
+ explain the significance of the distribution of ashes on Ash Wednesday.
+ explain that prayer, fasting, and almsgiving help us die to sin and rise to new life.
+ plan to live Lent in the spirit of Jesus.
+ explain that we turn to God in prayer in a special way during Lent.
+ prepare to celebrate the Sacrament of Penance and Reconciliation during Lent.

LENT   **GRADE 7**   LENT   **GRADE 8**

Lent

FOCUS: In this chapter, you will be helping your child to understand that Lent is a time for spiritual renewal through prayer, fasting, and almsgiving.

The season of Lent is God's annual invitation to us to leave behind the exile of sin and move more steadily through the desert of prayer and penance with Christ to the promised land of Easter. Lent, with its discipline of prayer, almsgiving, and penance, is an excellent opportunity to grow in faith. With him, we fast and pray; through him, we find strength to give of ourselves and our goods to those in need; and in him, we rise at last, triumphantly renewed, on Easter Sunday—a sure pledge of our final glorious Resurrection at the end of life's journey.

Scripture in This Lesson

Matthew 6:5–6 Jesus Teaches About Prayer.
2 Corinthians 5:20—6:2 Ambassadors for Christ

Catechism of the Catholic Church

613–617, 1067–1068, 1168–1171, 1434–1438

In this chapter, help your child to

- describe Ash Wednesday as the beginning of a spiritual journey we call Lent.
- explain the significance of the distribution of ashes on Ash Wednesday.
- describe Lent as a spiritual journey.
- explain that Lent is an annual reminder of our Baptism and a time to pray in a special way for catechumens (individuals preparing for Christian Initiation at the Easter Vigil).
- plan for spiritual renewal through Scripture reading and through prayer, fasting, and almsgiving.
- identify the Sacrament of Penance and Reconciliation as a means to a deeper relationship with Christ.

Key Terms for Your Information

- abstinence—denying oneself food, drink, or other pleasures; during Lent, Catholics over age 14 abstain from eating meat on Ash Wednesday and Fridays
- almsgiving—giving aid to those who are poor
- fasting—limiting the amount we eat for a period of time to express sorrow for sin and to make ourselves more aware of God's action In our lives
- Lent—the 40 days before Easter during which we prepare, through prayer, fasting, and giving aid to those who are poor, to change our lives and to live the Gospel more completely

Lent

FOCUS: In this chapter, you will be helping your child to understand that Lent is a time to change our hearts and live more like Christ.

Lent is an annual reminder that we are called to imitate Christ in prayer, sacrifice, and service to our fellow human beings. It is a season of intensified effort to live out the Paschal Mystery with Jesus Christ, to identify with him in the work of salvation. As we reflect prayerfully on the Savior's passion and death during these 40 days, let us joyously renew our baptismal commitment with all those who are about to enter the saving mysteries of Christ for the first time.

With them, let us embrace anew the sublime mystery of life in Jesus Christ:

> We were indeed buried with him through baptism into death, so that, just as Christ was raised from the dead by the glory of the Father, we too might live in newness of life.
> For if we have grown into union with him through a death like his, we shall also be united with him in the Resurrection.
>
> *Romans 6:4–5*

Scripture in This Lesson

Philippians 3:12 Possessed by Christ
2 Corinthians 5:20—6:2 Ambassadors for Christ

Catechism of the Catholic Church

1095, 1434–1439

In this chapter, help your child to

- explain the importance of Lent in the life of the Church.
- describe the history of Lent and its connection with the baptismal catechumenate.
- create a personal plan for conversion based on prayer, fasting, and almsgiving.
- identify the Sacrament of Penance and Reconciliation as a means to a deeper relationship with Christ.

Holy Week

FOCUS: In this chapter, you will be helping your child to understand that Jesus suffered and died for love of us.

The cost of discipleship is high; the relationship between a disciple and a master is demanding. But a disciple's love for the master is so great that he or she freely submits to the master's teachings and views. This submission respects and trusts the master's wisdom. The disciple believes and responds with deep faith and total submission and is thereby drawn to share in the mystery of the master's life.

To follow Jesus means to be transformed. It means one chooses to live the mystery of the cross, to accept suffering and difficulties in humble awareness that Christian self-denial is the pruning knife that frees us to grow in God's life. The liturgy is our ritual entering into the Paschal Mystery of Christ's death and Resurrection. United with the Lord Jesus, we learn to see and touch God even in the agony of suffering. Our faithful following of Christ along the Way of the Cross prepares us for meaningful participation in the Eucharist.

Scripture in This Lesson
Matthew 25:40 What We Do to Others We Do to Jesus.

Catechism of the Catholic Church
571–573, 617–618, 2669

In this chapter, help your child to
+ describe the Way of the Cross.
+ identify Holy Week as a time to follow Jesus on the Way of the Cross.
+ pray the Way of the Cross.

Key Terms for Your Information
+ Resurrection—the bodily raising of Jesus Christ from the dead on the third day after he died on the cross
+ tomb—a place in which to bury someone who has died

Holy Week

FOCUS: In this chapter, you will be helping your child to understand that Jesus suffered and died for love of us.

The richest part of the Church's liturgical year is the Easter Triduum. Its rituals call forth a faith response from us as we contemplate the saving power of Jesus. Our openness to the mysteries revealed can lead us closer to the risen Christ. The Easter Triduum is a reminder of the journey we are making, which will carry us through death to glory in Jesus. When we approach the signs and symbols of the Easter Triduum with faith, we can be moved to turn our lives over to Jesus.

If there is ever a time when we are faced with our solidarity in sin, our shallowness, our emptiness, it is during the Easter Triduum. If there is ever a time when we are surrounded with love unimaginable, caught up in the ecstasy of our unity with the suffering servant, awed with the sign of our immortality, it is during the Easter Triduum. We are ransomed; we are loved. We contemplate not only Christ's death and Resurrection, but also the wonder of our own share in it.

Scripture in This Lesson
Luke 22:14–22 The Last Supper
John 13:1–15 The Washing of the Disciples' Feet

Catechism of the Catholic Church
618, 1067–1068, 1168–1171

In this chapter, help your child to
+ identify the events in the life of Jesus that are commemorated during Holy Week.
+ describe Holy Week as a time to prepare for Easter by recalling Jesus' sacrifice for us.
+ tell the story of Jesus' Last Supper.
+ describe Holy Thursday as our commemoration of Jesus' gift to us in the Eucharist.
+ identify ways to serve others in the spirit of Jesus.

Holy Week

FOCUS: In this chapter, you will be helping your child to understand that Jesus suffered and died for love of us.

Our Lenten journey comes to an end during Holy Week, coming face-to-face with the reality of human suffering. Human suffering is real and painful. It can also transform us. Suffering can lead to growth; death leads to new life. This pattern shines through the mystery of the cross, the mystery of God's love transforming evil, hatred, and pain into new hope, new life.

Driven by limitless love for his Father and for us, Jesus accepted his passion freely, obediently, trustingly, and humbly. Through such obedience, he stood directly opposed to the evil of sin, or humanity's desire to be self-sufficient and self-directed. In his person, he reconciled all of us to God. For Christians, suffering is in relation to Jesus, in him, and through him. We expect to be transformed by the mystery of the cross, the mystery of suffering, the mystery of Resurrection with Jesus in redemptive love.

Scripture in This Lesson

Matthew 21:1–11 The Entry into Jerusalem
John 13:12–15 The Washing of the Disciples' Feet
Philippians 2:5–11 Christ's Humility and Exaltation

Catechism of the Catholic Church

571–573, 617–618,1674, 2708

In this chapter, help your child to

* tell the story of Jesus' triumphant entry into Jerusalem.
* describe Palm (Passion) Sunday as the beginning of our Holy Week journey with Christ.
* identify Holy Week as a time to intensify our preparations for Easter.
* describe the liturgies of the Triduum.
* name the Sorrowful Mysteries of the Rosary.
* follow Jesus during Holy Week by praying the Sorrowful Mysteries of the Rosary.

Holy Week

FOCUS: In this chapter, you will be helping your child to understand that during Holy Week, we follow Jesus on his Way of the Cross.

The cost of discipleship is high; the relationship between a disciple and a master is demanding. But a disciple's love for the master is so great that he or she freely submits to the master's teachings and views. This submission respects and trusts the master's wisdom. The disciple believes and responds with deep faith and total submission and is thereby drawn to share in the mystery of the master's life.

To follow Jesus means to be transformed. It means one chooses to live the mystery of the cross, to accept suffering and difficulties in humble awareness that Christian self-denial is the pruning knife that frees us to grow in God's life. The liturgy is our ritual entering into the Paschal Mystery of Christ's death and Resurrection. United with the Lord Jesus, we learn to see and touch God even in the agony of suffering. Our faithful following of Christ along the Way of the Cross prepares us for meaningful participation in the Eucharist.

Catechism of the Catholic Church

571–573, 617–618, 2669

In this chapter, help your child to

* describe Holy Week as a time to follow Jesus on the Way of the Cross.
* explain how to pray the Stations of the Cross.
* identify ways we can imitate the virtues of Christ in our daily lives.
* pray the Stations of the Cross.
* pray to imitate Jesus' virtues today.

Holy Week

FOCUS: In this chapter, you will be helping your child to understand that during Holy Week, we follow Jesus on his Way of the Cross through the Easter Triduum.

As Lent ends and Holy Week begins, our efforts intensify as we contemplate the mystery of Christ's sacrifice for our salvation. The passion is the crowning point of Jesus' public life, the high point of his mission on Earth, the work that is central to all his other works. No other mystery of Jesus was prophesied in such detail—and Jesus most accurately fulfilled all that had been written about him.

Crushed by the enormity of the task before him and the burden of the world's sins, Jesus' human nature at first cried out to be relieved of the suffering he was to undergo. However, as love triumphed, he immediately added that all should be as his Father willed. Love for his Father and love for us was the driving force, the supreme motivation of his entire life. He left us a legacy of love by his words and his deeds.

Scripture in This Lesson
John 15:12 Love One Another.

Catechism of the Catholic Church
638, 654–655, 1168–1169

In this chapter, help your child to
+ describe the liturgies of Holy Week.
+ identify symbols of the Holy Week liturgies.
+ tell the Gospel of the suffering and death of Jesus.
+ reflect on ways to respond in love to Jesus' sacrifice for us.

Holy Week

FOCUS: In this chapter, you will be helping your child to understand that during the Easter Triduum, the high point of the Church year, we celebrate the Paschal Mystery of Jesus.

Our meditation on the suffering and death of Jesus can prepare us to embrace the reality of our own death, confident in Jesus' promise of eternal life. Our sacraments and rituals are permeated with sign and symbol of the deep mystery of life. Sometimes these symbols are so powerful that they move us deeply.

Such is the power of the Easter Triduum. If there is ever a time when we are confronted with our complicity in sin, our shallowness, our emptiness, it is during the Easter Triduum. Yet we also are enveloped in love unimaginable, share in the agony of the suffering servant, and thrill to the intimation of our immortality. We are ransomed. We are loved. We contemplate not only Christ's death and Resurrection, but the wonder of our own share in it. We are participants in the reenactment of the mystery: life through death.

Scripture in This Lesson
John 13:1–15 Jesus Washes the Disciples' Feet.
John 18:1—19:42 The Passion of Jesus

Catechism of the Catholic Church
638, 654–655, 1168–1169

In this chapter, help your child to
+ describe our celebration of Palm (Passion) Sunday.
+ identify symbols of Palm Sunday.
+ describe the Easter Triduum as the commemoration of our salvation in Christ.
+ discuss the power of symbols.
+ explain that we share in the Paschal Mystery through our Baptism.

Key Terms for Your Information
+ paradox—something that seems contradictory or opposite of the truth, but actually isn't
+ Paschal Mystery—the work of salvation accomplished by Jesus Christ through his passion, death, and Resurrection; it is celebrated during the Easter Triduum
+ vigil—the evening before a great feast

Holy Week

FOCUS: In this chapter, you will be helping your child to understand that during the Easter Triduum, we commemorate our redemption in Christ.

The Easter Triduum is a reminder of the journey we are making, which will carry us through death to glory in Jesus. For those who are willing to look, there are reminders all around us that we are on a journey—that we are passing through this world. The rituals used by the Church during the Easter Triduum are permeated with sign and symbol of the Paschal Mystery. When we approach these symbols with faith, they are powerful and can move us deeply.

If there is ever a time when we are faced with our solidarity in sin, our shallowness, our emptiness, it is during the Easter Triduum. If there is ever a time when we are surrounded with love unimaginable, caught up in the ecstasy of our unity with the suffering servant, awed with the sign of our immortality, it is during the Easter Triduum. We are ransomed; we are loved. We contemplate not only Christ's death and Resurrection, but the wonder of our own share in it.

Scripture in This Lesson
Mark 14:1—15:47 The Passion and Death of Jesus According to Mark
John 18:1—19:42 The Passion and Death of Jesus According to John

Catechism of the Catholic Church
1067–1068, 1168–1171

In this chapter, help your child to
+ describe our celebration of Passion (Palm) Sunday.
+ reflect on the Gospel of Jesus' Passion and death.
+ explain that the Easter Triduum is the commemoration of our redemption in Christ.
+ describe the rituals of the Easter Triduum and appreciate their meaning.

Key Terms for Your Information
+ Easter Triduum—the liturgical time during which we celebrate the Paschal Mystery; the three days that begin with the Mass of the Lord's Supper on Holy Thursday and end on Easter Sunday evening
+ elect—former catechumens who were called by the bishop at the Rite of Election to prepare for the Easter sacraments.
+ ritual—words and actions that help us remember and express our faith

Holy Week

FOCUS: In this chapter, you will be helping your child to understand that, during the Easter Triduum, we celebrate the Passover of Christ and our redemption.

When bringing the Chosen People out of Egypt, God decreed that they solemnly commemorate their deliverance from slavery. The Israelites obeyed by having a week-long celebration every year, the focal point of which was the ritual slaying and eating of an unblemished lamb. Like every devout Jew, Jesus faithfully observed this festival. By instituting the Eucharist in the context of a Passover supper, Jesus linked the Jewish sacrificial rite with the offering of his own life. Henceforth, he—the Lamb of God—was to be sacrificed and sacramentally eaten so that all humanity might pass from sin's servitude to God's liberating love.

Mindful that our religious roots grew from the rich soil of Judaism, Christians celebrate a special supper every Holy Thursday. As the new People of God, we celebrate our liberation from slavery to sin. Our prayerful thoughts are directed toward the final events of Jesus' last week on earth. The primary focus of Holy Thursday's service is not the meal itself, but the representation of Jesus' death and Resurrection.

Scripture in This Lesson
Luke 19:28–40 Jesus' Entry into Jerusalem
Luke 22:39–46 The Agony in the Garden

Catechism of the Catholic Church
638, 640, 651–655, 1168

In this chapter, help your child to
+ describe our celebration of Passion (Palm) Sunday.
+ prayerfully consider the meaning of Jesus' acceptance of the cross.
+ identify the connection between the Easter Triduum and the Jewish Passover.
+ describe the events celebrated and the rituals used during the Easter Triduum.
+ appreciate more deeply that Christ has saved him or her from sin and death.

Easter

FOCUS: In this chapter, you will be helping your child to understand that the disciples saw Jesus risen from the dead and had faith.

The Resurrection is the victorious completion of redemption. Jesus showed his mastery over sin and death—over every hostile power. We share in his Resurrection through the waters of Baptism and are raised to the new life of grace. As partakers of his divine life, we are empowered by his strength to overcome every attack of the evil one. We count on being united with him in perfect happiness for all eternity. Meanwhile, we have already begun to live in union with him here on earth. We are sent, as were the first disciples, to communicate the joy and peace of the Resurrection to all people.

The Sunday eucharistic celebration is our encounter with the risen Lord. The Christian community professes publicly our loving acceptance of Jesus. The Eucharist in turn strengthens our relationship with the Lord. It inspires us to go forth in the name of Jesus to give his peace and to perpetuate the work of salvation.

Scripture in This Lesson
John 20:24–29 The Risen Lord Appears to Thomas.

Catechism of the Catholic Church
638–647, 651–655

In this chapter, help your child to
+ identify Easter as the day we celebrate Christ's Resurrection.
+ tell the story of Jesus' appearances to Thomas and the disciples.
+ identify how Jesus praised those who believe in him without seeing him.
+ explain that the gift of faith is received at Baptism.

Key Term for Your Information
+ faith—a gift of God that helps us to believe in God and to live as he wants us to live

Easter

FOCUS: In this chapter, you will be helping your child to understand that on Easter, we rejoice and share our joy with others because Jesus is risen from the dead.

Life in Christ calls us to walk daily in newness of life, a life no longer enslaved to sin. Through his Resurrection, Jesus gave us new life and new hope; we no longer need to fear suffering and death. Belief in the Resurrection moves us from a limited, earthbound outlook to a radically different, eternity-oriented view of life. Thus, we come to see misunderstanding, betrayal, loneliness, and other kinds of suffering that mark segments of our journey as part of the Paschal Mystery.

The season of Easter is an invitation to renew our faith in Christ's Resurrection and to allow ourselves to be transformed by its power. We pray that the brightness of Christ's resurrected life will break through in us.

We pray with the Church during the Easter season:

> Father of mercy,
> hear our prayers that we may leave
> our former selves behind and serve you
> with holy and renewed hearts.
> > *Prayer after Communion*
> > *Saturday of Seventh Week of Easter*

Scripture in This Lesson
Matthew 28:1–8 The Resurrection of Jesus

Catechism of the Catholic Church
638–647, 651–655

In this chapter, help your child to
+ state that Jesus is with them as their risen Lord.
+ identify peace and joy as gifts that Jesus gives to those who truly seek him.
+ identify ways to bring peace and joy to others through kind words and actions.

Easter

FOCUS: In this chapter, you will be helping your child to understand that Easter Sunday and the season of Easter are a time of great joy because Jesus is risen.

The Resurrection is the victorious completion of redemption. Jesus showed his mastery over sin and death—over every hostile power. We share in his Resurrection through the waters of Baptism and are raised to the new life of grace. As partakers of his divine life, we are empowered by his strength to overcome every attack of the evil one. We count on being united with him in perfect happiness for all eternity. Meanwhile, we have already begun to live in union with him here on earth. We are sent, as were the first disciples, to communicate the joy and peace of the Resurrection to all people.

The Sunday eucharistic celebration is our encounter with the risen Lord. The Christian community professes publicly our loving acceptance of Jesus. The Eucharist in turn strengthens our relationship with the Lord. It inspires us to go forth in the name of Jesus to give his peace and to perpetuate the work of salvation.

Scripture in This Lesson
Luke 24:1–53 The Ascension

Catechism of the Catholic Church
638–647, 651–655

In this chapter, help your child to
+ identify Easter as the day we celebrate Christ's Resurrection.
+ tell the story of Jesus' appearances to Thomas and the disciples.
+ identify how Jesus praised those who believe in him without seeing him.
+ explain that the gift of faith is received at Baptism.

Easter

FOCUS: In this chapter, you will be helping your child to understand that at Easter, we celebrate the gift of peace given to us by the risen Lord.

The Resurrection is the victorious completion of redemption. Jesus showed his mastery over sin and death—over every hostile power. We share in his Resurrection through the waters of Baptism and are raised to the new life of grace. As partakers of his divine life, we are empowered by his strength to overcome every attack of the evil one. We count on being united with him in perfect happiness for all eternity. Meanwhile, we have already begun to live in union with him here on earth. We are sent, as were the first disciples, to communicate the joy and peace of the Resurrection to all people.

The Sunday eucharistic celebration is our encounter with the risen Lord. The Christian community professes publicly our loving acceptance of Jesus. The Eucharist in turn strengthens our relationship with the Lord. It inspires us to go forth in the name of Jesus to give his peace and to perpetuate the work of salvation.

Catechism of the Catholic Church
638–647, 651–655, 1010–1013, 2304

In this chapter, help your child to
+ tell the story of the first Easter.
+ identify peace as a gift given by the risen Lord.
+ explain that Jesus sends us to bring his peace to others.

Easter

FOCUS: In this chapter, you will be helping your child to understand that Easter is a season of great joy because we celebrate Jesus risen from the dead.

The Resurrection of Jesus is the victorious completion of redemption. Jesus is the new creation and master over sin and death, over every hostile power. As our Lord and Redeemer, he shares his Resurrection with those who follow him. We share in his death and Resurrection through the waters of Baptism, dying to sin and selfishness and then rising to the new life of grace. At the Easter Vigil service, the priest prays for us:

> God, the all-powerful Father of our Lord Jesus Christ, has given us a new birth by water and the Holy Spirit and forgiven all our sins.
> May he also keep us faithful to our Lord Jesus Christ for ever and ever.
>> *from the conclusion of the renewal of*
>> *baptismal promises during the Easter Vigil*

To be raised to this new life means that we accept and share in his own life, the life of Christ "sitting at God's right hand." We accept the reality that our life is being conditioned by God and not by the world.

Scripture in This Lesson
Luke 24   The Resurrection Narrative

Catechism of the Catholic Church
1163, 1168–1171

In this chapter, help your child to
+ describe Easter as our celebration of the new life that Jesus gives to us through his death and Resurrection.
+ explain that we began to share this new life of Jesus through our Baptism.
+ identify ways to live our new life in Christ by faith, hope, and love.

Easter

FOCUS: In this chapter, you will be helping your child to understand that we celebrate the Easter season with joy.

The Resurrection of Jesus is God's guarantee that those who trust the Father and follow his plan as Jesus did will have victory. In the upper room, Jesus appeared and showed his wounds. His Resurrection proved that love is stronger than death. Filled with joy, the apostles went out and preached, telling people that they had no need to fear because Jesus had triumphed over death. Because of the Resurrection, we know that God can transform our human weakness.

A band of frightened disciples had an experience of the risen Christ that radically changed them. Christ had broken the power of death. They could share his power; through Baptism, they would share eternal life with him. Today, the risen Christ is the companion of every Christian. He gives each one courage for his or her mission. Whenever a Christian stands up for truth, fights an unjust status quo, or speaks up for a neighbor despite opposition, he or she is joined with others who proclaim the Gospel of the risen Christ.

Catechism of the Catholic Church
638, 654–655, 1168–1169

In this chapter, help your child to
+ describe the Easter season as a joyful celebration of the Resurrection of Jesus.
+ explain the meaning of several Easter liturgical symbols.
+ identify ways to celebrate the 50 days of the Easter season.

Easter

FOCUS: In this chapter, you will be helping your child to understand that during the Easter season, we celebrate Jesus' Resurrection and our hope for eternal life.

Life is a series of beginnings. We finish one thing and move on to another. Renewal and re-creation are intrinsic to the spiritual life also. Initially, Christ summons us to new life in Baptism. He nurtures and restores that life through his sacraments. It is this call to newness of spirit that we celebrate at Easter time with joyful solemnity. By his death and Resurrection, Jesus proved himself once and for all master over sin and death.

Because of our Baptism, we too share in Christ's paschal victory and witness to his triumph. The symbols of Easter speak to us of our victory in Christ. We adorn our sanctuaries with Easter lilies, reminders of his radiant, risen body. We decorate eggs, tombs from which new life bursts forth. Christians bake bread or cake in the shape of a lamb or a cross, symbols of Christ's Paschal Mystery. Easter is a triumphant celebration of glorious new life made possible only in Christ Jesus.

Scripture in This Lesson
Hebrews 10:12–24 Jesus Offered One Sacrifice for Sins.

Catechism of the Catholic Church
1067–1068, 1168–1171

In this chapter, help your child to
+ describe the primary liturgical symbols of Easter.
+ identify how Easter symbols are present in the liturgy throughout the Easter season.

Key Term for Your Information
+ Liturgy of the Hours—the public prayer of the Church to praise God and to sanctify the day. It includes an office of readings before sunrise, morning prayer at dawn, evening prayer at sunset, and prayer before going to bed. The chanting of psalms makes up the major portion of each of these services.

Easter

FOCUS: In this chapter, you will be helping your child to understand that through the power of Jesus who rose from the dead, we too will someday rise to eternal life.

Life is a series of beginnings. We finish one thing and move on to another. Renewal and re-creation are intrinsic to the spiritual life also. Initially, Christ summons us to new life in Baptism. He nurtures and restores that life through his sacraments. It is this call to newness of spirit that we celebrate at Easter time with joyful solemnity. By his death and Resurrection, Jesus proved himself once and for all master over sin and death.

Because of our Baptism, we too share in Christ's paschal victory and witness to his triumph. The symbols of Easter speak to us of our victory in Christ. We adorn our sanctuaries with Easter lilies, reminders of his radiant, risen body. We decorate eggs, tombs from which new life bursts forth. Christians bake bread or cake in the shape of a lamb or a cross, symbols of Christ's Paschal Mystery. Easter is a triumphant celebration of glorious new life made possible only in Christ Jesus.

Scripture in This Chapter
Matthew 17:2 Jesus' Face Shown Like the Sun.
John 20:1 Mary of Magdala Came to the Tomb.
Psalm 118:24 Let Us Rejoice.

Catechism of the Catholic Church
638, 640, 651–655, 1163, 1168–1170

In this chapter, help your child to
+ identify the impact of the Resurrection of Christ on his or her life.
+ explain the meaning behind familiar Easter symbols.
+ identify ways to give witness to the power of the risen Lord by prayer and good deeds.

Pentecost

FOCUS: In this chapter, you will be helping your child to understand that at Pentecost, the disciples received Jesus' gift of the Holy Spirit, and the Church was born.

When Pope John Paul II wrote, in *Catechesis in Our Time*, about the Holy Spirit, he made three important affirmations about the role of the Spirit in the Church. First, the Spirit is our teacher within the Church, by acting in our minds and hearts to make us understand and love the depths of God's love. Second, the Spirit transforms us into people who are willing to proclaim the Lord Jesus, even to the extent of giving up our lives for him. Third, the charisms and gifts of the Spirit enlighten and strengthen us so that we can bear witness to Christ within our daily spheres of activity. They help us to build up the Church.

On the feast of Pentecost, we celebrate the gift of the Holy Spirit and its importance in our lives. We pray with the Church that the Holy Spirit will direct our use of every gift and that our lives may bring Christ to others.

Scripture in This Lesson
Acts of the Apostles 2:42–47 Communal Life

Catechism of the Catholic Church
729–732, 767–768, 1076, 1287, 2623–2625

In this chapter, help your child to
+ describe Pentecost as our celebration of the gift of the Holy Spirit and the birthday of the Church.
+ explain that the Holy Spirit helps the Church to share God's love.
+ identify himself or herself as a member of the Church.

Key Terms for Your Information
+ Church—the name given to the followers of Christ all over the world
+ Holy Spirit—the third Person of the Trinity, who comes to us in Baptism and fills us with God's life

---

Pentecost

FOCUS: In this chapter, you will be helping your child to understand that the Holy Spirit gives us light and love.

Christ promised to fill the hearts of his people with the Holy Spirit. On Pentecost, the gifts of the Spirit that filled the apostles and disciples made them a light to the world. When we are open to the transforming fire of the Spirit within us, God consumes whatever keeps us from bearing witness and enables us to bring his kingdom to others through acts of reconciliation, healing, and selfless concern.

The Church prays that the Holy Spirit will work through our lives to bring Christ into the world today:

> Father of light,
> from whom every good gift comes,
> send your Spirit into our lives
> with the power of a mighty wind,
> and by the flame of your wisdom,
> open the horizons of our minds.
> Loosen our tongues to sing your praise
> in words beyond the power of speech,
> for without your Spirit
> man could never raise his voice
> in words of peace or announce the truth
> that Jesus is Lord.
> *Alternative Opening Prayer, Pentecost*

Scripture in This Lesson
John 15:26–27 The Coming of the Advocate
Acts of the Apostles 2:1–4,14 The Coming of the Spirit

Catechism of the Catholic Church
729–732, 2623

In this chapter, help your child to
+ recall that the Holy Spirit came to the apostles on Pentecost.
+ remember that he or she received the Holy Spirit when he or she was baptized.
+ identify the Holy Spirit's power to transform our lives.
+ listen and pray to the Holy Spirit.

Key Term for Your Information
+ Holy Spirit— the third Person of the Trinity, who comes to us in Baptism and fills us with God's life

Pentecost

FOCUS: In this chapter, you will be helping your child to understand that at Pentecost, when the disciples received Jesus' gift of the Holy Spirit, they announced the Good News of Jesus to all the people.

On Pentecost, the two powerful symbols of fire and wind—signifying light and love, life and strength—accompanied the Holy Spirit's coming. The Spirit filled the apostles and disciples with his gifts, making them a light to the nations and a breath of new creation—true People of God.

The fire of the Spirit can transform the lives of those called to witness to the Lord. Those filled with the Spirit bring the Kingdom of God to others by their acts of reconciliation, healing, and selfless concern. Faithful to the teaching of the Lord, the Church asks the Spirit to work through us to bring Christ to the world today, just as the apostles and disciples did in their time and place. Through the love of God poured into our hearts by the Holy Spirit, we can face and endure any hardship or persecution, welcoming all who come to us and proclaiming the Kingdom of God in word and works.

Scripture in This Lesson
Acts of the Apostles 3:1–8 Peter Heals the Man at the Temple Gate.

Catechism of the Catholic Church
731–735, 1076

In this chapter, help your child to
+ describe the feast of Pentecost as our celebration of Jesus' gift of the Holy Spirit.
+ explain that the Holy Spirit helps the Church to continue the work of Jesus.
+ identify ways in which we can give witness to Jesus through our words and actions.

Key Terms for Your Information
+ Holy Spirit—the third Person of the Trinity, who is sent to us as our helper and, through Baptism and Confirmation, fills us with God's life
+ mission—the work of Jesus Christ that is continued in the Church through the Holy Spirit. The mission of the Church is to proclaim salvation through Jesus' life, death, and Resurrection
+ Pentecost—the 50th day after Jesus was raised from the dead. On this day, the Holy Spirit was sent from heaven, and the Church was born

---

Pentecost

FOCUS: In this chapter, you will be helping your child to understand that the effects of the Holy Spirit, seen in the apostles on the first Pentecost, continue to show forth in the Church today.

The Holy Spirit is with us always, but we are not always sensitive to his presence. Just as photographic film captures elusive and fleeting impressions when it is carefully exposed to light, the human heart detects delicate and seemingly imperceptible movements of grace when it is closely attuned to the Holy Spirit.

In George Bernard Shaw's play *St. Joan*, King Charles asks Joan why she is granted heavenly revelations and he is not. Joan answers, "They do come to you, but you do not hear them. You have not sat in the field in the evening, listening for them." The inspirations of the Holy Spirit illuminate the various ways we hinder God's action in our lives. Only if we come into the healing presence of our God, will we see ourselves reflected as we truly are. The more receptive we are to the Holy Spirit in our lives, the more we will experience the fruits of his presence.

Catechism of the Catholic Church
694–701, 731–736, 1076, 2623

In this chapter, help your child to
+ identify the Feast of Pentecost as our celebration of Jesus' promised gift of the Holy Spirit.
+ tell the story of Pentecost as found in the Acts of the Apostles.
+ describe the effects of the Holy Spirit in our lives.

Key Terms for Your Information
+ Fruits of the Holy Spirit—the signs of the Holy Spirit's action in our lives
+ Holy Spirit—the third Person of the Trinity, who is sent to us as our helper and, through Baptism and Confirmation, fills us with God's life
+ Pentecost—the 50th day after Jesus was raised from the dead. On this day, the Holy Spirit was sent from heaven, and the Church was born

Pentecost

FOCUS: In this chapter, you will be helping your child to understand that the Holy Spirit lives in us and makes us holy.

On Pentecost, the two powerful symbols of fire and wind—signifying light and love, life and strength—accompanied the Holy Spirit's coming. The Spirit filled the apostles and disciples with his gifts, making them a light to the nations and a breath of new creation. The fire of the Spirit can transform the lives of those called to witness to the Lord. Those who are filled with the Spirit bring the Kingdom of God to others by their acts of reconciliation, healing, and selfless concern.

Faithful to the teaching of the Lord, the Church asks the Spirit to work through us to bring Christ to the world today. Through the love of God poured into our hearts by the Holy Spirit, we can face and endure any hardship or persecution, welcome all who come to us, and proclaim the Kingdom of God in both our words and works.

Catechism of the Catholic Church
731–732, 767–768

In this chapter, help your child to
+ identify names given to the Holy Spirit and petitions that are offered to the Holy Spirit on the feast of Pentecost.
+ pray to the Holy Spirit and seek to follow his guidance.
+ reflect on the seven Gifts of the Holy Spirit and their importance in our lives.

Key Terms for Your Information
+ Pentecost—the 50th day after Jesus was raised from the dead. On this day, the Holy Spirit was sent from heaven, and the Church was born
+ Holy Spirit—the third Person of the Trinity, who is sent to us as our helper and, through Baptism and Confirmation, fills us with God's life. Together with the Father and the Son, the Holy Spirit brings the divine plan of salvation to completion.
+ Sanctifier—name for the Holy Spirit that stands for God's power to make us holy
+ Gifts of the Holy Spirit—the permanent willingness, given to us by the Holy Spirit, that makes it possible for us to do what God asks of us.

Pentecost

FOCUS: In this chapter, you will be helping your child to understand that the gift of the Holy Spirit sanctifies us and enables us to carry on Christ's work.

On Pentecost, the two powerful symbols of fire and wind—signifying light and love, life and strength—accompanied the Holy Spirit's coming. The Spirit filled the apostles and disciples with his gifts, making them a light to the nations and a breath of new creation. The fire of the Spirit can transform the lives of those called to witness to the Lord. Those who are filled with the Spirit bring the Kingdom of God to others by their acts of reconciliation, healing, and selfless concern.

Faithful to the teaching of the Lord, the Church asks the Spirit to work through us to bring Christ to the world today. Through the love of God poured into our hearts by the Holy Spirit, we can face and endure any hardship or persecution, welcome all who come to us, and proclaim the Kingdom of God in both our words and works.

Catechism of the Catholic Church
731–735, 1076

In this chapter, help your child to
+ describe the work of the Holy Spirit in forming the People of God.
+ identify the feast of Pentecost as our celebration of the gift of the Holy Spirit.
+ identify a situation to bring to the Holy Spirit in prayer.

Key Term for Your Information
+ Holy Spirit—the third Person of the Trinity, who is sent to us as our advocate and, through Baptism and Confirmation, fills us with God's life. Together with the Father and the Son, the Holy Spirit brings the divine plan of salvation to completion.

Pentecost

FOCUS: In this chapter, you will be helping your child to understand that on Pentecost, we celebrate the fulfillment of Jesus' promise to send us the Holy Spirit.

In *Catechesis in Our Time*, Pope John Paul II made three important affirmations about the role of the Spirit in the Church. First, the Spirit is our teacher within the Church, by acting in our minds and hearts to make us understand and love the depths of God's love. Second, the Spirit transforms us into people who are willing to proclaim the Lord Jesus, even to the extent of giving up our lives for him. Third, the charisms and gifts of the Spirit enlighten and strengthen us so that we can bear witness to Christ within our daily spheres of activity. They help us to build up the Church. On the feast of Pentecost, we pray with the Church that the Holy Spirit will direct our use of every gift and that our lives may bring Christ to others.

Scripture in This Lesson

John 14:15–21   The Spirit of Truth Remains in Us.
John 15:26–27   The Advocate Comes from the Father.
John 16:12–15   The Spirit Guides Us in All Truth.

Catechism of the Catholic Church

691–693, 727–741, 1076

In this chapter, help your child to

+ identify the feast of Pentecost as our celebration of the outpouring of the Holy Spirit.
+ discuss the meaning of the names Jesus gave to the Holy Spirit: Advocate and Spirit of Truth.
+ describe how the Holy Spirit helps us.

Key Terms for Your Information

+ Advocate—Jesus' name for the Holy Spirit. The Holy Spirit comforts us, speaks for us in difficult times, and makes Jesus present to us
+ Holy Spirit—the third Person of the Trinity, sent to us as our helper and, through Baptism and Confirmation, fills us with God's life. Together with the Father and the Son, the Holy Spirit brings the divine plan of salvation to completion
+ Pentecost—the 50th day of the Jewish festival Shav'u'ot (the festival of weeks) following Passover, commemorating the time when the first fruits were harvested and brought to the Temple. Pentecost also commemorated the giving of the Torah on Mount Sinai. Christians celebrate Pentecost 50 days after Jesus' Passover from death to life. On this day, the Holy Spirit was sent from heaven, and the Church was born.

Pentecost

FOCUS: In this chapter, you will be helping your child to understand that on Pentecost, we celebrate the beginning of the Church.

When the Spirit came at Pentecost, amid wind and fire and songs of praise, a new era began. In the outpouring of that Spirit, the Church as the community of believers was born and its mission launched. The disciples were empowered to proclaim Christ to the world. This mission bound them together with a common vision and a common dedication to one another.

The Spirit brought life and grace to a world that needed so much to be whole again. We, the Church, devote all we are to our one Lord. By one Baptism, we are plunged into a new life in him. And we become one family, bonded together forever.

Scripture in This Lesson

Luke 4:18–19   The Spirit of the Lord Is Upon Me.
Acts of the Apostles 4:23–31   The Spirit Helps the Disciples Speak Boldly.

Catechism of the Catholic Church

687–690, 702–741, 1076

In this chapter, help your child to

+ identify the feast of Pentecost as a celebration of the presence of the Holy Spirit in the Church.
+ discuss the activity of the Holy Spirit throughout the three periods of salvation history.
+ name ways in which the Holy Spirit works in the Church today.

Key Terms for Your Information

+ Pentecost—the 50th day of the Jewish festival Shav'u'ot (the festival of weeks) following Passover, commemorating the time when the first fruits were harvested and brought to the Temple. Pentecost also commemorated the giving of the Torah on Mount Sinai. Christians celebrate Pentecost 50 days after Jesus' Passover from death to life. On this day, the Holy Spirit was sent from heaven, and the Church was born.
+ salvation history—the story of God's loving relationship with his people, which tells how God carries out his plan to save all people

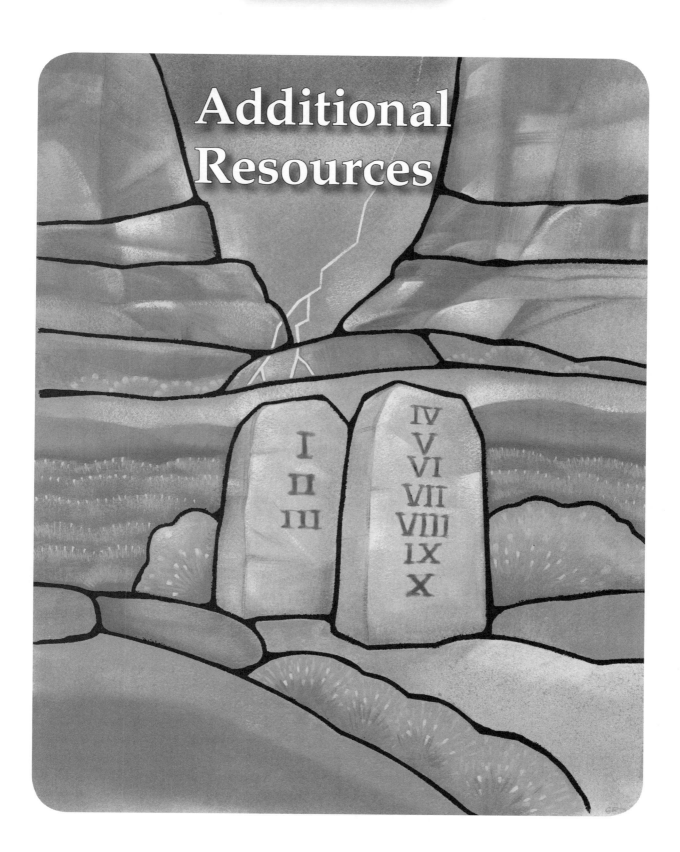

PART 3

Additional Resources

Overview of the Year in Our Church

We're all aware that there are natural rhythms to life. The seasons of the year cycle around, and we sense the times of beginning, growth, fullness, and dormancy. The Church has its own rhythms, feasts, and seasons, which are captured in the liturgical calendar that appears below. This "circle of life" in the Church presents the celebration of the whole mystery of Christ, from the anticipation of his birth and his Incarnation (God becoming human), to his death, Resurrection, ascension, and the expectation of his coming again. The Church invites us year after year to deepen the commitment we made in Baptism. We do so by immersing ourselves in the Paschal Mystery of Jesus as celebrated in the seasons and feasts, allowing ourselves to be shaped into the image of the one we come to know and follow. By conscientiously observing these seasons and feasts within your home, your family can grow naturally and easily in the Catholic way of life.

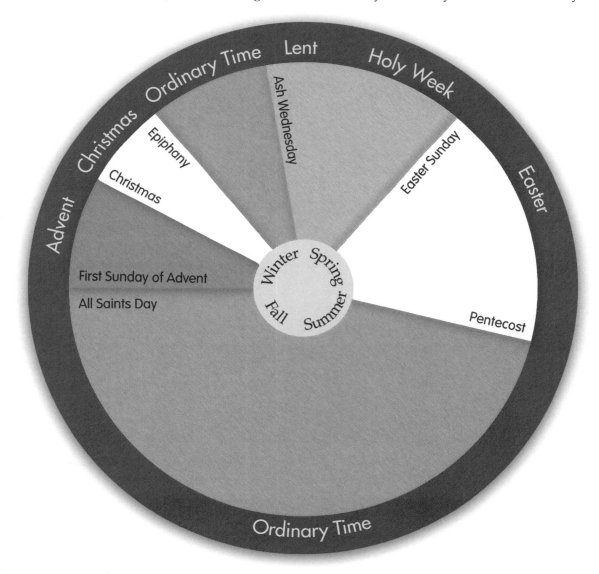

All Saints And All Souls Family Activity

All Saints and All Souls Days are celebrated on November 1 and 2. November can be regarded as a dreary month. In the Northern Hemisphere, winter approaches during this month. Leaves fall from the trees, temperatures drop, and daylight grows shorter. We are surrounded by signs of death in nature.

It is no coincidence, then, that we focus on those who have died, not only on these special days but also throughout the entire month of November. Many parishes keep a book of remembrance in their worship space in which parishioners are invited to write the names of loved ones who have died. Check to see if your parish has this custom; if so, add your loved ones' names to the book.

In preparation for this family activity, collect memorabilia (photos, videos, newspaper clippings, memorial cards, and other mementos) of members of your family or close friends who have died.

It may be possible that your child has never met these special relatives or friends. Be prepared to share some memories of what these people mean to you. Think of concrete ways that the memories of these people live on in your family today. (Examples: perhaps someone shares the name of a deceased family member or friend; you might have cherished items displayed in your home that belonged to the people; family members compare particular traits—kindness, sense of humor, reliability, and so forth—that one or more of your children has as well). You might also contact older family members and invite them to join you for this session, or ask them to help you collect photos or recount family stories.

Gather around your prayer center or another appropriate place. You may want to include a candle and a green plant or fresh flowers. Display the photographs and other items you have collected.

Using your own words, discuss the following points about the feasts of All Saints and All Souls.

+ Explain that our faith gives us the promise of a life with Jesus and God the Father in heaven and that we all remain connected because we belong to the Communion of Saints. Elaborate that we are one family together with Christ and that his love is not bound, even by death.

+ Begin your storytelling. Invite each member of your family to share memories of those who have died. Pass around their photographs if you have them, and share a few of your memories.

+ For those who have not yet known anyone who has died, help them to think of people in your community who have died and whom they might want to remember (neighbors, parishioners, someone at school).

+ When everyone has finished sharing, explain that one way of staying close to those who have died is by doing what you have just done—sharing memories about lost loved ones and reminiscing about their lives.

Telling stories is a wonderful way of keeping alive the memory of our loved ones. Another way is through prayer. We can help those who have died by praying for them, and they can help us through their intercession.

Close this special time of storytelling with spontaneous prayers of petition.

Keep up your family prayer space throughout the month of November. You may want to gather there as a family each night for a brief prayer. Encourage individual family members to spend time there privately.

Advent Family Activity

Work with your family to create an Advent basket, using the materials below. It can be a wonderful way of sharing the spirit of Advent with your friends and loved ones.

Materials
Medium-sized basket
Copy of Advent Basket Instructions
Candles—3 purple, 1 pink, 1 larger white
Wreath
Blank prayer cards in an envelope
Small cookie tin
Homemade or store-bought cookies
Christmas story, such as *The Gift of the Magi* by O. Henry or *The Stranger Child: A Legend* by Count Franz Pocci, laminated or bound

After your family has completed the Advent basket, follow the Advent Basket instructions to complete the activities for the first week of Advent. Invite other families to continue passing the basket throughout Advent.

Advent Basket Instructions
This Advent Basket has been created by the
_____ family to help those we love celebrate the season of Advent. We invite you to complete the following activities and then pass the Advent basket to the next family.

Activity 1: Work together to write a short prayer on one of the prayer cards. The prayer should be about your family's anticipation of Jesus. Feel free to decorate the card.

Activity 2: Set up the wreath and the candles. The candles should be arranged inside the wreath, with the white candle in the center. Go to **www.christourlife.org** for information about how to set up the Advent wreath and about which candle to light each week. Then pray together the prayer you wrote.

Activity 3: Share and enjoy the enclosed story and cookies with your family.

Activity 4: Return all items, including the prayer you wrote, to the basket.

Activity 5: Replace the cookies for the next family and pass the basket!

Tip Confirm beforehand which families would like to participate and provide a list of families with the basket so that everyone knows who should receive the basket next.

Christmas Family Activity

The sights and sounds and wonderful tastes and smells of Christmas are more than a delight for our senses. All our stories, songs, traditions, and family rituals convey somehow the meaning of the season. They invite us to pause and to reflect on what Jesus' birth means to us today. Jesus, the Son of God, became man to share God's life with us. Especially during this season of wonder and surprise, we see signs of that presence all around us.

Gather as a family near your Christmas tree.

You'll need the following materials:
a CD player
CDs with your family's favorite Christmas carols
drawing paper
crayons
Christmas cards your family has received (especially those that have some of the symbols mentioned below)

Explain in your own words how the Christmas season provides us with many signs and symbols that teach us about Jesus' birth. Describe a few of them.

- The trumpet is a sign of the angels' message to the shepherds.
- The candy cane is inspired by the shepherds' staff.
- The evergreen tree is a sign of everlasting life.
- A decorated evergreen tree (star or angel at the top, lights and ornaments in the branches, and a crèche scene at the bottom) represents the connection between heaven (top of the tree) and earth (bottom of the tree) that Jesus' birth made possible.

- The star at the top of a Christmas tree reminds us of the star of Bethlehem.
- Angels remind us of the messengers that greeted the shepherds with a song of praise.
- The ornaments remind us of the beauty that Jesus brought into the world.
- The crèche scene reminds us of Jesus' humble birth and the ordinary and extraordinary people who came to pay homage to him.
- Christmas candles represent the light of Christ born into the world at Christmas.

Together, look through the Christmas cards that your family has received and find as many of these symbols as possible. Ask each member to choose his or her favorite symbol and draw it with as much detail as possible. You may want to play some soft Christmas music in the background during this time. When everyone is ready, invite all to share their drawings and to talk about how these drawings remind them of the Christmas message.

After you have finished sharing, decide together where to display your family's artwork.

About 12 days after Christmas, we celebrate the feast of the Epiphany. The word epiphany means "to show or reveal." On the feast of the Epiphany, we celebrate that day when Jesus was revealed to the world, represented by the Magi (the three kings) who came from distant lands.

Gather as a family to celebrate the feast of the Epiphany.

Invite an adult or an older child to read the story of the visit of the Magi from the Bible, which is found in Matthew 2:1–12. After a silent moment of reflection, explain that in some cultures, the Epiphany is a traditional day of gift giving—a way of imitating the Magi who brought gifts to honor Jesus, the newborn king. Tell your family that we can also honor Jesus with the gift of doing something kind or helpful for another person, because when we serve others, we serve Jesus.

Have small slips of paper (one per person) and pencils ready. Then guide your family through the following activity:

✦ Invite each person to write his or her name on the paper, fold it in half, and place it in a basket or bowl.

✦ Pass the container around and have each person draw a name, keeping the name secret.

✦ Distribute an index card or a half-sheet of paper to each person and have crayons or markers available. Allow enough time for each person to think of a special act that can be performed as a gift to the person whose name he or she drew. Examples include doing an extra household chore, giving the person a special treat, or helping the person with a difficult task.

✦ When everyone has finished, invite each person to make a gift by writing or drawing a picture of what it is he or she will do. Instruct them to write on the other side of the paper the name of the person that they drew. As your family works on their pictures, play Christmas music in the background.

When everyone has finished their gifts, ask them to place their gifts in or near the crèche. Then invite each family member to go to the crèche scene and find his or her gift.

Bring your Epiphany celebration to a close with a snack that your family enjoys.

Lenten Family Activity

We have all heard the biblical phrase "To everything there is a season." Lent is the season of the year to take an honest look at our lives in order to become closer to God.

We prepare ourselves for Easter in prayer, fasting, and almsgiving. Each day we set aside a special time to pray so that we can better hear God's voice. Fasting can take many forms: we can fast from food by eating less than we normally do, by refraining from things we enjoy (such as a favorite TV program), or by making a conscious effort to avoid behaviors that separate us from God and from others (such as bad language or selfishness). Like prayer and fasting, giving alms focuses our attention on God by emphasizing our dependence on his gifts, which are to be shared with all. We give alms by donating time, money, or food to those who need it.

The following activity offers a way for your family to enter more deeply into the spirit of prayer, fasting, and almsgiving during the Lenten season.

As early in Lent as possible, invite your family to gather in your kitchen for a Lenten planning night.

> **For this time together, you will need the following:**
> a Bible
> the ingredients for making pretzels—
> a traditional Lenten food

In your own words, share what you know about our Lenten call. Emphasize that we are called to give alms as a way to focus our attention on our dependence on God and to share our abundance with those who are less fortunate.

When you are finished, read aloud the Gospel story of the Good Samaritan in Luke 10:29–37. When you have finished, allow time for your family to silently reflect on the story. Then bring the story into the present and share what it means to be a neighbor to others in the way that Jesus explains it. Discuss how your family might be a neighbor to others as Jesus defines it. Ask whether there is an individual, a family, or a group of people whom your family could

serve during Lent. Brainstorm possible activities in your area that you could do as a family, such as adopting an elderly person, giving time at a soup kitchen, or collecting blankets or other items for families at a homeless shelter.

Discuss with your family how prayer and fasting are an important part of our Lenten practice. Explain that a traditional Lenten food that symbolizes the practices of prayer and fasting is the pretzel. Share the history of the pretzel and what it symbolizes as a Lenten food.

In the Roman Empire, the early Christians fasted from milk, eggs, butter, and meat during the Lenten season. As an alternative, they made bread from the simplest ingredients: flour, salt, and water. The shape is meant to represent arms crossed over the chest, which was a common posture for prayer at that time. Pretzel is a German word that comes from the Latin *bracellae*, which means "little arms."

Invite your family to cross their arms and to imagine that they are praying just as the early Christians did.

Soft Pretzel Ingredients
1 package dry yeast
1½ cups warm water
1 tablespoon sugar
4 cups flour
1 beaten egg
coarse salt

When you are ready, mix the ingredients and let each family member make some "little arms."

Follow these directions:

+ Add the sugar to the water and stir.
+ Dissolve the yeast in the water.
+ Blend in the flour and turn the dough onto a lightly floured board.
+ Knead until smooth.
+ Cut slices of dough and roll into ropes.
+ Twist ropes into pretzel shapes and arrange them on a nonstick cookie sheet.
+ Brush pretzels with the egg and sprinkle coarse salt on top.
+ Bake at 425 degrees for 12–15 minutes or until golden brown.

While the pretzels are baking, invite an adult or older child to read Matthew 6:5–13. Listen to Jesus teach his disciples about prayer. Spend a few minutes sharing some ways that you can pray together during this Lenten season.

When the pretzels are done, invite everyone to sit at the table and place the pretzels in the center. Invite your family to pray silently for their own needs, for the needs of your family, and for the local and world communities. Then invite each member to take a pretzel and to mention someone for whom the family can pray. (Examples include an ill relative, an elderly neighbor, a friend at school or work who is having a difficult time.)

When all have finished praying, bring this time together to a close by praying the Our Father.

Throughout the Lenten season, you may want to serve pretzels at the beginning of a meal as a reminder of the need for fasting and prayer.

Holy Week Family Activity

At the heart of our faith is the greatest mystery of all—Jesus' suffering, death, and Resurrection. The story of Jesus' dying and rising is meant to be the pattern for our own lives. We absorb and take on that pattern by paying attention to and entering that story over and over again. During Holy Week, which is Palm Sunday to Easter Sunday, we tell and retell the story of Jesus, from his entry into Jerusalem to his last meal, trial, crucifixion, death, and Resurrection. This telling and retelling takes the forms of liturgy, ritual, and personal devotion. Holy Week is a time to enter into the most sacred days of our liturgical calendar.

Holy Week is filled with rich and powerful symbols. Although you probably are not accustomed to decorating your home for Holy Week as you do at Christmas, you can work together with your family to prepare for and honor Holy Week in your home. One activity is to prepare a Holy Week Table with symbols of Jesus' passion, death, and Resurrection.

Gather as a family on Palm Sunday (or Monday of Holy Week) around the table that you've designated as your Holy Week Table.

> **Work together to make five signs, each 8-by-11 inches:**
> 1. Palm Sunday
> 2. Holy Thursday
> 3. Good Friday
> 4. Holy Saturday
> 5. Easter Sunday

Arrange the five signs on the table and brainstorm a list of the symbols that represents each day. Work together as a family to gather these symbols. For ideas, see the examples below. Then follow the directions for special family rituals to conduct as you put your table together.

Palm Sunday (Luke 19:28–40): blessed palms

Holy Thursday (John 13:1–15): a basin, pitcher with water, towels

Good Friday (John 18:1–19, 42): a wooden cross, nails

Holy Saturday (Romans 6:3–11): a candle, holy water

Easter Sunday (John 20:1–9): a large rock (or rock candy)

Palm Sunday

Begin by arranging the palms that were blessed at Palm Sunday Mass. Leave a palm on the table and then lead a procession through your home, placing a palm (behind a crucifix, a sacred image, or other picture) in each family member's bedroom, as well as in the kitchen, dining room, and family room.

Play some inspirational music as you process through your home.

You might also encourage your child to make palm branches out of green construction paper to place on the table.

Holy Thursday

Obtain a basin, a pitcher, and a towel to symbolize Jesus' washing of the apostles' feet.

Fill the pitcher with water and place it with the basin and towel on your Holy Week Table by the Holy Thursday sign. Get your child involved by inviting him or her to place the symbols on the table.

Good Friday

Place on the table a wooden cross (or make a simple one out of two sticks and rubber bands) and three large nails to symbolize Jesus' crucifixion. You might lead your family in a short prayer of thanksgiving before or after you have placed the cross on the table.

Holy Saturday

Place a large white candle on the table to symbolize the light of the risen Christ, who triumphed over the darkness of death.

Fill a small bowl with water (you can get holy water from your parish Church) to symbolize the waters of Baptism for those who will be baptized on Holy Saturday.

Easter Sunday

To symbolize Jesus' Resurrection on Easter Sunday, send your child outside to find a good-sized rock to symbolize the stone that was rolled away from Jesus' tomb. If a suitable rock cannot be found, use rock candy.

After all of the symbols are in place, talk about ways that your family will celebrate Holy Week. Talk about what it means to serve others just as Jesus served his disciples by washing their feet. Think of concrete ways that each family member can serve someone else in the coming week. If you cannot make it to Church for Holy Week services, consider conducting a short family prayer service each day around your Holy Week Table. Also encourage your family members to take a private moment each day at the Holy Week Table to pray for the courage to follow Jesus on his journey of love to the cross and to his Resurrection.

Easter Family Activity

At the first Easter, Christ rose from the dead and appeared to many before he ascended into heaven. Jesus showed that on the other side of violent death and apparent abandonment, we can find peace and communion. After the Resurrection, Jesus offered his peace to the apostles when he appeared to them. Jesus' peace gives us the hope and comfort of knowing that God is with us even in the midst of our deepest hurts and greatest losses. As people whose faith has brought us to our own celebration of Easter, we are challenged to share this same peace with others.

The following activity invites you and your family to think about the meaning of peace and to consider ways to share the peace of Christ.

Gather with your family around your prayer table or some other appropriate place.

Prior to this activity, collect newspapers and magazines, several glue sticks, scissors, markers, and a large sheet of poster board. When your family has gathered, share in your own words how the disciples did not fully understand that Jesus had risen from the dead. Explain that the disciples were so surprised to see him standing among them that he had to prove that it was really him. Then he said, "Peace be with you."

Invite an adult or older child to read John 20:19–21.

Allow time for your family to reflect prayerfully on what they have just heard. Then invite them to imagine themselves in the room with the disciples. Ask them to consider how it would feel to see Jesus again and to hear him say "Peace be with you." After a few moments of contemplation, invite each family member to share his or her reflections.

With your family, discuss people today who are in need of the peace that the risen Jesus gives. They can be far away or just around the corner.

Then talk about where and when in your own lives your family is in need of peace.

When everyone is finished, spread out the newspapers and magazines and invite each person to look cut out pictures and words that portray peaceful living. Guide your family through the following activity directions:

+ Allow each family member to glue his or her cutouts onto the poster board.
+ Share with one another why you chose the pieces you contributed.
+ As a way of symbolizing our call to share the peace of Christ with others, invite an adult or older child to use a marker and write the word Peace in the blank spaces of your poster. Have the person write the word in as many languages as possible. You can choose from the list or add other words that are spoken in your family, neighborhood, or parish.

Arabic	SALAM
Cantonese	PENG ON
French	PAIX
Gaelic-Irish	SIOCHAIN
German	FRIEDEN
Greek	ERENE
Hawaiian	MALUHIA
Hebrew	SHALOM
Hungarian	BEKE
Italian	PACE
Japanese	HEIWA
Korean	PYOUNG-HWA
Latin	PAX
Lithuanian	TAIKA
Polish	POKOJ
Portuguese	PAZ
Russian	MIR
Spanish	PAZ
Swahili	SALAMU
Tagalog (Filipino)	KAPAYAPAAN
Vietnamese	HOA BINH

✦ Decide together where you will display your poster throughout the Easter season.

Close by praying the Peace Prayer of Saint Francis.

Lord, make me an instrument of your peace:
where there is hatred, let me sow love;
where there is injury, pardon;
where there is doubt, faith;
where there is despair, hope;
where there is darkness, light;
and where there is sadness, joy.

O Divine master, grant that I may not so much seek
to be consoled, as to console;
to be understood, as to understand;
to be loved, as to love.
For it is in giving that we receive,
it is in pardoning that we are pardoned,
and it is in dying that we are born to eternal life.
Amen.

As a follow-up to this activity, you may want to learn more about Play for Peace, a Chicago-based global organization working both to reduce violence and to build more peaceful communities throughout the world. If you have Internet access, you can learn more about the organization at **www.playforpeace.org.**

Pentecost Family Activity

Do you remember going to a pep rally back in high school? The idea was for the whole school to rouse the spirits of the football or basketball team before an important game. A traditional cheer, which you probably heard, was "We've got spirit, yes we do!"

Nothing great happens without spirit. At Pentecost, the Holy Spirit came to the disciples, giving them strength, confidence, and the boldness to teach others about the promise of salvation through Jesus Christ. At our Baptism, we receive the Holy Spirit in our lives in real and sometimes surprising ways. With the presence of the Holy Spirit, we are empowered and encouraged to live out our faith in our homes, in our parishes, and in our world.

For this family activity, you will need the following materials:

a Bible
heavy construction paper (one sheet per person)
colorful streamers (9 per person, 24 inches long, preferably yellow, orange, and red)
scissors
stapler
clear tape
crayons
permanent black markers
twine or heavy string

Gather in a place where you can comfortably lay out your materials and have room to work. Distribute the craft items. You may need to adjust the width of the streamers according to the size paper you use.

Ask your family if they know what a wind sock is. Explain that, since wind is invisible, a wind sock helps to determine the direction and speed of the wind. In other words, the only way we recognize the wind is by looking at its effect on different objects. Explain that on the feast of Pentecost, we celebrate the presence of the Holy Spirit in our lives and that since we cannot see the Holy Spirit, the only way we can recognize him is by the effects he has on people. Another word for *effects* is *fruits*. In Saint Paul's letter to the Galatians, 5:22–23, we are told what these fruits or effects of the Holy Spirit are:

Love:	the charity we express to others
Joy:	the happiness we receive from our faith
Peace:	the tranquility of our souls
Patience:	the ability to endure difficulties
Kindness:	the goodness we show people
Generosity:	the ability to share with others
Faithfulness:	the commitment we make to God
Gentleness:	the ability to act without harshness or anger
Self-control:	the ability to avoid acting on temptation

- Write one of the fruits of the Holy Spirit on each of the streamers.
- Write large so that each word can be easily seen.
- Decorate the construction paper with crayons and lay it horizontally.
- Tape the streamers to the inside of the bottom edge of the paper.
- Roll the construction paper to make a cylinder and staple it at each end.
- Cut a sufficient length of twine or heavy string for the handle.
- You can either make two small holes at the top of the cylinder and tie your string to make the handle, or knot the string at each end and tape the knots to the cylinder for a handle.

After each person is finished and you have admired one another's' work, gather in your prayer center or another appropriate place. Invite an adult or older child to read the account of Pentecost from the Acts of the Apostles 2:1–12.

After a moment of silence, explain that the two signs of the presence of the Holy Spirit were wind and fire. We can't see wind, but we see its effects. A Spirit wind sock is a reminder that the Holy Spirit blows through each of us, and the effects we see are the fruits that are manifested in our behavior.

Invite everyone to look closely at the fruits of the Holy Spirit on their wind sock and to silently reflect on which ones are most important to them right now. Take a few minutes to share your responses with one another.

Decide where you will hang your Spirit wind sock so that it will be a reminder of how we are called to live our faith. You can place it outdoors or inside near a window.

Close this time together by praying the Prayer to the Holy Spirit.

V. Come, Holy Spirit, fill the hearts of your faithful.
R. And kindle in them the fire of your love.
V. Send forth your Spirit and they shall be created.
R. And you will renew the face of the earth.
Let us pray.
Lord, by the light of the Holy Spirit
you have taught the hearts of your faithful.
In the same Spirit
help us to relish what is right
and always rejoice in your consolation.
We ask this through Christ our Lord.
Amen.

Additional Resources

At the back of the Student Book, you will find additional resources that you can use with your child.

Special Lessons: Some grades include additional lessons that you can use with your child.

Pullouts: Each grade includes one or more pullout sections that can be folded into booklets for convenient use. You may use these at any time, although you may want to match the pullout themes with corresponding chapter themes in the Student Book for reinforcement.

Learning Aids: Some grades include learning aids such as maps, timelines, and calendars that you can use to enhance a lesson or at any other time.

Punchouts: Some grades include punchout figures that can be used to enhance the lesson in the chapter to which it corresponds.

The charts that follow indicate the special lessons, pullouts, and punchouts for each grade, along with directions for how to use the special lessons and punchouts.

Grade 1 Poster and Punchout

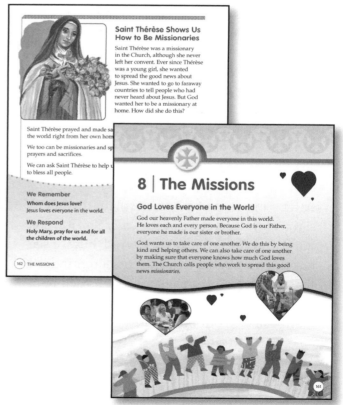

Grade 2 Special Lesson

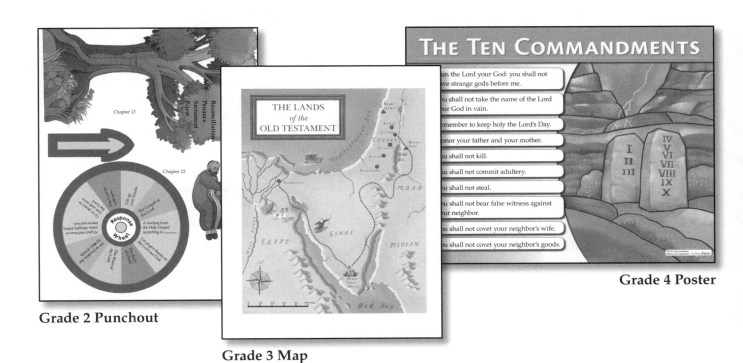

Grade 2 Punchout

Grade 3 Map

Grade 4 Poster

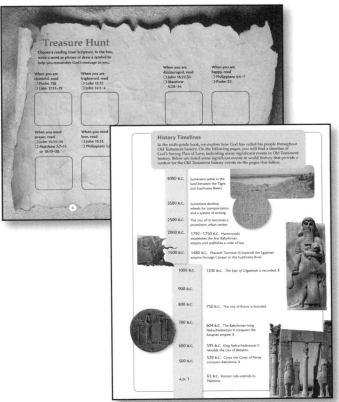

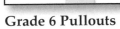

Grade 6 Pullouts

Grade 8 Special Lesson

Special Lessons
(none)

Pullouts (See page 237 in the Student Book.)
✦ The Way of the Cross booklet
✦ Scripture Prayer booklet

Learning Aids
(none)

Punchouts (listed in the order that they appear in the Student Book, following the Scripture Prayer booklet)

✦ **I Will Help Gift Cards** (Chapter 11)
Help your child remove the four I Will Help gift cards from the back of the book. Tell your child that these gift cards will help him or her give to others as a gift. They are promises to help. Have your child write on the gift cards the names of those he or she wishes to help and give the cards to those people. Tell these people that when they need help, they can call on him or her. Help your child to write the names.

✦ **VIP Badges** (Chapter 3)
Help your child remove the VIP badge from the back of the book. Explain that he or she can give a VIP badge to someone who brings God's love, care, or forgiveness. Say: *When you give a badge to your VIP, tell that person why he or she is a VIP to you.*

✦ **Puzzle** (Chapter 14)
Read the story of Jairus's daughter (Mark 5:21–24,35–43). Help your child to remove the puzzle of Jairus's daughter from the back of the book. Work together to complete the puzzle. When finished, invite your child to tell the story in his or her own words.

✦ **Guardian Angel Card** (Special Lesson 8—appears only in the Catechist Guide)

✦ **This card is used in a lesson on the feast of the Guardian Angels** (October 2), which is found only in the Catechist Guide. You may wish to use this card with your child on October 2 or at any other time. Explain how God, in his love, has given each of us a guardian angel to help us on our way to heaven. Help your child to learn the Guardian Angel prayer.

✦ **Lamb** (Chapter 18)
To reinforce the image of Jesus as the Good Shepherd, help your child remove the sheep punchout from the back of the book. Work together to glue a button for the lamb's eye. Draw a mouth with a crayon or marker. Glue cotton balls to the lamb's body until the lamb has a soft, wooly coat.

✦ **Angel, Mary, and Two White Strips** (Chapter 10)
Work with your child to remove the punchouts of Mary, the angel, and the two white strips above them from the back of the book. Show your child how to join the strips to make bases and then insert the figures. Tell your child to look at the figures as you tell the story in Chapter 10 of the angel visiting Mary.

✦ **Manger and Infant Jesus** (Chapter 11)
Work together to remove the manger and the infant Jesus punchouts from the back of the book. Fold back the two middle legs of the manger so that it will stand. As you read the story of the Nativity in Chapter 11, direct your child to place the infant Jesus in the manger at the part where Mary laid Jesus in the manger.

✦ **Fish** (Chapter 13)
Remove the fish punchout from the back of the book and have your child write his or her name on the fish as a reminder that he or she is called to be Jesus' helper.

✦ **I Am with You Tabernacle** (Chapter 19)
Help your child remove the I Am with You Tabernacle punchout from the back of the book and fold the doors. Tell your child to place this punchout somewhere as a reminder of Jesus' great gift of himself in the Eucharist.

✦ **Cross** (Chapter 1)
Tell your child that you are going to give him or her a reminder of how Jesus died, rose, and is still with us. Explain that it is a reminder that Jesus loves us and is our friend. Hand him or her the cross. Together, reflect about how Jesus died and rose and is still with us. Have your child put the cross in a special place where he or she will see it often.

✦ **Prayer cards** (Chapter 7)
Help your child remove the two prayer cards from the back of the book and have him or her decorate them. Place the mealtime prayer reminder on the table where you eat and the morning and night prayer reminders where your child sleeps.

✦ **Joy heart** (Chapter 9)
Remove the Joy heart punchout from the back of the book. Allow time for your child to color the heart. Tell your child to place this heart where it will help him or her to remember to bring joy to others.

✦ **Butterfly** (Chapter 20)
Have your child remove the butterfly from the back of the book and color it. Encourage your child to make the butterfly beautiful as a reminder of Jesus' glorious new life. Staple the butterfly to the end of a straw. Talk about how butterflies symbolize new life.

✦ **Jesus button** (Chapter 1)
With your child, remove the Jesus button. Tell him or her to wear it as a sign of friendship with Jesus. Encourage your child to tell others the story of Jesus and the children when he or she shows the Jesus button to others.

✦ **God Is My Father button** (Chapter 3)
Remove the God Is My Father button from the back of the book and invite your child to wear it as a reminder that God is our loving Father and we are his children

✦ **Christian Fish button** (Chapter 5)
Remove the Christian Fish button from the back of the book and present it to your child. Explain that we Christians are like little fish. At Baptism, we became children of God through the waters of Baptism. Just as fish must stay in the water to live, we must try to be like Jesus if we want to live the new life he gave us at Baptism.

✦ **Mary button** (Chapter 23)
Help your child to remove the Mary button from the back of the book. Invite him or her to write YES on it. Tell your child to wear the button as a reminder to be like Mary by saying yes to God.

✦ **Glory to God pendant** (Chapter 25)
Remove the Glory to God pendant from the back of the book and invite your child to decorate it. Provide some yarn to loop through the hole at the top so that it can be worn as a necklace.

Special Lessons

The Missions (page 161)

FOCUS: In this lesson, you will be helping your child to understand that missionaries spread the good news of God's love to people far and near.

The life of a Christian is a life in the Spirit. It is a life so responsive to the Word of the Father that it reveres each person as created in the image of God and redeemed by Christ. When Jesus asked Peter if he loved him, he gave Peter a definite criterion to determine whether his avowed love was true: the sign of Peter's love of the Lord would be the love with which he welcomed and cared for his sheep. It would lead all people to unity in Christ.

Christ's desire to unite all people in his love motivates those who love him to dedicate themselves to making his prayer for unity a reality. As good ministers of Christ, all the faithful gladly apply themselves to bringing his love to others.

All Christians have the mission to lead others to Jesus and, by their good works and the example of their lives, perceive the bond that unites all people. As members of God's family, we are interdependent. As followers of Jesus, the first missionary, we ought to be sensitive to the needs of others and feel a responsibility to help them. Works of charity and mercy are the most striking evidence of the Christian life.

Scripture in This Lesson

John 21:15–17 Jesus and Peter

Catechism of the Catholic Church

849–851, 854, 856

In this chapter, help your child to

+ identify the needs of our brothers and sisters throughout the world.
+ describe the missionary spirit and our call to spread the Gospel.
+ identify ways to help the missions.

Key Terms for Your Information

+ missionaries—people who work to spread the Good News.
+ patroness—a female saint who takes care of and prays for a particular person, place, or thing.

Pullouts (see page 199 in the Student Book)

+ First Communion Pullouts
+ Manger Figures
+ Christmas Songs
+ Easter Eggs/Basket
+ Scripture Prayer booklet "I Am the Good Shepherd"

Learning Aids

(none)

Punchouts (listed in the order that they appear in the Student Book, following the Scripture Prayer booklet)

✦ **My Morning Offering** (Chapter 16)
Have your child remove the Morning Offering card from the back of the book. Invite your child to decorate it. Discuss where he or she might place this card to remember this special prayer every morning.

✦ **Cross** (Chapter 2)
Have your child remove and fold the cross from the back of the book. Invite your child to display the cross in your home as a reminder of Jesus.

✦ **Paschal Candle** (Chapter 3)
Help your child remove the Paschal candle from the back of the book. Have him or her color the flame and the chi-rho (the Greek letters that designate Christ).

✦ **Top Ten CDs** (and God's Laws of Love cover) (Chapter 5)
Have your child remove the Top Ten CDs and the cover from the back of the book. Help him or her tape or staple the cover for the CDs. Instruct your child to write his or her name on the cover and color it. These CDs will help your child remember Key Terms for Your Information for the Ten Commandments.

✦ **Finger Puppets** (Chapter 7)
Work with your child and any siblings or friends to perform a play about caring, using the finger puppets found in the back of the book. Work together to remove the finger puppets and mount them on craft sticks. Talk about examples of ways we can show we care about ourselves, others, and the world. Choose one of the ideas to role-play with the puppets.

✦ **Zacchaeus and the Tree** (Chapter 13)
Have your child remove the punchouts of Zacchaeus and the sycamore tree from the back of the book. Insert the tab of the Zacchaeus figure into the slit of the tree so that the figure moves up and down. Tell your child that this tree will help him or her remember the parts of the Sacrament of Reconciliation. Have your child practice until you can tell what each word in the tree means.

✦ **Response Wheel** (Chapter 22)
Help your child remove the Response Wheel from the back of the book and attach the spinner with a metal fastener. Tell your child the responses can all be found in their Mass booklet (which comes with the Grade 2 Student Book). The responses are on pages 6, 11, 14, 17, 21, and 24 of the booklet. Practice the responses with your child. Spin the spinner and have your child give the response to the prayer on which it stops. Use the wheel until your child knows all the responses to the prayers.

Special Lessons
(none)

Pullouts (See page 229 in the Student Book.)

✦ Reconciliation booklet
✦ My Rosary booklet
✦ Gifted with Faith booklet

Learning Aids
✦ Map of the Lands of the Old Testament
✦ Map of Palestine in the Time of Jesus

Punchouts (listed in the order that they appear in the Student Book, following the Scripture Prayer booklet)

✦ **Made By God with Love** (Chapter 1)
Create Made by God with Love badges. Have your child remove the badge from the back of the book. Ask your child to print his or her name on the badge and color it. Use masking tape or a pin to attach the badge to your child's clothing or backpack. Tell your child to wear the badge all day as a reminder that God calls him or her by name.

✦ **Alleluia** (Chapter 20)
Help your child remove the Alleluia button from the back of the book. Tell your child to wear it as a reminder that he or she has God's life and will live forever.

✦ **Cross** (Chapter 3)
Help your child remove the cross from the back of the book. Have him or her hold the cross as you say: *The cross is a special sign for Christians. It reminds us to try to be like Jesus. We should use our Christian vision to see God calling us to know, love, and serve him. Then we will love God above all else and love others as Jesus loves us.* Roll a piece of masking tape to stick to the back of the cross so that your child can wear it.

✦ **My Talent Gift Box** (Chapter 2)
Help your child remove the My Talent Gift Box from the back of the book. Have him or her write one talent on the front of the box. On the back of the box, have your child write how he or she might use that talent for others. Allow time for your child to decorate the box.

✦ **Jesus** (Chapter 21)
Have your child remove the Jesus punchout from the back of the book. Tell your child to attach it to his or her mirror in their room so that each time they look into it, he or she will be reminded to reflect Jesus.

✦ **Reconciliation Badge** (Chapter 23)
Help your child remove the Reconciliation badge from the back of the book. Encourage him or her to wear it after receiving the Sacrament of Penance and Reconciliation.

✦ **Tablets** (Chapter 7)
Help your child remove the tablets from the back of the book. Read together the keywords of the Ten Commandments.

✦ **Morning Offering** (Chapter 11)
Work together to carefully remove the heart punchout from the back of the book. Help your child to assemble the base for the heart as directed on the punchout page. Tell your child to use this heart as a reminder to pray the Morning Offering.

Special Lessons

(none)

Pullouts (See page 221 in the Student Book.)

✦ Act of Faith card
✦ Jesus card
✦ VIP shield
✦ Christ candle
✦ My Way of the Cross booklet
✦ I Celebrate the Sacrament of Reconciliation booklet
✦ Walking with Jesus booklet
✦ Along the Way of Holiness
✦ Advent calendar

Learning Aids

(none)

Punchouts

(none)

Special Lessons

Feast Day—May 13: Our Lady of Fatima (page 181)

FOCUS: In this lesson, you will be helping your child to understand that Jesus gave us his Mother to be our Mother.

Not only did Jesus give totally of himself for our redemption, but he also gave us the person most precious to him—his Mother. Actually, Christ's words on Calvary simply confirmed the fact that Mary is the Mother of us all. She did not become so just because Jesus entrusted her to John; rather, she is our Mother because she is the Mother of Jesus.

Christians throughout the centuries have proclaimed the praises of Mary, who gave Christ his human heredity, characteristics, and talents. Mary, who was "favored" and "blessed among women" (Luke 1:28, 42) was assumed into heaven and crowned by her divine Son, Jesus Christ, as Queen of Angels and Saints, Queen of Apostles and Martyrs, Queen of Confessors and Virgins, and "most honored of all creation" (Saint Germanus).

Though we honor Mary under many titles, the most significant and the most meaningful to us is Mother. It was, after all, because of her divine maternity that she received other graces and titles; it was because of that motherhood that we can boast of her as our Mother.

Catechism of the Catholic Church

963

In this lesson, help your child to

+ describe Mary's appearance at Fatima.
+ explain that Mary is our Mother and that she offers guidance and help.

Pullouts (See page 223 in the Student Book.)

+ The Seven Sacraments
+ We Are a Family game
+ An Act of Consecration cutout
+ Morning Offering cutout
+ A Prayer for My Family cutout
+ Kindness badge
+ Lent is a Time for Reconciliation
+ My Reconciliation booklet
+ Celebrating the Eucharist booklet
+ Life with Christ booklet

Learning Aids

(none)

Punchouts

(none)

Special Lessons

Feast Day—December 8: Our Lady of Guadalupe
(page 191)

FOCUS: In this lesson, you will be helping your child to understand that Mary, the Mother of God, wants to help us as our Mother.

Not only did Jesus give totally of himself for our redemption, but he also gave us the most precious earthly possession he had—his Mother. We read in the *Dogmatic Constitution on the Church:*

> This motherhood of Mary in the order of grace continues uninterruptedly from the consent which she loyally gave at the Annunciation and which she sustained without wavering beneath the cross. (62)

On the hill of Calvary, John, the "beloved disciple," heard Christ say "Behold your mother." At that moment, representing all of humanity, John received a most incomparable mother to love and be loved by. On the hill of Tepeyac, Juan (John), the "beloved little son," heard Mary say "I am your merciful mother." At that moment he too represented all of humanity and received a merciful, loving mother who wanted to aid her children in every way possible. Though we honor Mary under many titles, the most meaningful to us is Mother. It was, after all, because of her divine maternity that she received all other privileges; it is because of that motherhood that we can boast of her as our Mother.

Catechism of the Catholic Church
969, 971, 975

In this lesson, help your child to
- retell the story of Mary's apparitions to Juan Diego.
- describe Mary's gift of her true image.
- explain that we are to respond to Mary's love for us by living as true followers of her Son.

Key Terms for Your Information
- Aztec—American Indian people of central Mexico, whose empire was at its height during the 16th century; they were conquered by Spain in 1521, at which time Catholicism was introduced to the native people
- Guadalupe—name given to Mary as she appeared in Mexico; a shrine to her in Spain
- Juan Diego—the Aztec to whom Mary appeared
- Tepeyac—a hill outside Mexico City
- tilma—a garment similar to a Roman toga

Feast Day—March 19: The Month of Saint Joseph
(page 193)

FOCUS: In this lesson, you will be helping your child to understand that Saint Joseph, foster father of Jesus, is a great saint.

Though we have little historical information about Saint Joseph, we know that he was from the royal line of David. He was chosen by God to be Mary's husband and the legal father and guardian of her Son, Jesus Christ. Joseph shouldered his responsibilities with generosity and love, trusting firmly in the Lord.

As head of the Holy Family, Joseph did for Jesus and Mary all the things that a loving husband and father does. He protected them from harm and did not spare himself in doing so, even when it meant traveling in the dark of night across unfamiliar desert sands to escape Herod's threat of murder. On returning from Egypt, he led his family to Nazareth in Galilee, where they could live without fear. There he plied his craftsman's trade, which provided a level of comfort comparable to that of the ordinary villager. Saint Joseph can intercede for us so that with God's help, our homes can be places of love, security, and joy—places where God dwells.

Just as God called Saint Joseph to care for the human life of Jesus, Pope Pius IX looked to him to protect the Mystical Body of Christ, the Church, at a time when the Church was being attacked by enemies and endangered by false philosophies. In every age, we need Saint Joseph's help and protection for the Church, and Joseph is ever ready to help us in any need: physical, temporal, or spiritual.

Scripture in This Lesson

Luke 2:1–7   The Birth of Jesus
Luke 2:25–35   The Presentation in the Temple
Luke 2:41–51   The Boy Jesus in the Temple

Catechism of the Catholic Church

488, 531–532

In this lesson, help your child to

+ identify titles given to Saint Joseph.
+ describe Joseph's place in salvation history.

Key Terms for Your Information

+ legend—story that is for the most part fictional, but may have some basis in historical fact
+ espousal—marriage contract; the man and wife did not live together until after the second part of the marriage, the procession to the groom's house

May: The Month of Mary (page 194)

FOCUS: In this lesson, you will be helping your child to understand that Mary, our Mother, is a powerful intercessor.

A gift is often a sign of love, a sign that someone wants to deepen his or her relationship with another. God has given each of us gifts that show profound love for us. God's greatest gift, of course, is Jesus, who revealed God's loving plan—a call to be one with him and with one another. The last gift Jesus gave us as he hung dying on the cross was Mary, his Mother. Jesus gave her to us to be our Mother. Mary, who brought Jesus into the world, prays for us and helps us become followers of Jesus who bring his love to others.

It is easy to place unquestioning confidence in those we love. Those who love Jesus have great confidence in him and recourse to Mary's intercessory power. Every May we turn to Mary in a special way to ask her intercession and to learn from her life how to experience the Lord's love in our daily joys and sorrows. To express our love and honor, we address Mary with many beautiful titles. One of these is Mother of Perpetual Help.

Catechism of the Catholic Church
494, 968-971, 1172

In this lesson, help your child to
✦ explain why Mary is called Mother of Perpetual Help.
✦ describe Mary's motherly love and concern for him or her.

Jonah: A Fish Story (page 195)

FOCUS: In this lesson, you will be helping your child to understand that God loves everyone, including repentant sinners.

Jonah was a disobedient prophet who tried to escape a distasteful mission. God called him to preach repentance to the people of Nineveh, the capital of Assyria, which was Israel's chief enemy. Jonah boarded a ship headed in the opposite direction. A violent storm arose. Realizing that he was the jinx that caused it, Jonah encouraged the sailors to cast him overboard. A huge fish swallowed Jonah. From the depths of darkness, Jonah cried out to God. Three days later he was spewed out on shore. Finally accepting God's will for him, Jonah went to Nineveh, where he called the people to repent.

A sublime lesson can be gleaned from this humorous fish story. Jonah represents the extreme nationalism and narrow-minded intolerance of the Jewish people during the fifth century. The book provides a mirror for its readers to see themselves as they were: petty, selfish, unreasonable, unwilling to admit that God's love extends to all. The story taught the author's contemporaries that God was not their exclusive property, that racial and liturgical privileges were not the greatest of glories, and that God loved everyone—even the despised Assyrians.

Perhaps a greater mystery than a three-day survival in the belly of a fish is the fact that God chose this reluctant prophet as the instrument of salvation for the Gentiles. Jonah prefigures Christ. Jesus himself refers to Jonah's stay in the fish's belly to prepare the people for his Resurrection, which was for all people.

Scripture in This Lesson
The Book of Jonah

Catechism of the Catholic Church
219

In this lesson, help your child to
✦ identify Jonah as a story intended to give a message.
✦ explain that happiness is gained only when we follow God's will.
✦ express an understanding of the greatness of God's love, which embraces all people.

Key Term for Your Information
✦ Nineveh—the capital of Assyria, Israel's enemy

Judith: A Brave Woman (page 197)

FOCUS: In this lesson, you will be helping your child to understand that all things are possible for those who are faithful to God.

Judith may or may not be a real person. The name itself means "Jewess" and might refer to the Jewish people as a whole. The Book of Judith is an example of haggaic midrash, an early form of Jewish scriptural interpretation. The theme of the Book of Judith is the certain victory of God over the forces of evil, and its purpose is to encourage and reanimate the confidence of the Jewish people. The story's symbolism lies in a vast army intent upon destroying Israel and making paganism supreme over the earth. The author of Judith united the four empires of Assyria, Babylon, Media, and Persia under the leadership of Nebuchadnezzar to form a composite symbol of God's enemy. From a storytelling perspective, this makes the Book of Judith a literary read, while imparting important values of the faith.

The important thing to remember about the Book of Judith is the truth that God always has been and always will be victorious over the forces of evil. We need only put our trust in God and God will protect and defend us from evil and its myriad forces. In the footsteps of valiant women such as Esther, Judith, and Mary, we walk confidently into the future.

Scripture in This Lesson
The Book of Judith

Catechism of the Catholic Church
64, 489

In this lesson, help your child to
+ describe the Book of Judith as a story intended to reveal truths about God.
+ explain that confidence in God enables us to accomplish great things and assures deliverance from evil.

Job: A Man of Suffering (page 199)

FOCUS: In this lesson, you will be helping your child to understand that faith in God helps us cope with the mystery of suffering.

The Book of Job belongs to Wisdom Literature, although Job's author is not concerned with broad generalities or with many wisdom lessons. Rather, the author addresses one problem—the suffering of the innocent.

The basic theme of the Book of Job is the mystery of unmerited suffering of the just person. The solution to suffering given by Christ on the cross and in the parable of Dives and Lazarus was unknown to Job. If he had known what we know about the theology of reward and punishment, he might not have protested as he did. As it was, Job had the task of defending God's justice to a world that believed that here on earth the good are rewarded and the evil are punished.

The author had Job conclude that the question of suffering was too deep for him, because human beings could not penetrate the secrets of God's providence. When Job finally submits to God's inscrutable ways in humility and trust, God rewards him by restoring his family, his property, and his health.

It is Jesus who reveals that suffering is not always the result of personal sin. Since the crucifixion, suffering born in Christian faith brings the fullness of the kingdom. We are able to transform suffering into something meaningful by uniting ourselves with the suffering Christ and accepting it. Through it, we can grow as loving, patient people.

Scripture in This Lesson
The Book of Job

Catechism of the Catholic Church

164, 309, 1500–1501

In this lesson, help your child to

+ describe the Book of Job as a story intended to teach that even the just may suffer.
+ explain that he or she can bear sufferings better through a deeper awareness of God's power, presence, and wisdom.

Grade 6: Esther: Queen of Courage and Faith (page 201)

FOCUS: In this lesson, you will be helping your child to understand that those who love and trust God are saved.

The Book of Esther was written to inspire faith in God by teaching about God's providence in saving the people from destruction. It also explains the origin, significance, and dates of the Jewish feast of Purim, a joyous celebration that recalls the story of Esther and God's saving hand. In order to encourage and edify the readers, the author wrote about an otherwise unrecorded event in Jewish history: a pogrom against the Jews of the dispersion, which failed because of the intervention of a woman. The heroine is Esther, a beautiful and good Jewish woman, who risked her life to intercede for the lives of her people. Esther's courageous action and obedience foreshadow Mary's yes on behalf of the world. Esther and Judith both prefigure Mary.

A day for the massacre of the Jews was selected by lot (pur), but with God's help, Esther and her uncle Mordecai were able to reverse the king's decree of execution and the Jews were able to slaughter their enemies. This sounds vindictive—and so it was—but it must be remembered that Christ's precept of love of enemies had not yet been taught.

Once again, in the Book of Esther, the dramatic techniques of the storyteller remind the people that God's loving care continually watches over them if they serve faithfully or turn to God repentantly. We need never doubt God's love, even in the worst situations.

Scripture in This Lesson

The Book of Esther

Catechism of the Catholic Church

64, 489

In this lesson, help your child to

+ identify Esther as the instrument through which God saved the Jewish people from destruction.
+ describe Esther's faith and courage.
+ explain that God watches over us and is always willing to help us if we ask.

Pullouts (See page 245 in the Student Book.)

+ Map of Palestine
+ With Christ We Die and Rise
+ Reconciliation booklet
+ Prayer leaflets
+ Scripture Prayer booklet

Learning Aids

+ History timeline
+ God's Saving Plan of Love timeline

Punchouts

(none)

Special Lessons

(none)

Pullouts (See page 223 in the Student Book.)

✦ Map of Palestine
✦ Making Sunday Special
✦ Reconciliation booklet
✦ Scripture booklet

Learning Aids

(none)

Punchouts

(none)

Special Lessons

Reconciliation (page 215)

FOCUS: In this lesson, you will be helping your child to understand that an informed conscience and the examination of conscience help in Reconciliation, an essential part of Catholic life.

The Bible teaches us that people sin repeatedly and God absolves repeatedly. God forgives with love and tenderness those who are repentant and discloses that we are also to forgive the sinner and offer reconciliation. Christ personifies the Father's forgiveness. Whenever Jesus sees true sorrow for sin, he not only forgives the penitents but also restores them to the community.

Sin offends God and wounds the sinner, but it also harms the community. We who follow Christ celebrate the Sacrament of Penance and Reconciliation, in which we repent and ask pardon of both God and community. By doing penance, we try to heal the pain we have caused. Conversion of heart requires looking at ourselves honestly in the light of God's law and the teachings of Christ. God alone knows the cure for our sinful hearts and, through grace, draws us to conversion and heals us.

Scripture in This Lesson

Luke 7:36–50 A Penitent Woman
Luke 15:11–24 The Lost Son
Luke 19:1–10 Zacchaeus
Luke 22:54–62 Peter's Denial

Catechism of the Catholic Church

1427–1433, 1440–1470, 1780–1794

In this lesson, help your child to

+ explain that the first step in healing is self-knowledge.
+ describe how to examine his or her conscience.
+ describe the role of conscience.
+ explain how to form his or her conscience.
+ review the process of the rite of Reconciliation.
+ explain that reconciliation involves a decision to turn to God by seeking forgiveness through the Church.

Key Terms for Your Information

+ absolution—forgiveness or pardon for sin
+ conscience—the power of the intellect to decide whether an act is good or bad
+ contrition—sorrow for sin with the intention not to sin again
+ penitent—a person who seeks forgiveness, often through the Sacrament of Reconciliation

Celebrating Eucharist (page 225)

FOCUS: In this lesson, you will be helping your child to understand that the Eucharist is the sacrifice of Christ and a sacrament that nourishes us and unites us with Christ and with one another.

God chose the Jewish people to play a special part in the divine plan of salvation and led them to adore the one true God. Under God's guidance, their priests avoided human sacrifice, offering instead only the most perfect animals and the best farm produce. God's only Son became the perfect sacrifice by his death on the cross. Christ commissioned the apostles and their successors to honor his sacrifice in an unbloody manner to the end of time. At the Last Supper, he instituted the Eucharist as both sacrifice and sacrament and revealed his real presence in this sacrament. Thus, the Eucharist is the mystical representation of his sacrificial death and also the banquet of his Body and Blood by which he nourishes us and remains with us.

Although the Eucharist is sacrifice and sacrament, sometimes one aspect is emphasized. For example, in the 16th century, when Protestantism denied that the Mass was a sacrifice for the remission of sin, the sacrificial aspect was emphasized. In other times, when there has been widespread forgetfulness of God and the divine goodness, the Church stressed the Mass as a sacrament of divine mercy. The Second Vatican Council teaches both aspects of the eucharistic celebration. What is essential is that in the Eucharist, Christ offers himself to his heavenly Father and unites us, the community of believers, in his sacrifice. Also essential is the fact that in the Mass, all who share in Christ's Body and Blood are nourished with his divine life and become one.

Scripture in This Lesson
1 Corinthians 10:16 The Cup of Blessing
Luke 22:19–20 The Last Supper

Catechism of the Catholic Church
1324–1405

In this lesson, help your child to
+ describe the rites and traditions of the Eucharist.
+ explain how various eucharistic customs came about.
+ explain the importance of the Eucharist.

Pullouts (See page 279 in the Student Book.)
+ Map of Palestine
+ Reconciliation booklet
+ Scripture Prayer booklet
+ My Parish booklet

Learning Aids
+ Events in World History timeline
+ Journey of the Church Through Time timeline

Punchouts
(none)

Using the *What Catholics Should Know* Section of the Student Book

Our Catholic Tradition provides us with a multitude of resources for deepening our relationship with God. The *What Catholics Should Know* section of the Student Book places these resources at your fingertips so that you can help your child become more familiar with them. The *What Catholics Should Know* section includes the following:

+ Prayer and How We Pray
+ Formulas of Catholic Doctrine
+ Celebrating and Living Our Catholic Faith
+ Making Good Choices
+ The Bible
+ Showing Our Love for the World

Here are some of the ways you can use the *What Catholics Should Know* section:

+ You can use this section of the Student Book at any time with your child to review some of the basics of the Catholic faith that are appropriate for his or her age.
+ With your child, review this section over the summer, after you have completed the chapters in the book.
+ Use the various lists in this section to quiz your child's knowledge of the Catholic faith.

Using the Glossary in the Student Book

You can help to develop your child's Catholic vocabulary by using the Glossary in the back of the Student Book. The Glossary is cumulative over the eight grades, containing over 300 words relating to our Catholic Tradition. Consider using the Glossary in the following ways:

+ In the text of the Student Book, vocabulary words (Words Your Child Should Know) are printed in bold type. Each time you come across a boldface word, have your child locate that word in the Glossary and read the definition.

+ In the chapter review, vocabulary words are listed under the heading Words Your Child Should Know. Once again, have your child locate these words in the Glossary to review their definitions.

+ Use the Glossary to quiz your child on Words Your Child Should Know for a chapter or a unit.

+ Over the summer months, choose a word (or several words) from the Glossary each week and have your child memorize each definition.

+ Improve your own Catholic vocabulary by reviewing words from the Glossary on a regular basis.

+ Read to your child a definition of a word from the Glossary and have him or her guess the word.

Using the Prayers on the Inside Covers of the Student Book

Traditional prayers are like family heirlooms, passed down from generation to generation. These prayers provide us with words to speak to God when we are at a loss for our own words. Likewise, they enable us to join others in communal prayer, sharing common words. The inside covers to your child's Student Book contain traditional Catholic prayers that are appropriate for your child's age. Consider using these prayers in the following ways:

1. Begin and end the time you spend with your child working on chapters by praying selected traditional prayers.

2. Help your child to take to heart (memorize) the prayers over the course of the year.

3. Periodically quiz your child on various traditional prayers to see if they can recall the words and whether he or she understands the meaning.

4. Select prayers that your family can pray together on special occasions.

5. Encourage your child to pray selected prayers as his or her own morning or night prayer.

6. Learn traditional prayers with which you are not familiar.

Using *Catholic Prayer for Catholic Families*

Catholic Prayer for Catholic Families contains all of the prayers taught in the *Christ Our Life* series. It also offers hints and suggestions for making prayer an everyday activity. Use this resource to do the following:

+ enrich your own understanding of prayer.
+ learn various methods of praying.
+ learn the words of traditional prayers with which you are not familiar.
+ become more familiar with prayers and forms of prayer that you will be helping your child to learn.
+ nourish your own prayer life.

Using the *Christ Our Life* Web site (**www.christourlife.org**)

The *Christ Our Life* Web site is your online partner in faith formation, providing you with family activities and resources to assist you.

To help you find everything on the site, use the comprehensive Search feature, available from every Web page. The *Christ Our Life* Web site, **www.christourlife.org**, offers a wealth of information and resources for parents, including the following:

+ Sunday Connection—This free subscription service delivers weekly background information and activities for the Sunday readings. E-mails are automatically sent each Monday, allowing you a week for preparation.

+ 3-Minute Retreats—These help nurture everyday faith with peaceful music and prayer. A new retreat is offered each day.

+ Articles—A variety of articles about Catholic Tradition topics will help you to grow in your own understanding of the Catholic faith. Topics include Prayer and Spirituality, Scripture, Sacraments and Liturgy, the Saints, Catholic Social Teaching, and Church Tradition.

Web site membership is free and allows you access to all of these features. Join our online community to discover everything **christourlife.org** has to offer.

A Family Prayer

Children	**Adults**
Praise be to God	who made us a family.
Praise be to God	for the love that we share.
Praise be to God	for sending us Jesus.
Praise be to God	for teaching us to care.
Help us, Lord Jesus	fill our lives with your Spirit.
Help us, Lord Jesus	teach us how to forgive.
Help us, Lord Jesus	grant us wisdom and patience.
Help us, Lord Jesus	in your grace may we live.
Come, Holy Spirit	fill our lives with your gifts.
Come, Holy Spirit	help us serve other's needs.
Come, Holy Spirit	teach us faith, hope, and love.
Come, Holy Spirit	guide our thoughts and our deeds.
Be with us, God	we ask Mary to help us.
Be with us, God	we look to Joseph for aid.
Be with us, God	may we respect one another.
Be with us, God	may our hope never fade.
Hear us, Lord Jesus	watch over our family.
Hear us, Lord Jesus	help our faith to grow strong.
Hear us, Lord Jesus	come and dwell in our hearts.
Hear us, Lord Jesus	to you we belong.
Spirit, we praise you	you invite us to know you.
Spirit, we praise you	may we walk in your light.
Spirit, we praise you	may we find you in all things.
Spirit, we praise you	all day and all night.

A Parent's Prayer

Loving God,
You are the giver of all we possess,
the source of all of our blessings.
We thank and praise you.

Thank you for the gift of our children.

Help us to understand and patiently listen
to them, and to learn from our mistakes.
Give us the patience and wisdom to be
honorable guides for them.

Help us to set boundaries for them, and yet
encourage them to explore.
Give us the strength and courage to treat
each day as a fresh start.

May our children come to know you,
the one true God, and Jesus Christ, whom
you have sent.

May your Holy Spirit help them to grow in
faith, hope and love,
so they may know peace, truth, and
goodness.

May their ears hear your voice.
May their eyes see your presence in all
things.
May their lips proclaim your word.
May their hearts be your dwelling place.
May their hands do works of charity.
May their feet walk in the way of Jesus
Christ, your Son and our Lord.

Amen.

Going Through a Chapter With Your Children

By following the step-by-step process outlined on pages 32–34 and summarized in convenient format below, you can go through the chapters of the Student Book individually with each child, helping him or her to grow in faith. Convenient charts in Part Two of this guide provide you with brief background on the content and outlines of the important concepts for your child to learn. Then, follow these simple steps:

Before You Begin

+ Read over the assigned chapter in the Student Book on your own to become more familiar with its content. Be sure to look for any Note to Parents features related to the chapter/unit and read these ahead of time as well.

+ Look over the background information provided in Part Two of this guide (pages 40–169). Prepare any materials that you will need: a Bible, the *Christ Our Life* Children's Book, writing utensils, crayons and/or markers.

Working on the Lesson

+ Begin by gathering together in the place that you've set aside for this special time.

+ Join together in an opening prayer.

+ Work together on the pages of the chapter in the Student Book.

+ In addition to reading the text, work with your child to complete any activities in the chapter.

+ Keep in mind the information from the charts in Part Two that tells you what to help your children know or do in each chapter.

+ Help your child to take to heart (memorize) key words from the Glossary as well as the prayers included on the inside covers of the Student Book.

+ For features titled A Moment with Jesus, invite your child to close his or her eyes as you slowly and prayerfully read the text. Pause for a few moments of silence with your child as you both pray quietly.

+ Additional activities and assessments (quizzes) for each chapter are available on Blackline Masters at the *Christ Our Life* Website (www.christourlife.org). To download these resources, talk to your parish catechetical leader/director of religious education about an access code from Loyola Press.

+ End this time together with prayer.